Solomon Northup

Solomon Northup

The Complete Story of the Author of *Twelve Years a Slave*

David Fiske, Clifford W. Brown, and Rachel Seligman

 PRAEGER

AN IMPRINT OF ABC-CLIO, LLC
Santa Barbara, California • Denver, Colorado • Oxford, England

Library of Congress Cataloging-in-Publication Data

Fiske, David (David A.), 1954–
   Solomon Northup : the complete story of the author of Twelve years a slave / David Fiske, Clifford W. Brown, and Rachel Seligman.
        pages cm
   Includes bibliographical references and index.
   ISBN 978-1-4408-2974-1 (hardcopy : alk. paper) — ISBN 978-1-4408-2975-8 (ebook)   1. Northup, Solomon, 1808–   2. Slaves—United States—Biography. 3. African Americans—Biography.   4. Plantation life—Louisiana—History—19th century.   5. Slavery—Louisiana—History—19th century.   6. Northup family.   7. Hampton family.   8. Stanton family.   9. Slaves' writings, American. 10. Northup, Solomon, 1808– Twelve years a slave.   I. Brown, Clifford W. (Clifford Waters), 1942–   II. Seligman, Rachel.   III. Title.
   E444.N87F57   2013
   306.3'62092—dc23
   [B]   2013011536

ISBN: 978-1-4408-2974-1
EISBN: 978-1-4408-2975-8

17   16   15   14   13   2   3   4   5

This book is also available on the World Wide Web as an eBook.
Visit www.abc-clio.com for details.

Praeger
An Imprint of ABC-CLIO, LLC

ABC-CLIO, LLC
130 Cremona Drive, P.O. Box 1911
Santa Barbara, California 93116-1911

This book is printed on acid-free paper ∞

Manufactured in the United States of America

This book is dedicated to the many African American victims of kidnapping who, unlike Northup, were never rescued and lived out their remaining days as slaves. May their stories some day be told.

Contents

Maps and Illustrations

Foreword

I have been aware of my great-great grandfather's story since high school. My mother, Victoria Northup Linzy Dunham, Alonzo Northup's granddaughter, gave me and my brothers and sisters copies of *Twelve Years a Slave* (facsimiled from the first edition) at an early age—but, like many young people I did not pay a lot of attention to family history. Later on, I regrettably lost the book. With all the responsibilities of raising a family, as well as holding a responsible position outside the home, I let Solomon's story fade into the background. In 1999, our local newspaper carried a story about Union College's Solomon Northup exhibit. I was curious, contacted the College, and as a result, was invited to participate in the final program where I was asked to read a moving passage from Solomon's book. When Saratoga Springs started Solomon Northup Day shortly thereafter, my family attended in force, including my 90-plus year-old mother then living in California. These annual events enabled our family to reconnect to its past and appreciate the importance of the Solomon Northup story. I am very pleased that there is now a renewed interest in my ancestor, that the Fiske, Brown, and Seligman biography of him is being published, and that even Hollywood will present its version. As a result, our whole family will have an enhanced understanding of our ancestor's story and its importance—and so will lots of other Americans.

It is a story worth remembering. There are many lessons in Grandpa Northup's book, but to me the most important one is about persistence and determination in the face of extraordinary adversity. His life was horribly interrupted at the age of 33, but with remarkable persistence he survived the ordeal and finally made it back to his family. A literate person, he produced a bestseller and shared his story with audiences throughout the country. It also appears that he worked on the underground railroad to help others who had experienced some of the ordeals with which he was familiar. His courage and perseverance should be an inspiration to all humans who face life's obstacles and tragedies. We are all proud of him and Anne, and hope that others will benefit from knowing his story.

Carol Linzy Adams Sally
Great-great granddaughter of Solomon Northup

Preface

The genesis of this book can be traced back about 15 years, beginning with the separate moments when each of the authors was introduced to the remarkable saga of Solomon Northup. For David Fiske, it was a visit to the Old Fort House Museum in Fort Edward, New York, in the 1990s. The museum is located in a house that Northup and his wife Anne once resided in, and features a permanent exhibit dedicated to his story. This visit sparked a passionate interest in Northup that has led to years of research into the unknown aspects of his life. For Rachel Seligman, it was a friend's suggestion that *Twelve Years a Slave* was essential reading for anyone wanting greater knowledge of local history. That encounter with the story engendered a large-scale exhibition project at the Mandeville Gallery at Union College in 1999 (where Seligman was the director/curator). Seligman, in turn, brought the story to Clifford Brown, professor of political science and then chair of the Mandeville Gallery Advisory Committee. Throughout the creation of the exhibition, and ever since, Brown has continued to be a source of research and a clearinghouse for information on Northup. For all three authors, Northup's story—that of a free black man lured away from his home in Saratoga Springs, kidnapped, enslaved for 12 years in rural Louisiana before being rescued, and then returned to his family in upstate New York—was so compelling that it continues to exert an unflagging hold over them.

Northup tells his own story in *Twelve Years a Slave*, a richly detailed, suspenseful narrative, and a seemingly impossible saga that nevertheless rings with an unwavering authenticity. He was an educated man with a lively interest in the ways of the world, and was able to sustain his curiosity and engagement with life despite his horrifying plight. This is evident in every page of his narrative, with its extensive descriptions of the people, places, and activities with which he was engaged. Because he remained a keen observer throughout his ordeal, his compelling saga reveals to us myriad details of the ordinary routines of daily life on Louisiana plantations in the 1840s and 1850s, as well as vivid descriptions of the life of a slave experiencing the dictates of harsh, arbitrary, and brutal masters.

Despite his situation—one that must have seemed an inescapable nightmare—Northup was able to maintain a degree of hope for his future. How was this possible? Would any of us today be able to do so? What explains his ability to stay engaged and interested in the workings of the plantation and in the lives of his fellow slaves? What accounts for his continued hope in the face of the seeming hopelessness of his situation? Northup's resourcefulness and inner strength provide valuable lessons.

Northup was eventually freed. Although it was sadly commonplace for free black citizens to be kidnapped into slavery, it was an extremely rare and remarkable occurrence for anyone to be rescued, as Northup was. With his freedom came opportunities to share his story with the world, and not surprisingly, he seized these opportunities, not only through the written narrative, but also through a series of public tours, theatrical reenactments, and other activities. His aim was to shed light and spread awareness in the North about the "peculiar institution" of slavery. He became an active abolitionist, helping others escape slavery. His book (published not long after Harriet Beecher Stowe's wildly popular *Uncle Tom's Cabin*) was also extremely well received and sold 11,000 copies in its first month. It has been reprinted numerous times since then, has been reworked for children, and is referenced in countless texts about slavery. It has been filmed as a PBS film *(Solomon Northup's Odyssey)*, and, as of this writing, a major motion picture is in the works.

The version the authors read was the edition published by Louisiana State University Press in 1968, edited by Joseph Logsdon and Sue Eakin. This edition included not only Northup's original text, but also extensive research documenting the specific events (using Northup's detailed descriptions) and revealing the exact locations and the histories of those mentioned in the story. This rich research material is included in their edition through front matter and footnotes that expand the depth of information about the people, places, and events described by Northup. This edition then became the inspiration for the exhibition at the Mandeville Gallery, an interdisciplinary exhibition space in the center of the Union College campus. Union College is a small liberal arts college in Schenectady, New York, about 22 miles south of Saratoga Springs—the city from which Northup was lured south and into slavery. Union College was also connected to the story in a more direct way, because Northup enlisted a Union College alumnus, David Wilson (Class of 1840), to help him write his book. The Mandeville Gallery seemed a logical place to present this historical exhibition, with so many local connections and so much rich material for students of American Studies, History, Political Science, Sociology, Literature, and Music.

Conceived as a visual retelling of Solomon's narrative, the exhibition used the extant documentation, photographs, prints, letters, advertisements, and objects, as well as contemporary images of places described by Northup. With the help of numerous Union College faculty and students, as well as regional scholars, historians, and archivists, the visual material was compiled and organized to tell the story. The exhibition opened in January 1999, and received thousands of visitors. It traveled subsequently to numerous venues throughout the upstate New York area and beyond. In addition, extensive programming, as well as a companion exhibition of contemporary art, helped illuminate links between literature, music, history, and sociology, to name a few. Lectures, panel discussions, concerts, readings, and symposia—involving scholars from around the country, including Sue Eakin and Joseph Logsdon— allowed a deeper exploration into such issues as the phenomenon of kidnapping free black citizens. The exhibition had the unexpectedly wonderful result of connecting the college with a group of Northup's descendants, who can trace their lineage back to his son, Alonzo. At the closing event for the exhibition, a family reunion of sorts took place, with over 30 members of the Northup family attending.

The exhibition awakened (or *reawakened*) considerable interest in the Northup narrative in the Saratoga area, and a number of the historians and scholars (some of whom worked on the exhibition) have continued to investigate the local details with energy and determination. David Fiske's research on Northup provides the foundation for our revelations about his life after slavery, and two unpublished manuscripts by Clifford Brown detail the kidnapping and rescue. The Union College exhibition also led to the creation of Solomon Northup Day in Saratoga Springs, which renewed regional interest in the story.

Much credit must be given to Eakin and Logsdon for their extensive research and the high quality of that research. The information they gathered for their book is exceptional and allows us to focus this volume on what occurred before and after Northup's period of enslavement. Furthermore, they were both very supportive of the exhibition project, contributing content to the show and participating in the programming with lectures and panel discussions. Sadly, neither is alive today to see the continued interest in Northup's story and the current wave of scholarly and popular interest.

The kidnapping of free blacks and their sale into slavery was a practice far more extensive than most people today realize. The fear of being kidnapped was one of the harsh realities of free black life in every part of the United States from the late 18th century until the Civil War. As Northup's story illustrates, northerners as well as southerners participated in this grim, but often highly profitable business. Most of the men, women and children who were abducted into slavery were never heard from again. As Northup himself stated, "I doubt not hundreds have been as unfortunate as myself; that hundreds of free citizens have been kidnapped and sold into slavery, and are at this moment wearing out their lives on plantations in Texas and Louisiana." It is indeed an incredible thing that we have Northup's narrative to help shed light on this aspect of the history of slavery and to give us such a vivid and complete picture of how such a thing came to pass. *Twelve Years a Slave* engages our imaginations and our curiosity; its compelling and harrowing events stir us to continue to dig further into the story and uncover more details about the people connected to these events, in an attempt both to answer the remaining mysteries surrounding Northup and to try to understand further the larger questions and issues surrounding this chapter in American history.

A great many individuals and organizations have assisted the authors in their research, and we cannot hope to name them all here. However, we would like to extend special appreciation to the following: Terry Adkins, Dick Andress, John Anson, Kenneth Aslakson, Peter Baldes, Erica Ball, Leonard Bellanca, Marva Belt, Mary Beth Betts, Terri Blasko, Brookside Museum, Marilyn Brownell (for the excellent maps that appear in this book), Karen Campola, Warren Cardwell, Richard Carver, Christopher Clarke-Hazlatt, Reverend Peter Coffin and Tanya Brice Coffin, Tom Colarco, Bruce Connolly, Dennis Darius, Katie De Groot, Heather Buanno Dukes, Sue Eakin, Ellen Fladger, Fort Edward Historical Association, Carol Fortsch, Heath Fradkoff, William Furgeson, David Gerhan, Amy Godine, Ron Grant, Robert Gullo, Eileen Hannay, Historic New Orleans Collection, The Historical Society of Washington, D.C., Kim Hoffend, Elizabeth Holahan, Field Horne, Mary Huth, Shirley Iverson, Lea Kemp, Harvey Kimball, Lauren Krizner, Brad Lewis, Library of Congress research staff, Joseph Logsdon, Nancy Martin, Tony Mathison, Paul McCarty, Khayree Miles, A. T. Miller, Michael Millman, Renee Moore, Mystic Seaport Museum, New York City Public Library research staff, New York Historical Society, New York State Archives, New York

State Library research staff, Charles Northup, Don Northup and Lois Merkley, Donna Northup, Howard Northup, John Northup, Warren Northup, Office of Historic Alexandria, Ford Peatross, William Poole, Radcliffe Maritime Museum, Wendyanne Ramroop, Gail Redmann, Rhode Island Historical Society, Ruth Rosenburg-Naparsteck, Vicky Rushbert, Carol Linzy Adams Sally, Saratoga County Clerk's Office, Saratoga County Historian's Office, Saratoga Room of the Saratoga Springs Public Library, Saratoga Springs Historical Society, Akin Sawyerr, Caroline Seligman, Wendy Shadwell, Ellen Sherman, Fred Shroyer, Alan Singer, Victor Snythe, Patrick Sorsby, Christina Sorum, Special Collections of Union College's Schaffer Library, Jean Stamm, Geoffrey Stein, Summer Research students of Union College, Sonia Taub, Kay Tomasi, Stephen Tyson, UNITAS of Union College, Carolyn Vacca, Warren County (NY) Records Center, Margaret Washington, Washington County (NY) Historical Society, Donna Wells, and Whitehall Historical Society.

Authors' note: Through the years, Northup's name has often been misspelled. In quotes used in this work, we have used the spellings used in the original materials.

Our book begins with an overview of Northup's kidnapping, enslavement, and rescue. Subsequent chapters provide details of his life prior to being kidnapped; his abduction, enslavement and eventual rescue; and his activities after his return. The narrative in Chapter 1 is based faithfully on Northup's own account in *Twelve Years a Slave*. He presented it in the first person; we present it in the third person. We have tried in places to capture the drama of the original, but there can be no substitute for Northup's own voice in *Twelve Years a Slave*.

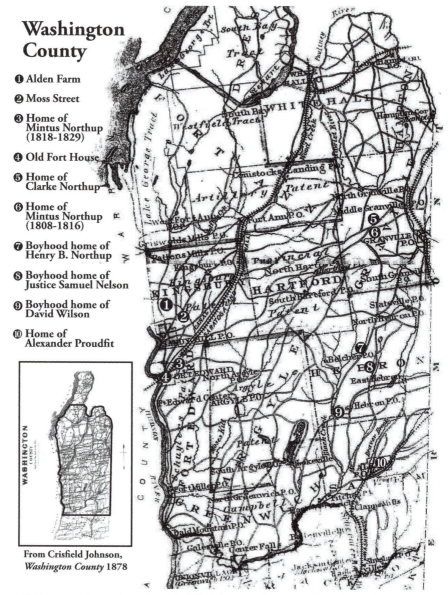

Washington County

❶ Alden Farm

❷ Moss Street

❸ Home of
Mintus Northup
(1818-1829)

❹ Old Fort House

❺ Home of
Clarke Northup

❻ Home of
Mintus Northup
(1808-1816)

❼ Boyhood home of
Henry B. Northup

❽ Boyhood home of
Justice Samuel Nelson

❾ Boyhood home of
David Wilson

❿ Home of
Alexander Proudfit

From Crisfield Johnson,
Washington County 1878

1. This map shows locations in Washington County, NY, where the Northups lived and worked. (Base map from Crisfield Johnson's *History of Washington Co., New York*, published by Everts & Ensign in 1878. Adapted by Marilyn Brownell.)

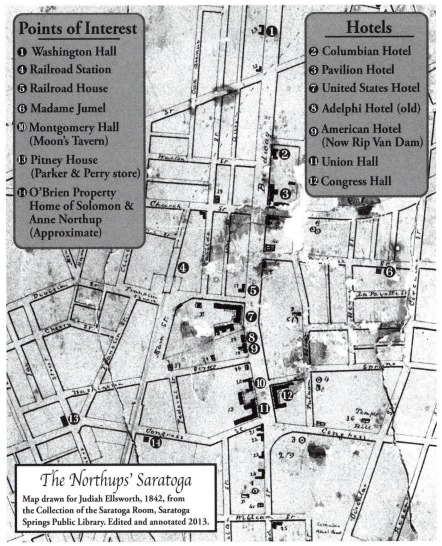

Points of Interest

❶ Washington Hall
❹ Railroad Station
❺ Railroad House
❻ Madame Jumel
❿ Montgomery Hall
   (Moon's Tavern)
⓭ Pitney House
   (Parker & Perry store)
⓮ O'Brien Property
   Home of Solomon &
   Anne Northup
   (Approximate)

Hotels

❷ Columbian Hotel
❸ Pavilion Hotel
❼ United States Hotel
❽ Adelphi Hotel (old)
❾ American Hotel
   (Now Rip Van Dam)
⓫ Union Hall
⓬ Congress Hall

The Northups' Saratoga

Map drawn for Judiah Ellsworth, 1842, from
the Collection of the Saratoga Room, Saratoga
Springs Public Library. Edited and annotated 2013.

2. Map of Saratoga Springs, New York, showing places that were part of the lives of Solomon and Anne Northup. (Base map from the one "Drawn for Judiah Ellsworth, 1842." Courtesy of the Saratoga Room, Saratoga Springs Public Library. Adapted by Marilyn Brownell.)

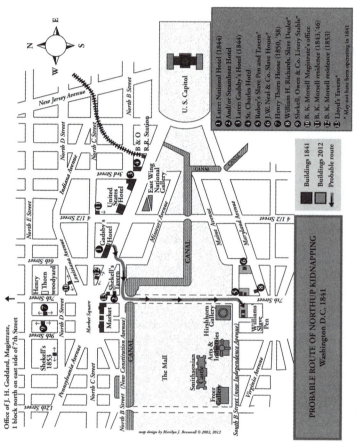

3.1. This map of a portion of Washington, D.C., shows the likely route of Northup's kidnappers, when they took him from Gadsby's Hotel to Williams' Slave Pen. (Marilyn Brownell)

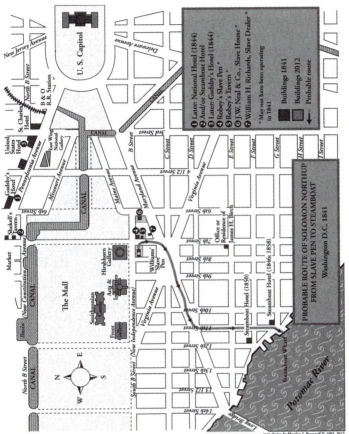

3.2. This map shows the route used to take slaves from Williams' Slave Pen to the wharf on the Potomac River. (Marilyn Brownell)

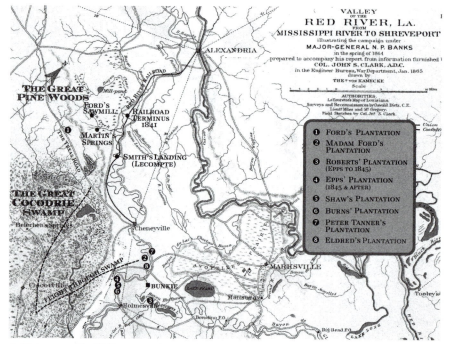

4. This post-Civil War map shows the area in Louisiana where Northup was held in slavery, and identifies many locations mentioned in Northup's book. (Base map courtesy of David Rumsey Map Collection, www.davidrumsey.com. Adapted by Marilyn Brownell.)

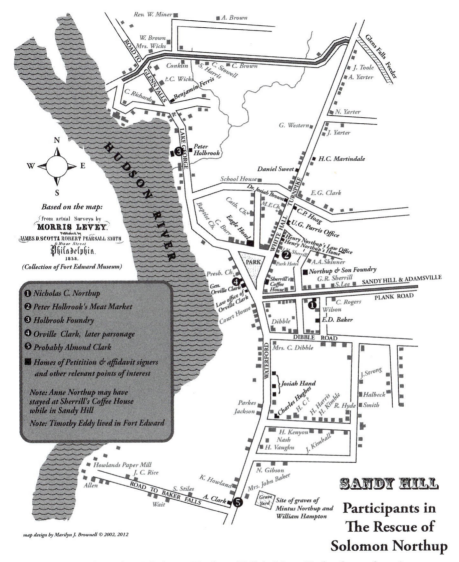

Rev. W. Miner · A. Brown

ROAD TO GLENN FALLS

W. Brown
Mrs. Wicks

Conklin · C. Stowell · C. Brown

?.C. Wicks · S. Harris

C. Richards · Benjamin Ferris

LAKE GEORGE

Glens Falls Feeder

J. Toole
A. Yarter

N. Yarter

G. Western · J. Yarter

H.C. Martindale

❺

Peter
Holbrook

Daniel Sweet

School House

Dr. Josiah Brown

Cath. Ch.

M.E. Ch.

E.G. Clark

C.P. Hoag

U.G. Parris Office

Baptist Ch.

C. Burr

Eagle Hotel

WHITE HALL

TURNPIKE

Henry Northup's Law Office
Henry Northup's Home

❷ Sherrill

A.A. Skinner

PARK

Park Hotel

HUDSON RIVER

N
W · E
S

Based on the map:

from actual Surveys by
MORRIS LEVEY.
Published by
JAMES D. SCOTT & ROBERT PEARSALL SMITH
6 Minor Street
Philadelphia.
1853.
(Collection of Fort Edward Museum)

❶ *Nicholas C. Northup*
❷ *Peter Holbrook's Meat Market*
❸ *Holbrook Foundry*
❹ *Orville Clark, later parsonage*
❺ *Probably Almond Clark*

■ *Homes of Petitition & affidavit signers
   and other relevant points of interest*

*Note: Anne Northup may have
stayed at Sherrill's Coffee House
while in Sandy Hill*

Note: Timothy Eddy lived in Fort Edward

Presb. Ch.

Gen.
Orville Clark **❹**

Law office of
Orville Clark

Court House

Northup & Son Foundry
G.R. Sherrill
S. Lee

SANDY HILL & ADAMSVILLE

PLANK ROAD

Sherrill's
Coffee
House

❶
Wilson

C. Rogers

E.D. Baker

Dibble

DIBBLE   ROAD

WATERFORD

Mrs. C. Dibble

Josiah Hand

Charles Hughes

H. C.?

H. Harris
H. Kimble

R. Hyde

J. Strong

Halbeck

Smith

Parkes
Jackson

H. Kenyon
Nash

H. Vaughn

J. Kimball

N. Gibson

Mrs. John Baker

Howlands Paper Mill
J. C. Rice

Allen

ROAD TO BAKER FALLS

Wait

S. Stiles

K. Howland

A. Clark

❺

Grave
Yard

Site of graves of
Mintus Northup and
William Hampton

map design by Marilyn J. Brownell © 2002, 2012

SANDY HILL

Participants in
The Rescue of
Solomon Northup

5. This map of Sandy Hill (now Hudson Falls), New York, shows locations connected with the Northups, and also the residences of individuals who assisted with Solomon's rescue. (Base map from a map by Morris Levey, published by James D. Scott and Robert Pearsall Smith in 1853. Adapted by Marilyn Brownell.)

1

Twelve Years a Slave: An Overview

He awoke in darkness and in chains. The severe headache of last night had subsided, but wasn't completely gone, and he still felt faint and weak. Uncomprehending, dazed, he tried to collect his thoughts and survey his surroundings in the gloom from the rough bench on which he was now sitting up. Where was he? Why was he here? Was this still part of his nightmare or was it real, some colossal misunderstanding, some terrible mistake? What was happening? He was handcuffed and his ankles fettered. He was attached to a ring in the floor. His money and papers were gone from his pockets. Someone had taken his coat and hat. He yelled, but the sound of his own voice seemed strange. Aside from this, the only noise was the clink of his chains.[1]

Where were Brown and Hamilton? Why had they let this happen to him? They must not know that he was there. Surely they were looking for him. They would get him out. They understood the city and its ways. They would rescue him. His thoughts began to focus. He was clearly in a cell. He had committed no crime. There was no reason to hold him. But someone had put him there. Why? There must be a reason. What were the possibilities? Slowly, awareness began to emerge from incomprehension. Slowly, the recollections and the uneasiness and the vague doubts began to materialize and focus. Could he have been kidnapped?

He had been warned. He knew about the practice. He even knew that it was not uncommon. Free blacks, American citizens like him, would fetch a good price on the open market if they could be abducted, cowed, chained, and transported to the slave states—as much as a thousand dollars. This was done fairly frequently, especially in southern Pennsylvania, or along the Ohio River, regions close to slave territory. There were vigilante societies in the major cities of the north to warn and protect free blacks subject to such depredation, but he was from Saratoga, far from slave territory. Kidnapping was certainly not common there. It seemed remote. But he had indeed been warned. He was told that if he went south it could happen to him. He had even been warned about Hamilton and Brown. But the warnings had not rung true. After all, they had been so considerate, so accommodating, so generous to him and he had come to trust them during the week they'd spent together on the trip to Washington, D.C. But where were they now? Surely they were looking for him. As his mind began to focus more clearly, however, the doubts began to gather and focus again: could they have done this to him?

He had met the two men about a week ago on a street in Saratoga Springs, New York. They told him their names were Abram Hamilton and Merrill Brown. They worked for a circus, or so they had said. The circus was in Washington and they had taken a break from their duties to travel to New York, paying their way by giving nightly entertainments, and they needed someone to play music. They had heard that he was a violinist, a fiddler, and was well known in Saratoga and nearby parts. Would he go with them to New York City? They'd offered him good wages. He could easily do the job. It was the slack season in that well-known resort—he could use the cash. His wife was away, his children taken care of, and he would be home soon.

So he had agreed. He would accompany them to New York and play at their performances. But after reaching New York, they had wanted him to continue on. They were headed to that circus in Washington; would he come along? It would only add a few days to his trip. They talked a good line. They offered him even better wages. He had traveled a bit himself up north, to Canada, and enjoyed it. He had never been to Washington. It appealed to his sense of adventure as well as to his pocketbook. And so he said yes again. Before leaving New York, they had considerately taken him to get papers certifying his status as a free person. Then they conducted him south. Arriving at Washington, the three of them stayed at its leading hotel (although he himself had to sleep in the humble accommodations reserved for blacks). They paid him a generous sum that evening for his time to date and he had gone to bed with a pocket filled with money.

The next day they strolled around the capital city witnessing the solemn ceremonies accompanying the funeral of President William Henry Harrison. Afterward they tavern-hopped. And then it all began to happen. Not long after a drink, the headache started. He began to feel ill. Back at the hotel, the sight of food made him nauseous. Brown and Hamilton commiserated with him, suggested he go to bed, and predicted he'd feel better in the morning. But things got worse during the night. He could not sleep. In total darkness, he groped his way to the kitchen for some water, then slowly struggled back to his room. The pain was intense. The headache became unbearable, stressing him to the edge of madness. In the agony, awareness was blunted, and consciousness receded. At some point during his ordeal, deep into the night, he became dimly aware that men had entered his room. Mention was made of a physician, and they maneuvered him, compliant, out into the night. And then the night had closed in on him.

Sitting now in the cell, with these recollections forming in his mind, he was seized momentarily with a sense of betrayal, and then of hopelessness and despair and then a growing, persisting sense of injustice. How could they have done this to him? How could this have happened? How could he have let it happen? How could he, a free citizen of New York, one who'd grown up there, whose parents had also been free citizens, a recognized person in the community with a wife and family and a person who had wronged no one, nor violated any law—how could he be treated this way? If things were as they seemed, where was the justice? The humanity?

Day was dawning. He could not see the daylight but he heard the sounds: the distant crowing of a cock, carriages rumbling on the pavement, the sounds outside the building of a city waking up and moving into another day. Suddenly there were footsteps overhead, followed a few minutes later by the turning of a key in the lock. Two men entered the cell. One looked sinister and repulsive. This man was clearly in charge; the other was obviously a lackey. As he later found out, the first was James H. Birch,[2] a leading Washington slave trader and the second was Ebenezer Radburn, the keeper of the slave pen.[3]

"Well, my boy, how do you feel now?"
"I am sick. Why am I here?" he demanded.
"I bought you. You are my slave. And I am sending you to New Orleans."
"I am not a slave. I am a free man. My name is Solomon Northup."

He was alert enough by now to speak loudly and boldly. "Solomon Northup," he repeated. "I am a free citizen of New York. I have a wife and family. Please remove these chains! I've done nothing wrong. Why this treatment? Who sent me here? Those villains will pay for it! Take off these chains!"

The words made no impression on Birch, who responded with threats, which quickly escalated into violence. Birch used whips and paddles until it was pointless for him, fettered as he was, to continue defiance. He fell silent. The beatings continued until he was nearly senseless again. And then once more he was alone and in darkness, sore and aching. He was kept in solitary confinement for several days, although at some point they removed the fetters and opened a small, high window. They gave him a piece of shriveled fried pork, a slice of bread and a cup of water twice a day. It was made clear to him that the whippings would continue if he maintained his claim to freedom. He was even threatened with death if he did so. Under full physical control, he had no options. He was eventually let out of the cell and allowed to mingle with the other slaves in the yard of what he soon learned was Williams' Slave Pen, a notorious Washington institution. All he could do was wait passively and listen to the stories of the other slaves.

After two weeks or more in captivity, he was awakened in the middle of the night, ordered to roll up his blanket, and told to prepare to leave. He had no realistic choice. Besides, he could not easily escape from where he was, so perhaps his chances might be better somewhere else. He did what he was told. It was the end of April 1841. He was about to begin an extraordinary journey lasting nearly 12 years.

* * * * * *

There are numerous slave narratives, including most famously that of Frederick Douglass. There are many scholarly and literary accounts that describe the "peculiar institution." But the importance of Solomon Northup's story is that it comes from the perspective of a person who grew up free and therefore had the assumptions and values of a free society before he entered slavery. Northup had also developed many skills in a technologically advanced region of the country. He was the legatee of several cultures, including that of antebellum upstate New York, part of the New England diaspora, with its emphasis on shrewdness, self-sufficiency, innovation, and what Northup calls "industry." From this perspective Northup confronted each day's challenges, and his perspective was bound to differ, if only in nuanced ways, from that of someone raised in a culture of subservience.

Not only a narrative about slavery and the rural culture of the antebellum South, Northup's account is a story about survival and the triumph of the human spirit over great adversity: despite all he endured, he never lost his sense of self, his awareness of who he was, the injustice of his situation, and his resolve to escape. Moreover, though he was a shrewd observer of slavery and southern institutions, he was also a participant and a victim, and he became emotionally attached to other victims, feeling their suffering, sensing what aspirations their circumstances allowed, sharing their hopes and fears. Despite this, he never lost perspective and his ability to observe and evaluate. With the outlook of one whose soul is free, he judged his fellow participants in the drama, both black and white, and showed how they, too, were conditioned by the institution of slavery.

He eventually succeeded in getting a letter home that led to his rescue. He returned north and produced a book about his life, assisted by David Wilson, a local author from the county where he had grown up. Although it will never be possible to disentangle the precise contributions of each to the book, it is very clear that it is Northup's tale, not that of his editor. Told from Northup's perspective, the narrative line is his. His factual assertions check out. The value judgments about people and institutions are Northup's. Most of all, it is his literalism that structures and styles the tale. Wilson states in his introduction to *Twelve Years* that Northup "carefully perused the manuscript, dictating an alteration wherever the most trivial inaccuracy has appeared."[4] This attention to detail regarding people, places, processes, and events makes the story ring true, and creates a work of timeless value.

* * * * * *

JOURNEY SOUTH

Upon leaving the slave pen, Northup and four other slaves under Birch's control were marched through the streets of Washington to the Potomac, and loaded onto a steamboat. Accompanied by Birch, the group was carried to a river landing, traveled by coach to Fredericksburg, and then by train to Richmond, where they were lodged overnight in another slave pen. The following day, Birch put them on a two-masted brig, the *Orleans*, which promptly sailed for Louisiana. Although regaining freedom was constantly on his mind and he'd largely recovered physically from the beatings, Northup had seen no chance during this trip to escape from the experienced slave dealer.

But escape was still very much his central focus. On board, he met two other free blacks who had been kidnapped. The trio, furious at the injustice of their situation and desperate from the grim prospects they faced, concocted a plan to free their fellow captives (who were not kept in very secure conditions), enlist them to help seize control of the ship, and then sail it to New York. Murdering the officers (following the *Amistad* model) was considered an option. The plan evaporated when one of the conspirators fell ill and died of smallpox, leaving Northup and his remaining partner with too small a margin of safety to proceed with a reasonable chance of success.

As the ship neared New Orleans, Northup struck up an acquaintance with an English crew member, who agreed to mail a letter for him upon reaching port. Northup used this opportunity to write a brief account of his circumstances to a life-long acquaintance, attorney Henry B. Northup.[5]

Arriving at New Orleans in late May 1841, Solomon was taken to a slave pen run by Theophilus Freeman, Birch's partner. His name had already been changed to "Platt" to hide his identity, and he was to be known by this name for the next 12 years. Hundreds of miles from home, still under physical control, now subject to further control under the laws of a slave state, and deprived of any means of proving his free status, Northup fell into despair. He also became extremely sick. He had contracted smallpox from the man who died en route, and nearly succumbed to it. For nearly a month, he remained in New Orleans, either in the slave pen or the hospital. Escape was still on his mind, despite increasingly slim chances: if he were sold to someone from New Orleans, maybe he could eventually slip onto a ship headed north, but even this hope was dashed. Toward the end of June, he was sold to William Prince Ford of Rapides Parish in central Louisiana.

LIFE AS A SLAVE

Ford and his newly purchased slaves steamed up the Mississippi and then up the Red River to Alexandria. There they debarked, traveled 12 miles by train, and then walked 9 or 10 miles to Ford's plantation. Surrounded by forests and swamps, and by a society replete with safeguards against the escape of slaves, Northup was in a network of geographic and social restraints making flight nearly impossible. The letter he'd written brought no rescuer. With no realistic chance of immediate escape, all he could do was try to survive.

Ford, according to Northup, was a decent human being. He owned slaves and had no moral qualms about it, but he treated his slaves humanely. Northup saw evidence of this on the day of his own sale when Ford had offered (unsuccessfully) to buy the daughter of a slave he'd purchased so mother and daughter could stay together. Northup quickly sensed that if he worked hard, Ford would treat him well, and so he turned to his tasks.

Ford, at the time a well-to-do plantation owner and operator, had recently built a saw mill a few miles from his home. Northup was sent there. He spent the summer piling lumber and chopping logs. He had been a woodsman, among other occupations, in New York: he could stack a crib and handle an axe. Professionally, he felt right at home. His work became a momentary escape, and he plunged right into it, performing tasks well, exceeding expectations, and earning recognition. Ford noticed. By summer's end, the mill had a large quantity of lumber to transport to market about six miles away. This was an expensive proposition by wagon, and Northup suggested Ford raft the lumber downstream to its destination, which could be done quickly and cheaply. Since it had never been tried in this location, there was some risk. Conditions here were different, but Northup had rafted lumber on the Champlain Canal and on the lake itself, and he felt confident after inspecting the route. Overriding the qualms of his superintendent, Ford let Northup try. The venture was a success, and Ford gave him charge of the lumber shipping from then on. He became an instant celebrity.

Shortly thereafter, Ford's wife asked her husband to buy a loom for weaving cloth for winter garments. When Ford said he didn't know where one could be bought, Northup offered that he was a "jack of all trades," and suggested building one. This project was also a success, and over the winter he built several more. Shifting gears, he applied his carpentry skills to the efficient planing and chiseling of tongue-and-groove boards to refurbish the house. These successes were little victories for Northup, and even if they did not constitute fighting back, they were something of a substitute. He'd found a way to carve out a role for himself in this new and heavily constrained environment. In some limited way, he could achieve success and recognition. He still had his sense of self. Opportunity of escape was minimal for the time-being, but at least he could survive and maintain some self-respect.

SOLD TO ANOTHER MASTER

Then disaster struck. Ford, in his generosity, had signed a promissory note for his brother. The note came due, the brother could not pay, Ford had to make good, and was forced to liquidate some of his assets, including Northup. Without much warning, he became the property of John M. Tibaut (referred to by Northup as Tibeats), a carpenter who had worked for Ford and to whom he owed money.[6] Northup was worth more than the debt, and Ford retained a chattel mortgage for the difference. Ford probably felt he was doing Northup a favor by selling him to a carpenter instead of to an owner who would use him in the fields. He was, however, badly mistaken.

Tibaut was a narrow-minded, quick-tempered, and spiteful man. With no home, he drifted from one plantation to another as jobs opened up, struggling on the edge of financial ruin. He had few possessions besides Northup. Moreover, he had no standing in the community and was universally disliked.[7] Perhaps most importantly, he was not particularly smart—less well trained and less clever than Northup. This was an explosive mixture: a slave with self-esteem who was smart, energetic, and resourceful (and with a good reputation in the area), now owned by a white man who was the opposite in all respects and who knew it. Northup respected Ford; he did not respect Tibaut. Ford appreciated Northup; Tibaut resented him and was jealous.

The clash was not long in coming. They were building a weaving house for Ford on his wife's plantation—perhaps to hold one of the looms Northup had made. From the start, Tibaut had taken out his frustrations on Northup with a constant flow of nasty criticism. He had never complimented him for anything. On this occasion, he ordered Northup to obtain some nails from Ford's overseer, "a Mr. Chapin" (whose actual name was Chafin),[8] and use them to attach clapboards to the building. This Northup did early the next morning. When Tibaut arrived, he was in a foul mood, complained about the clapboards, yelled about the length of the nails Northup had obtained, and flew into a rage when Northup tried to explain that he had only been doing what Tibaut had asked. The explanations did not mollify Tibaut—indeed they angered him, and he rushed for the whip.

Northup had not been whipped since leaving New Orleans the previous year. His blood rose. No doubt all his frustrations surged in memory, boiled to the surface, and focused his emotions on Tibaut. Fear turned to anger. When Tibaut ordered him to strip, Northup looked him in the eye and refused, point blank.

THE FIRST FIGHT

Furious at the defiance, Tibaut, lash in hand, grabbed Northup. The response was an explosion. Northup fought back, quickly tripping Tibaut and hurling him to the ground. Now Northup had the upper hand. Enraged, he seized the whip and thrashed Tibaut, ending with a kick that sent him rolling. This must have given Northup immense satisfaction. It seemed but primitive justice, requiting a year's frustration at his enslavement and his treatment. But what he had done was a serious, perhaps capital crime, and as his passion cooled he realized the dangers he faced.

The yells and screams rapidly brought an audience. Chafin came running. Grasping the situation, he sided with Northup, whom he knew well, further infuriating Tibaut. Humiliated, Tibaut swore he would have satisfaction and that things were not over yet. After a brief conversation with Chafin, Tibaut departed the scene.

Chafin, much agitated, told Northup in no uncertain terms to remain where he was and not to leave. He predicted trouble, and it was not long before trouble came. Tibaut returned with two overseers from nearby plantations, and the three of them grabbed Northup, tied him up, put a rope around his neck, and dragged him to a nearby tree. Chafin, about to witness a lynching, hesitated, then made up his mind. He stepped back into the house, and emerged with a gun in each hand. "Whoever moves that slave another foot from where he stands is a dead man . . . he does not deserve this treatment. . . . In the absence of William Ford, I am master here. . . . My duty is to protect his interests. . . . Ford holds a mortgage on Platt. If you hang him, he loses his debt."[9]

The three slunk away. Chafin, not convinced the matter was over, sent for Ford. He came as fast as he could, released Northup, commiserated with him, and set about trying to solve the problem. Presently Tibaut returned; he and Ford negotiated. Northup, under the protection of Chafin, continued working on the weaving house for a few days until it was finished, and then Tibaut hired him out to Peter Tanner, owner of a large plantation, where he'd work under another carpenter. By now, the story had spread across the area that "Platt," the slave already known for rafting the lumber down the bayou, had now whipped his master. Tanner, although he threatened Northup with perdition for disobedience, actually seemed highly amused by the whole story of Tibaut's whipping. Northup worked productively for Tanner about a month. But then he returned to working with Tibaut, back on Mrs. Ford's plantation. Things proceeded without incident for a short while, but when Chafin left the premises for a day's absence, Tibaut's temper exploded once more.

THE SECOND FIGHT

Northup was planing some wood, when Tibaut told him he was not shaving deep enough. Northup shaved deeper, whereupon Tibaut yelled that Northup had now planed it *too* deep. Confused, Northup stopped work, plane in hand, waiting for Tibaut to calm down. This infuriated Tibaut even more. Swearing at the top of his lungs, he seized a hatchet and charged Northup. Before he could land a blow, however, Northup sprang at him, grabbing the hatchet by the handle and Tibaut by the throat. He wrestled the hatchet from Tibaut, cast it beyond his reach, and took him to the ground. Tibaut broke free, seized a nearby stake, and once more attempted to attack Northup. Again Northup leapt at him, brought him to the ground, grabbed the stake, and threw it beyond reach. Tibaut again wriggled free and leaping up, rushed to grab a nearby broadaxe, but this was under a heavy plank and before he could free it, Northup was on him again, pinning him onto the plank to immobilize arm and axe. They stayed deadlocked—Northup on top and Tibaut pinned underneath, his hand still on the axe. The stalemate was broken when Northup seized Tibaut by the throat and choked him violently. Tibaut turned purple in the face, relaxed his grip on the axe, and went limp.

Northup could easily have killed him and nearly did. But his survival instinct intervened. Something inside reminded him: to kill Tibaut was to die himself. Yet to let him live meant Tibaut would surely kill *him*. He paused, but there was no time to debate the point: Northup released Tibaut, and fled.

FLIGHT

By the time Tibaut recovered his senses, Northup was gone, running as fast as he could into the woods that soon gave way to bayous and then to swamp. As his adrenalin surged back, Tibaut with renewed rage rushed to a neighbor's plantation, reappearing with a posse and a pack of dogs. In full bay and with fresh scent they pursued Northup into the woods and then the swamp. But, unlike many slaves, Northup could swim. With a good head start, he crossed the small streams on foot, then swam down a larger one into and across a small lake, breaking the trail of scent and evading his pursuers, although they came close enough that he heard the dogs and the shouts of the men. But the deeper he went, the more confused they became, and after about four hours they abandoned the chase.

Now Northup was in the middle of the Great Cocodrie Swamp. Fearing water moccasins, Northup with care—and a stick—could avoid *them*, but a bigger problem was a two-legged species. What was he to do? He proceeded south, away from the plantation, throughout the afternoon and into the night until the dangers of travel in the darkness convinced him to halt. Fear had driven him in flight, but now, as reason and judgment reasserted themselves, he paused and considered his situation. He couldn't stay in the swamp very long as a fugitive. He certainly could not return to where he came from, even if Chafin was back—there were limits to Chafin's ability to help, because Tibaut, by law, owned Northup. And so he decided to seek aid from the one man who had an actual say in the matter and whom he trusted: Ford. He turned around and proceeded toward Ford's summer home. The moon and the stars of the clear night gave him his compass.

Next morning, he emerged from the swamp onto drier ground. The swamp vegetation gave way to brush and then to pine, and Northup, soaking wet, clothes torn and tattered, reached the higher ground of the Great Pine Woods. He made his way through it, traveling northwest, now using the sun for a guide. At a clearing he spotted two men. With no pass, he could legally be overpowered and detained. Furthermore, he was quite a sight. Boldly, he strode up to the person in charge and demanded, "Where does William Ford live? Which is the way to his place?" The direction was pointed out to him. He walked on purposefully, reaching Ford's without further incident. Appalled by Northup's story, Ford gave him shelter, food, and the opportunity to rest and recover. Ford informed Tibaut that he either had to sell Northup, lease him out, or face action by Ford to repossess him. The following day, Randal Eldred, owner of a nearby plantation, appeared, saying he had leased Northup from Tibaut, and that they were to proceed to the "Big Cane Break," some 30 miles south. And so Northup embarked on another adventure.

THE BIG CANE BREAK

The Big Cane Break was a virgin forest of large spreading oak, bay, sycamore, and cypress trees, with a dense thicket of wild cane growing in between. The forest and the cane were to be cleared to make way for a plantation. Eldred and a carpenter named Meyers, for whom Northup had worked at Tanner's, accompanied them. Northup and another slave chopped up logs and built two cabins, one for themselves, the other for Eldred and Meyers. This done, they proceeded to the main tasks: felling trees, cutting them up, and hacking down the cane to clear the land. They were joined by a crew of female slaves who wielded axes as effectively as the men. After a month, Eldred told Northup he had done a good job and offered him a few days off so he could return to Ford's plantation for a visit. Getting a pass from a reluctant Tibaut (who had suddenly appeared, probably to collect the money from the lease of his slave), Northup departed for Ford's. After a few days there, he started back to the Cane Break, but was met on the way by Tibaut, who announced he had sold him to Edwin Epps. It was April 9, 1843. Northup had been in captivity two years, almost to the day.

SERVING EDWIN EPPS

His value had increased. Whereas Ford had paid $900 for him in New Orleans, Epps paid Tibaut $1500, a healthy return on Ford's investment. Payment was in cash, so Epps would own him outright. With Ford's chattel mortgage retired, his first master no longer had a role in Northup's fate. Northup was now again fully on his own.

Under Ford, Northup had worked primarily at the sawmill; under Tibaut, as a carpenter. With Epps, he was to work primarily as a plantation slave in the fields and in support of operations there. Epps at the time lived on Bayou Huffpower, where he leased a cotton plantation from his wife's uncle. A former overseer, Epps had about nine slaves, including Northup. He was a hard, but efficient, taskmaster who drove his slaves severely. He was cunning and vindictive. He was quick to resort to the lash, and life with him was a constant challenge. He was also very insecure, and by no means near the top of the social hierarchy. He drank to excess. He forced his affections on Patsey, one of his slaves, and made her life miserable. Unlike Tibaut, however, he owned property, was active in community affairs, had a family, and survived economically, carving out a reasonable life despite many setbacks.

Arriving in April 1843, Northup was ordered to make an axe helve, which he did, using a standard northern curved design, which Epps apparently had never seen before and was much interested in when its advantages were explained. Being spring, the corn needed cultivating and the cotton needed "scraping." Northup was initially set hoeing corn, a task familiar to him from working on farms in New York. He was then assigned to work with other slaves at scraping cotton, a multi-stage process, using mule-drawn plows and hand-wielded hoes to remove the weeds and grass between the young plants, shape the ground along the rows, and cull the weaker sprouts. Northup worked a few months at these occupations, no doubt demonstrating a high level of proficiency, before becoming very sick, requiring the attention of a physician, belatedly and reluctantly summoned by Epps. When Northup was recovering, he was set to work picking cotton, a task totally new to him, and at which he proved to be quite clumsy. He was whipped to no effect until Epps finally concluded that he was not suited for this job. He had resisted whippings by Tibaut. Now he submitted to them, having no choice in this larger, more organized operation.

Epps reassigned him to cutting and hauling wood, drawing cotton from the field, and other routines supporting the plantation's work. He had presumably demonstrated talent in most agricultural tasks (other than picking cotton) and he was therefore a valuable slave, even on a cotton plantation. Epps grudgingly recognized Northup's unusual talents, and eventually he was made a driver, a person in charge of other slaves when they performed organized tasks like planting, hoeing, scraping, and harvesting.

For two years, Northup participated in the routines of plantation life on Bayou Huffpower, working in the fields and laboring with others to provide food for the plantation—growing vegetables and rounding up hogs and cattle from the nearby swamps where they "pastured." He also played music. Epps, at the urging of his wife, bought Northup a fiddle. He played frequently for the family and often at dances elsewhere. His circumstances were challenging and often repelling, but he coped, adapted, and survived.

In 1845, Epps bought a plantation on Bayou Boeuf about two miles south of Mrs. Ford's plantation where Northup had worked for Tibaut. The household moved there, and the cycle of planting, cultivating, and harvesting commenced again. However, 1845 was a very bad year for Epps: his cotton crop was destroyed by caterpillars, and there was no harvest. In September, having no immediate use for Northup and other slaves, Epps and several planters decided to take a drove of them south 140 miles to St. Mary's Parish, near the Gulf of Mexico, hoping to lease them out to sugar planters.

JOURNEY TO SOUTHERN LOUISIANA

That fall a large caravan set out with four owners and 147 slaves to make the journey south. Northup, given the job of quartermaster, took charge of the blankets and provisions. After an interesting, but often unpleasant, journey through many towns and over the Grand Coteau (a vast prairie of grassland in central Louisiana), they reached their destination where Northup was hired out to William Turner, owner of a large sugar plantation with its own sugar processing house. Initially, Turner put Northup to work doing repairs at the sugar house, but then he was sent into the fields where he quickly became proficient with a cane knife, holding his own with the best of the others. After a spell at this, he was transferred back to the sugar house and made a driver, supervising the slave labor force that moved the product through the plant and operated the machinery. He remained in St. Mary's Parish for four months, until January 1846.

It was the custom to pay slaves for their work on Sundays, and since the sugar harvest and processing continued seven days a week, Northup received $10 for his Sunday employment during the months he was there. He also played the violin at a large party on the way back, and the participants took up a collection that netted him another $17. These sums made him feel like a millionaire. The route home took him through Centerville on the Rio Teche, which was served by steamboats. Northup, ascertaining that one of the captains was a northerner, asked to be stowed away on his vessel and taken to free territory. The captain considered the request carefully, but finally refused, stating that it was too risky for him personally.

WITH EPPS AGAIN

Beginning his sixth year of slavery that spring, Northup entered once more the cycle of planting, cultivating, and harvesting to which he'd become accustomed. His savings from the trip south and his further earnings from playing the fiddle enabled him to improve his living conditions and, in a sense, settle in. The slaves on Bayou Boeuf did not receive generous rations, but were allowed to supplement them by hunting and fishing. This was not easy, however, since daytime was occupied by their labors. Hunting at night after an exhausting day was not an easy proposition. That summer, Northup had the idea of building a fish trap which would catch fish unattended. He designed and built one of his own invention, and from then on had a fairly steady supply of fish for himself and for companions.

That fall, Northup was hired out to a nearby sugar plantation, owned by a Mr. Hawkins, with a large sugar mill on its premises. He was employed as a lead cane cutter in the field and also worked in the mill. He probably also participated in the planting of sugar. He worked there during sugaring time for three successive years. Thus passed 1846–1848, with Northup working alternatively at Epps's cotton plantation and at Hawkins's sugar plantation. Fiddling engagements provided enjoyable respites from the hard routines of slave life. After 1848, he worked fairly steadily for Epps alone.

RENEWED HOPE OF ESCAPE

Throughout the years, Northup pursued efforts to escape as occasions arose. In 1849, after watching carefully for an opportunity, he managed to take a sheet of paper from a packet bought by Mrs. Epps. He made ink and a quill pen, and drafted a letter home. But slaves were not allowed to post letters without written permission from their masters. He needed someone to mail his letter, and hid it for a long time while awaiting an opportunity. A white man named Armsby came to the area, seeking work as an overseer. He was turned down by Epps and others, and ended up working in the fields, apparently a rarity for a white man. Northup approached him, felt him out, and finally offered to pay him to mail the letter. Armsby, however, told Epps instead, who then confronted Northup with Armsby's allegations. Northup was able to talk himself out of danger by convincing Epps that Armsby was lying. Immediately afterward he burned the letter and was back to square one. It was a full three years before another opportunity arose.

In June 1852, Epps began to build himself a new house. Among the carpenters hired for this job was Samuel Bass, originally from Canada, who had spent many years in Illinois and other northern states. Because Northup was a carpenter, he was taken out of the field and assigned to work with Bass on the house. Bass lived in Marksville, but stayed on the Bayou Boeuf while working on the job. He was well known along the Bayou as an eccentric, a harmless and generous character who held opinions contrary to those of the community, and who was fond of expressing them. His manner of expression, however, was inoffensive and even humorous, and arguments with him were regarded more as entertainment than as serious controversy. He was a good carpenter, a hard worker, and a reliable employee, so he was well-regarded and respected.

He loved arguing with Epps, and on more than one occasion Northup overheard their conversations about slavery, race, and the Constitution. Sizing up Bass as a person he might be able to trust, Northup decided to approach him and take the risk of sharing his own story. He asked Bass where he came from, and when Bass said he was from Canada, a place he assumed Northup had never heard of, Northup responded that he had been there, naming several Canadian towns he'd visited. Bass, impressed, asked how Northup had managed to visit Canada, and the story came out.

HELP FROM SAMUEL BASS

Bass was very sympathetic. He agreed to write to acquaintances of Northup's in Saratoga asking them to obtain papers attesting to Northup's free status and asking them to send those papers to Northup at nearby Marksville, where Bass could pick them up. In addition, Bass wrote directly to Custom House officials in New York City, asking them to send confirmation of Northup's free status. These letters were posted on August 15, 1852.

Bass estimated that it would take at least two weeks for the letters to reach Saratoga, two weeks for a reply to reach Marksville, plus some time in between for the correspondents to act. He expected nothing would be heard before six weeks had elapsed. In the meantime, he and Northup consulted secretly about how to proceed if free papers arrived from any of these sources.

Bass returned to Marksville in mid-September, but there were no answers to his letters. Then 6, 8, 10 weeks passed with no response. Severe disappointment came on the heels of what had been high hopes. It was now the first of November, work on the house was finished, and Bass was about to leave. He told Northup that he would return the day before Christmas, and if there were no developments, he would take a further step to secure Northup's freedom.

It was a long two months of anxious waiting. Northup's hopes had risen once again. What might Bass propose? Would he be disappointed again? Northup had all but given up on the letters. Perhaps they had been misdirected, the intended recipients were all dead, or none cared about his fate. He worried. He seemed distracted to his fellow slaves. The days passed.

On Christmas Eve 1852, Bass reappeared and spent the night with Epps in the new Great House. Early the following morning he secretly approached Northup. There had been no reply to the letters. Bass, however, was resolved to go to Saratoga himself. He had some carpentry jobs to complete first, which would take three or four months, but he expected to have substantial money when they were done. He promised to head north on Solomon's behalf in April. And so Northup entered the annual Christmas celebration with growing hopes once again that his days in slavery might eventually come to an end. In the meantime, he had to carry on. During the week between Christmas and New Year's Day he had several engagements to play at parties. These kept him busy and kept his mind off his uncertain, yet hopeful, circumstances. But reality soon set in again.

* * * * *

He'd overslept. It hadn't happened in years, but he was exhausted from all the merriment of the past week. He had been right in the middle of it. He and his fiddle. He'd really made it sing this year, and he had loved doing it, but some dances went on until dawn and he had played away all night with no sleep. He had felt the spirit of the dances themselves, the energy, the joy, the laughter, yes, the freedom. He'd felt all of this to the bottom of his soul, and it carried him from height to height, but now it was over. He was drained.

So this morning he just hadn't heard the horn. The sun wasn't up yet, so maybe if he hurried he could get to the field before Old Hog Jaw noticed. He rushed out of the cabin leaving his dinner and water gourd, but Epps was already out on the piazza surveying his domain. "This is a PRETTY TIME OF DAY to be getting up," he yelled.

He ignored the comment and continued running to the field. It was winter, but there was still cotton to gather, the fourth and final harvest. Despite the fact that he'd never been any good at picking cotton, he got his row up fast and drew even with his fellow slaves. But to no avail. Epps presently arrived with his lash. He ordered him to strip and gave him 15 stripes—a small count by Epps's standards, but enough to make his back sting. Epps asked him if he thought he could get up IN THE MORNING from now on. He yelled back that HE COULD. It was one hell of a way to start a new year.

The next day was Sunday, and depression set in again. Here he was, stuck where he had been for more than a decade, bored by the routines, dealing with the frustrations, angry at the injustices, and worried that nothing would change. Yes, Bass had promised to go to Saratoga on his behalf come spring, and he sounded sincere, but what if something happened in the meantime to upset his plans? April seemed a long time away. What if something happened to Bass? Would hopes be shattered again as they had been so many times before? Or what if Bass inadvertently spilled the beans? Would the secret be discovered? Would discovery leave him even worse off? So much had gone wrong in the past. Would more go wrong again? With a sore back and these melancholy thoughts, exhausted and emotionally drained, he spent a restless day brooding over his fate.

Monday morning he did not oversleep, but it was bitterly cold outside. He was up early and out in the field, trying to pick cotton with near-frozen fingers. The harvesting was not going very quickly. Epps arrived, observed this, and swore at his slaves, saying that nothing was getting done. When someone complained about the cold, Epps replied that he would take care of that—he knew how to WARM THEM. He would get his whip. Yes, he would warm them all right, they would be HOTTER THAN HELL by the time he was finished with them. He went back to the Great House to fetch it.

They turned back to the cotton. But no sooner had they done so than their attention was diverted by a carriage that wheeled up a couple hundred yards away, and they gazed at it curiously. Two white men emerged and walked toward the field, one at a distance behind the other. This was strange. Visitors never came at this time of day. The two walked purposefully as if on some specific business. What were they doing here? The first man headed right to them and the half dozen or so slaves stared at him as he approached. Solomon didn't know him, though he could identify every planter in the area. Who on earth was he? What was his business here?

Without revealing that he was actually the Sheriff of Avoyelles Parish, the man walked up to one of the slaves and asked, "Where's the boy they call Platt?"

"Thar he is master," the slave replied, gesturing to him and twitching off his hat. Now he was really puzzled, wondering what could be wanted of him by this total stranger.

"Your name is Platt, is it?"

"Yes, Master."

Pointing back to the companion, now standing only a few dozen feet behind him, the sheriff demanded, "Do you know that man?" He looked across the short distance between them and stared at the man. Memories flashed through his head and recognition came almost instantly. With exploding emotion, he exclaimed, "Henry B. Northup! Thank God, Thank God!"

It was January 3, 1853. Northup had been a slave 11 years, 8 months, and 26 days. Bass's letters to Saratoga had finally been answered.

2

Early Life

THE NORTHUPS

Solomon Northup and Henry B. Northup came from two different families that had long been interconnected. Solomon's father, Mintus, was a slave of Henry's great uncle, Captain Henry Northup, and as was customary, he was given the surname of the family he belonged to.

The American stories of both the black and white Northups, apparently, began in Rhode Island. Stephen Northup, the immigrant ancestor of the white Northups, arrived in 1643 with Roger Williams (who was then returning from England with the colony's first charter).[1] He lived first in Providence, and then moved to North Kingston. In 1699, his son Stephen built a house there that is still standing. Stephen's son, Henry, was the father of Immanuel Northup, a prosperous farmer with seven slaves at the time of the 1740 state census. One of Immanuel's sons was Henry who went to sea from Newport, became a captain, and was a Loyalist during the American Revolution. He owned Mintus, although how that came about is unknown.[2] After the Revolution, Captain Henry and other family members moved to upstate New York, but maintained close ties with relatives in Rhode Island.[3]

Mintus and Susanna Northup

Cemetery records indicate that Mintus was born in 1778.[4] Strong evidence shows he was still a slave when he came to New York with Captain Henry.[5] Although a Tory, Henry decided to remain an American, becoming a farmer in midlife. He followed several relatives to New York after 1790,[6] and settled in Hoosick Falls, where he owned several hundred acres of land at the time of his death, though it may not all have been cultivated.[7] Working on Henry's farm in these circumstances would have allowed Mintus to develop the skills to become a successful independent farmer when emancipated on September 1, 1798, by the terms of Henry's will.[8]

What did Mintus do immediately after being freed from slavery? It was fall, and agricultural employment prospects were numerous, but short-term. Possibly he remained in the Hoosick area, or went to Granville in Washington County to work on the farm of Henry's nephew, Clarke.[9] Mary Knowles, Clarke's wife, was a Quaker preacher, and Clarke may also have been a Quaker. Granville had a small but active group of Friends at that time.[10] Given his family's Quaker values, it is not surprising that Clarke would be receptive to employing an African American; he may have done so soon after Mintus's manumission. Mintus could have been in Granville for a few years.[11]

The date of Mintus's marriage is unknown. His wife's name was probably Susanna, but her family name is also unknown.[12] Solomon describes his mother as a "quadroon," or three-quarters white. She was probably not a slave of Captain Henry, since there is no record of his freeing her. She was free when she married and may always have been free.[13] Mintus might have known her from Rhode Island or he might have met her in New York.

Sojourn in the Adirondacks

Mintus moved to Essex County in the Adirondacks in 1804 or shortly thereafter. He was probably married before the move. He was certainly there before 1807 when Solomon was born. Moving there may have been an opportunity for him to exercise his newfound freedom. He and Susanna lived in a part of the town of Schroon (sometimes given as "Scaroon") that later became the town of Minerva.[14] According to Mabel Jones, a Minerva Town Historian, settlers—originally from Massachusetts and Rhode Island—came to the area in 1804 from Granville and Hartford in Washington County.[15] Given the Granville connection, Mintus and Susanna probably knew these settlers directly or through Clarke Northup. They may have accompanied them or followed them later The family remained there until 1808 or 1809. By 1810, they were back in Granville.

Life in the Minerva area was challenging. It was remote and isolated, separated from other parts of the county by high mountains, and connected to them only by "imperfect communication."[16] The pioneers "found a rugged wilderness in which to establish their homes. . . . "[17] Some early settlers harvested timber, while others farmed. In both cases, logging would have been the initial task. Log cabins were the only housing (even at the town's incorporation in 1817, it comprised only "a few log cabins scattered over its wide surface").[18] Mintus and Susanna probably lived in a log cabin, built—by custom—with the help of neighbors. Bartering was common, and each household raised its own produce, supplementing it with local fish and game. New clothes and shoes would have been homemade.[19]

Mintus, by then an experienced farmer, presumably went to the Adirondacks to clear land for a farm. Acreage would have been cheap, but, situated between mountains, the region was marginal farming territory. The town was later described as: "one third mountain, one third feasible land, and the residue rough and stony. A large portion of the soil is cold and hard and only moderately productive. . . . " With hard work, "the soil that in many places failed to respond luxuriantly to the early farmer's labors, was cultivated where possible to rise the necessary grains and vegetables for the current wants of the community."[20] Farming was possible, but conditions were inferior to those in Hoosick and Granville. That Mintus and Susanna persevered for several years is a tribute to their tenacity.

The Move to Granville

Around 1808[21] Mintus and his family left the Adirondacks and moved to Slyborough, in the town of Granville "where for some years he labored on the farm of Clark [sic] Northup."[22] Solomon's only sibling, Joseph, was probably born there. The family lived in Granville for about eight years, until 1816. Clarke Northup had learned the tanning trade[23] and may have done some tanning in Slyborough. If so, Mintus may have been more than a laborer, taking serious responsibilities on the farm, while Clarke engaged himself in tanning (Map 1 gives the Washington County locations where Solomon Northup lived during his youth and early marriage).

Granville was settled out of New England, and its farming culture reflected those origins. Clarke found farming there very congenial, remaining in Granville his whole life. It was a much more productive and prosperous agricultural region for Mintus than Minerva had been. In Granville, Mintus and a young Solomon were probably exposed to many good farming practices. Quakers at that time (like the Shakers) were considered excellent farmers: "wherever there were settlements of the Society of Friends, agriculture flourished."[24]

The farm of John Holmes Northup, Clarke's brother, was in Hebron, a few miles south of Slyborough. John, Henry B. Northup's father, was a farmer and blacksmith, who specialized in making agricultural equipment, especially plows. The brothers, who came from Rhode Island about the same time, were close, and the two families likely saw a lot of each other and assisted each other when planting and harvesting required extra labor. Mintus and his family may have participated in such mutually beneficial exchanges, and they may therefore have spent considerable time at John's farm.[25]

Henry B. Northup, about two years older than Solomon, stated "he knew Mintus Northup . . . from [his] earliest recollection. . . . [and] knew the children of said Mintus, viz, Solomon and Joseph . . . [and] was well acquainted with said Solomon . . . from his childhood."[26] Solomon and Henry almost certainly played together as children and worked together as older children on the two farms. They may have attended school together when young.[27] When Nicholas Carr Northup, Henry's brother, lived in Sandy Hill (now Hudson Falls) and Mintus Northup lived in nearby Fort Edward, the families maintained close contact. Henry himself almost certainly remained friends with Solomon and his family when he, too, moved to Sandy Hill.[28] When Henry went to Louisiana to rescue Solomon, they had known each other their whole lives and were close acquaintances.[29]

The Move to Kingsbury

Mintus and family moved to Kingsbury in Washington County in about 1816,[30] and rented or leased the Alden Farm near the village of Moss Street.[31] The years preceding Mintus's move to Kingsbury had been prosperous in Washington County, its economy stimulated by the War of 1812: "the war was a most excellent thing for the financial interests of the county, especially as the demands created by the necessities of the general government changed . . . stagnation to an unusual business activity."[32] In the agricultural sector, a boom in flax and wool production continued after the war.[33] The year 1816 itself, however, was the disastrous "year of no summer" when crops failed throughout the world after the explosion of a volcano in Java in 1815 filled the atmosphere with ash. Mintus's first year in Kingsbury would have been challenging, especially for a renter. This may be the reason he stayed there for only two years.

The Move to Fort Edward

Around 1818, the family relocated to neighboring Fort Edward, where the Federal Census shows them living in 1820. Solomon said his father's "whole life was passed in the peaceful pursuits of agriculture."[34] Known as a diligent and hardworking person, he was "respected as a man for his industry and integrity, as many now living who well remember him are ready to testify."[35] Orville Clark, a prominent citizen of Sandy Hill, confirmed this, characterizing Mintus as "a respectable man in the community in which he resided."[36]

Five children of John Holmes Northup, including Henry B., moved to Sandy Hill, and the family continued its acquaintance with Mintus's family. John Henry Northup, Henry B.'s nephew,[37] remembered that when he was a child, Mintus "came to Sandy Hill and made little beds in the garden for each of us children."[38]

Mintus "acquired, by his diligence and economy, a property qualification to entitle him to the right of suffrage."[39] Before 1821, this would have meant an estate of at least $100; afterward, an estate of at least $250. Before 1822, *all* citizens had to own property worth $100 to vote. In 1822, a new state constitution eliminated the property qualification for whites and raised it for blacks.

Though Mintus and his family were well-received by the Fort Edward community, they were subject to the prejudices of the time; although citizens, free blacks did not enjoy the same advantages as whites. During the 1821 convention that raised the property qualification for black voters, a speaker described the limited civil rights of blacks:

> Are the negroes permitted to a participation in social intercourse with the whites? Are they elevated to public office? No sir—public sentiment forbids it. [Though county clerks were required to make lists of potential jurors], "Was a negro ever returned upon that list? If he were, no jury would sit with him. Was a constable ever known to summon a negro as a juror . . . ? . . . Never. . . . [Blacks, even if willing, could not serve in the state militia. Nor would any] white man . . . invite him to a seat at his table, nor in his pew in the church.[40]

The sentiments expressed in these debates may have included hyperbole; nevertheless they reflected the feelings of many whites.

Governor Washington Hunt (instrumental in Northup's rescue) described the status of the state's free blacks in 1851:

> Although the free people of color enjoy a certain degree of liberty, they are commonly treated, both in the free and slave states as an inferior race, and deprived of the social and political rights without which freedom is but an empty name. Even in our own State they are excluded from the most essential privileges of citizenship. Debarred from all participation in public employments, rejected from most of the institutions of learning, and religion, governed by laws which they have no share in framing, having been denied the right of suffrage by a vast popular majority, shut out from social intercourse, and condemned to a life of servility and drudgery, their condition amongst us is deplorable in the extreme . . . . [41]

Mintus could vote, but he probably had little opportunity to participate fully in civic life. This was the social environment in which Mintus and Susanna lived and in which Solomon grew up. It was certainly better than slavery, as Solomon repeatedly testifies; but it was not the full freedom enjoyed by most white citizens.

Mintus died on November 22, 1829, at the age of 51, and was buried in the Baker Cemetery in Sandy Hill. Solomon, married less than a year, was 22 at the time. Susanna outlived Mintus and moved to western New York. She died while Solomon was in Louisiana.

SOLOMON'S EARLY YEARS

The best evidence suggests that Solomon was born on July 10, 1807, and married on December 25, 1828 (both dates are one year earlier than those given in *Twelve Years*).[42] The family probably left Schroon when Solomon was one or two years old, left Granville when he was about nine, and left Kingsbury when he was about 11. He lived with his parents in Fort Edward for about 10 years before marrying Anne Hampton when he was 21.

From birth until his marriage, Northup lived on a farm and was "principally engaged with my father in the labors of the farm."[43] Farming activities would have involved the planting and harvesting of crops, such as wheat, corn, rye, oats, and other cereals, and could have included cultivating vegetables and raising livestock. By adulthood, Northup would have been thoroughly exposed to agricultural and husbandry practices.

Schooling

By Solomon Northup's own account he could read and write; he mentions reading books as an adolescent.[44] There are episodes in Louisiana where these abilities are part of the narrative.[45] His signature exists in clear, if inelegant, cursive script. Henry B. Northup, in an affidavit related to the rescue, says Northup "could read and write." Because a demonstration of this ability could have been part of an identification process to satisfy a court that Solomon was who he claimed to be, Henry would not have stated it without knowing it to be true.

Northup had access to schooling and possibly to books at home. He states that his father gave his children "an education surpassing that ordinarily bestowed upon children of our condition," by which he probably meant children of African descent. Moreover, John Henry Northup, who knew Mintus, wrote in a letter to his grandmother that Mintus "gave his boys a common school education,"[46] suggesting that Mintus made sure that Solomon and Joseph went to school, which not all parents did at that time. Solomon also began to play the violin at an early age, recalling it as "an amusement that was the ruling passion of my youth."[47]

There were schools (likely private) in Granville from the 1780s on.[48] The common (public) school system of the state was created by the Legislature in 1812. Although separate provisions applied to New York City and Albany, other towns were invited to participate in a matching grant scheme by which the state shared the expense of establishing schools. The aim was to enroll all children between the ages of 5 and 15, inclusive. The system began operation in 1813 under the direction of Gideon Hawley and functioned throughout most of the years Northup was age-eligible. From the very beginning, the system emphasized teacher recruitment, quality, and screening, as well as obtaining quality books.[49] The state provided supporting funds, set standards, and examined and licensed teachers. Local school districts enjoyed much discretion regarding curriculum. A major aim of the system was state support for indigent children.

Blacks often attended the same schools as whites, because "the laws of the State of New York never prohibited the attendance of Negroes at the District and Common Schools."[50] Moreover, the Legislature was moving toward supporting black education. In 1809, it passed a law requiring slave owners to have their young slaves taught to read.[51] School districts had the option of establishing separate schools for blacks, provided the facilities were equal to those for whites (which, in practice, was not always the case).[52] This was probably not done for the relatively few black children in Washington County, and Northup almost certainly would have attended school with the white children in his community, possibly including Henry B. Northup.

Granville, where Northup lived until he was nine years old, began participating in the common school system in 1813, when Northup was six, and by 1814, it had created 19 school districts. A large number of children of eligible age were soon attending the common schools.[53] In addition, Granville had a "normal school" for educating teachers,[54] which probably meant Granville (and perhaps Washington County) had little trouble recruiting teachers. The common school system in Kingsbury was established in 1813, with 12 school districts. It had been operating for three years by the time the Northups lived there (Northup was about nine years old when they arrived). The common school system in Fort Edward started in 1818, when seven districts were delineated. The school commissioners' report for 1819 stated that seven schools were taught in the town, with periods varying from three to eleven months; that the number of children taught was 261; that school-age children numbered 353.[55] Three-quarters of the eligible children had at least some schooling that year. In 1819, Northup was 12 years old, living in Fort Edward, and could easily have been one of the pupils. The opportunity for him to have attended school was real, and the probability that he did so was great.

The quality and extent of Solomon's schooling is unknown. One historian observed, "Four, or at most five or six, months in the district school gave the farmer's children but the rudiments of an education. Country scholars learned reading, writing, and arithmetic fairly well. Spelling and writing was taught in the schools especially well . . . "[56] The books used in Fort Edward in 1819 were "Webster's spelling book and grammar, Morse's geography, Pike's arithmetic, and the English Reader."[57] Northup probably completed exercises in reading, spelling, math, and geography. "The schools were ungraded; there were many classes; the methods of teaching were primitive; and yet it is certain that pupils who had a mind to study got a very good common school education . . . "[58] State supervision of the school system helped ensure that his teachers were competent.

With respect to Northup's reading books at home, it should be recalled that in Granville, where he lived until he was nine, the family was closely associated with that of Clarke Northup, a Quaker family from Rhode Island. New England Quaker families were literate, emphasized education, owned books, and came from a culture of sharing—and the Clarke Northups were not the only Quakers in Granville at that time. In short, Northup likely had access to printed resources.

MARRIAGE TO ANNE HAMPTON

On Christmas Day in 1828, Solomon Northup married Anne Hampton, daughter of William Hampton, a free black citizen of Sandy Hill. She was of African, Native American, and white ancestry. Solomon lovingly concludes that "the union of them all . . . in her origin, has given her a singularly pleasing expression, such as is rarely to be seen."[59] It is likely her mother was Hannah Hampton, a woman of color. Anne was reportedly born in 1808, and grew up in what was described as a respectable Sandy Hill family, whose head of household met the property qualification for voting.[60] She had five brothers.[61]

In her teens, Anne worked as a domestic servant in the home of Alexander Proudfit in nearby Salem, New York. He was a Presbyterian minister, a trustee of Union College, and a leading citizen of Salem.[62] Writing in *Twelve Years,* Northup says, "Anne still holds in grateful remembrance the exceeding kindness and excellent counsels of that good man."[63] Proudfit later moved to Saratoga Springs, and possibly continued to sponsor Anne there.[64] She also resided, presumably as a domestic, with Mr. Baird, proprietor of the Eagle Tavern in Sandy Hill. It was probably there that she developed her kitchen management skills, which she later used across the street at Sherrill's Coffee House, and even later at hotels in Saratoga and Glens Falls, where in many cases she ran the kitchen.

The marriage was filled with vicissitudes and separations, but the evidence suggests that she remained loyal to Solomon and was proud to be his wife. Northup speaks of Anne with great affection in *Twelve Years.* They had three children: Elizabeth, Margaret, and Alonzo.

After marriage, Anne and Solomon lived at the Old Fort House in Fort Edward. This historic building, now a museum, has a room dedicated to Northup's memory.[65] They lived there for about 18 months, from December 1828, through the spring of 1830, during which time Northup worked as a laborer on the newly opened Champlain Canal, as a rafter on this canal, as a rafter on Lake Champlain, and as a woodsman. During his extended absences, Anne may have continued working at the Eagle Tavern or at Sherrill's Coffee House. She may also have worked locally as a domestic servant.

EMPLOYMENT PROSPECTS AND HABITS OF MIND

When Northup left his father's farm and entered the labor force, he confronted challenges faced by almost anyone in his time who did not own a farm, have a large amount of capital, or enjoy promising family connections. He lived in preindustrial upstate New York. Farm work was available, but it was seasonal and had to be supplemented with winter work.[66] Employment in the lumber industry (a major regional business) was also seasonal and dovetailed well with agriculture in this respect, but it was often not steady or fixed in place: as woodlots were cleared, work migrated, and employment often had to be sought at new locations. Most businesses were owner-operated with few employees, although the highways, waterways, and soon the railroads provided steadier employment for some.

Given these circumstances, those desiring year-round employment would expect to have several different jobs during the year, most requiring different skills. In addition, a range of skills was required to enhance a person's ability to keep employed when a job expired (as most would). It is not surprising that Northup developed skills in many areas. This would have been the norm in the rural upstate economy of his time. Specific skills developed in one area, such as farming, would not necessarily carry over to another area, such as lumbering; but developing good skills in any area would create a cast of mind that would make it easier to acquire skills in another.

Throughout Northup's account of his experiences, there are examples of the resourcefulness and "industry" (to use his word)[67] that he developed living in the economic and cultural circumstances of the New England diaspora. These were based on a cast of mind that included: alertness to new opportunities; curiosity about how things work; belief that practices and processes can always be improved, and a constant search for ways to do so; and a conviction that all knowledge is potentially useful and handy. It was also important to recognize the value of building, maintaining, or just participating in a good network of shared information. Additional useful habits of mind included flexibility and imagination in approaching new tasks; confidence in facing problems, both technical and economic; and pride in accomplishment, especially with challenging tasks.

These habits of mind that Northup acquired and exercised were basic survival skills shared throughout the economy and society in which he grew up. They were to become even more important for Northup in the economy and society to which he was transported.

Work Repairing the Canal

During the winter months immediately after his marriage, Northup worked on the Champlain Canal, doing maintenance or repair work.[68] There was a range of unskilled, semiskilled, and skilled job opportunities for Northup on the canal, including dredging work or bank repairs, carpentry on the wooden aqueduct channels, or masonry work on the towpath bridges and lock walls. He "labored" with other workers, so the work was likely unskilled or semiskilled. Northup, however, was sufficiently well-paid or sufficiently frugal to amass enough capital to go into business for himself.

Rafting

When spring arrived in 1829, Northup took his savings, bought a pair of horses "and other things necessarily required in the business of navigation," and became a rafter—a contractor who floated rafts between locations, and probably built them as well. Initially, he rafted on the Champlain Canal from Whitehall to Troy, a distance of about 65 miles.[69] Later he rafted on Lake Champlain itself.

The late 1820s were a time of extensive lumbering in the Upper Hudson region and along the shores of Lake Champlain.[70] Logs were dragged or sledged to water-powered saw mills located along the streams throughout the area. In 1829, the year Northup began rafting, there were more than 500 such mills in this region, a total that may have represented the industry at its peak.[71]

Although logs could be—and were—moved great distances by water and then processed, it was often more efficient to saw them into lumber (flat boards and planks) or hew them into timber (square posts and beams) near where they were cut, build rafts of them, and then raft the product along the waterways to market. In the late 1820s and 1830s, when Northup was in this business, an enormous amount of cut wood was rafted on the streams flowing into Lake Champlain and on those flowing into the major rivers. Some of the wood from the Champlain littoral was rafted to Canada; most of the rest was sent to Albany or Troy after the Champlain Canal opened in 1823. Much wood produced to the south of Lake Champlain also went down to Albany or Troy. Soon after the canal's opening (and that of the Erie Canal in 1825), Albany's role as the chief lumber market in upstate New York was solidified.[72] Northup was participating in a thriving industry with many opportunities right in the region where he grew up. While in the business, he rafted both north and south. Although cutting and sawing wood could be done in the winter, rafting could only be done during the eight months when neither the canal nor Lake Champlain was frozen.

Successful rafting took considerable skill, acquired largely through experience, and Northup implies that he acquired this skill "on the job" during the summer of 1829. [73] Northup mentions rafting "timber" in New York[74] and "lumber" in Louisiana,[75] but probably had experience with both in New York.

Each raft would have a set of oars on the front and back for steering and maneuvering, and a small crew was required to operate them. Northup refers to hiring "several efficient hands" to help him, no doubt for this purpose.[76] While going through the canal itself, the raft would be towed by the team of horses he had purchased, with another crew member handling them. The crew's operations were directed by the pilot, Northup himself. Small loads of other products might be carried on the rafts, and larger rafts had a shanty with bunks and a stove. While Northup rafted on the canal between Champlain and Troy, his crew probably did not need a shanty. Later, when he rafted to Canada on the Champlain, they almost certainly used one.

There was very little rafting on the Hudson, but a great deal on Lake Champlain. Rafts could be poled, rowed, sailed, or pulled behind steamboats in the absence of a towpath. Northup rafted many times through the Champlain Canal, made several "voyages" on Lake Champlain, and visited Canada.[77] He also states that he went to Rochester and Buffalo during this period, which suggests that he traveled the Erie Canal at least once.[78] This was probably for work, not pleasure.

Rafting required carpentry skills, navigational skills, supervisory skills, and entrepreneurial skills—all considerable, and much more than those needed by a simple laborer. Northup doesn't elaborate on his achievements in boastful terms, but does say he became "perfectly familiar with the art and mysteries of rafting," and allows himself a rare lapse in decorum in *Twelve Years* when, looking back, he compares himself to the "simple-witted lumbermen [no doubt both black and white] on the banks of the Bayou Boeuf."[79]

Cutting Wood

In the winter of 1830, with the canal closed, Northup "entered into another contract with Medad Gunn, to cut a large quantity of wood."[80] There is some confusion here as to whether this was done right after his inaugural year of rafting, as the text implies, or somewhat later.[81] Either way, he developed experience as a woodsman. Since he had a contract, it is highly probable he hired and supervised a small crew to do this cutting, Northup working with them on the job.

Northup gives no details as to what he did, but woodcutting was a serious profession that required a great deal of skill:[82]

There is probably no industry which involves so many varied details as the business of lumbering; none which requires so close attention at every stage of the work; and none in which intelligence, strict economy, and, above all, thorough experience, are so necessary to profitable results. Failures have been so many that no one should undertake it who has not within him these specified requisites to success.[83]

In a typical operation, the first task was to build a camp for the crew. This was usually a log cabin with bunks, a necessity during the winter months. An access road was then cut to bring in supplies and haul out logs. When cut, logs were stacked and then sledged to a river or mill after there was sufficient snowfall for the sledge. Felling a tree with an axe and dropping it precisely was an important skill because each tree was potentially unique in balance and trees falling on other trees (standing or cut) could create major problems. Bucking, or cutting the logs with an axe, required different skills, as did removing the limbs. An experienced axeman would be expected to have the ability to do all three.

It was also dangerous work, not so much because of the axe, but because of the tree: falling limbs can kill a man; widowmaker trees resting on other trees can do the same; a tree being felled can twist and hit the axeman; a tree can lodge and then spring back at the stump, killing the axeman; and a load of logs can shove a team down a steep grade resulting in an accident.[84] A successful lumberman had to be skillful, careful, and constantly aware of his surroundings and their dangers. Northup talks of only one season of cutting wood, although there may have been others in subsequent years. In any event, even one winter in the woods in charge of a crew would have honed many skills and been a major growth experience for a young man.

Farming in Kingsbury

In 1830,[85] the Northups took up farming, and they rented or leased the Alden Farm that Mintus had run previously. Northup gives no reason, but he does say moving was a joint decision, and it is entirely possible that it was done at Anne's initiative. Rafting and lumbering would have kept Northup away from home for long periods, and possibly both wanted to spend more time together, especially if they planned a family. During summers at least, they would live and work together.

The 1830 Census shows their Kingsbury household had two male and three female "free colored persons," which may have included

Northup's mother and brother. Northup's account of their four years in this location[86] consists of three sparse paragraphs, though he describes it as a busy time:

> That year I planted twenty-five acres of corn, sowed large fields of oats, and commenced farming upon as large a scale as my utmost means would permit. Anne was diligent about the house affairs, while I toiled laboriously in the field.[87]

It would have taken much work to plant, cultivate, and harvest 25 acres of corn. Northup bought a team of oxen, to be used for plowing and harrowing. With the type of plow commonly used (such as those made contemporaneously by John Holmes Northup),[88] a farmer with a team of oxen could plow up to two acres a day[89] (a recent technological breakthrough). Northup's acreage, assuming he had this implement, would require two weeks to plow, and several days to harrow smooth with the homemade A-frame spiked harrows of the day.[90] Seeding was done by hand, hill by hill. The whole family had to participate. After field preparation, planting would have taken at least another two weeks. If work started in early April, the corn could be planted by the end of May. After it sprouted, the corn would have to be cultivated (in early June) to prevent weeds from ruining the crop, a task that could be done with certain types of plows, or with hoes. In the fall, the ears would have to be picked and the leaves and stalks preserved for fodder.[91] The ears would be husked and a lot hulled. Some would be set aside as seed corn, some retained for animal fodder, some ground for food, and the rest sold. Twenty-five bushels of corn per acre was considered a good yield.[92] Rotation was understood as necessary, especially for corn, and Northup would have had to rotate his crops with peas, clover, or buckwheat to grow corn on a sustained basis.

Oats were easier. Again, the field would have to be plowed and harrowed, but six acres could be seeded by hand in a day. Next, the field would be harrowed and rolled. An ox-drawn roller could be fashioned from a large tree trunk. Oats did not require cultivating, but at harvest time the field would have to be scythed down by hand,[93] gathered into sheaves, taken to a threshing location, trampled or flailed, and the grain separated from the straw. Some grain would be retained as seed stock, some used as animal fodder, some ground for food, and some sold. New York farms during this period could expect to produce about 50 bushels of oats per acre each year.[94] Oats were an important part of Northup's production schedule. He could have planted oats before planting his corn, for an early summer crop. He could have begun immediately after planting corn, for a mid-to-late summer crop.

In either case, he might have plowed some acreage the previous fall and simply harrowed it in the spring.

In addition to seasonal work, there was always "counter-cyclical" work on the farm: "all types of repair work on tools, fences, ditches, barns, and houses."[95] Northup may also have worked in the woods during winter, although he does not say so. He might have done some rafting in late fall. He had one enjoyable source of extra cash. During winters, Northup says that he had "numerous calls to play on the violin. Wherever the young people assembled to dance, I was almost invariably there. Throughout the surrounding villages my fiddle was notorious."[96]

Anne's activities would have been equally intense. Elizabeth was born in Kingsbury in 1831 or 1832, and Margaret arrived in 1833 or 1834.[97] A farm-wife's duties were extensive, especially while caring for two young children. Anne would have fed the livestock; kept chickens; milked the cow; made butter, cheese, soap, and tallow candles; planted and maintained a vegetable garden; preserved food; dressed meat; stacked wood; washed clothes; hauled water; made and mended clothes; helped with the crops; and possibly ground grain—in addition to cleaning, cooking, housekeeping, and caring for the relatives and children.[98] Moreover, she spent much time in winter running the kitchen at the Eagle Tavern or Sherrill's Coffee House.

They were a hardworking family, and Northup states that "with fiddling, cooking, and farming, we soon found ourselves in possession of abundance, and, in fact, leading a happy and prosperous life."[99] Yet, in 1834 they moved to Saratoga Springs. Why, then, did they envision leaving Kingsbury?

They would not have felt particularly isolated. Northup's fiddling took him to surrounding towns where he could make acquaintances. Anne's work off the farm brought her into contact with many people in Sandy Hill. While it's not possible to know how well this African American family was received in their own neighborhood, years later, the leading citizens of Sandy Hill came together to effect Northup's rescue, which speaks well for both Northup's reputation and the community's decency. The close relations between the white and black Northup families may have been helpful to Solomon and Anne; the text suggests no overt social issues at this time.[100]

Northup, however, does mention economic issues: "I resolved to enter upon a life of industry; and notwithstanding the obstacle of color, and the consciousness of my lowly state, indulged in pleasant dreams of a good time coming . . . "[101] He also refers to his father as "laboring under the disadvantages of which my unfortunate race is subjected," and also as "never seeking employment in those more menial positions which seem to be especially allotted to the children of Africa."[102] Northup was clearly aware of racial barriers to economic advancement. Whether he sensed such in his farming circumstances or location, is not known.

Racial issues aside, he may have reached a plateau in terms of the farm's economic possibilities. The "structure and composition of farms in the Hudson Valley environment limited the output a family could expect from its toil."[103] Saint Jean de Crèvecoeur observed, "I do not mean that everyone who comes will grow rich in a little time; no, but he may procure an easy, decent maintenance by his industry. Instead of starving, he will be fed. Instead of being idle, he will have employment."[104] Northup may have wanted more than this. Martin Bruegel recounts the following:

> Traveling through an area at the foot of the Catskills in 1788, Alexander Coventry observed that "the inhabitants are very poor, but seem industrious." . . . As an assessment of the rural condition, the statement summed up the lives of the majority among the inhabitants in the Hudson Valley countryside: they engaged in multiple activities to secure a decent competence.[105]

This may characterize the Northups' lives in Kingsbury. They had a decent "competence" and were "happy and prosperous," but they probably could not envision much advancement. Agriculture in the area was beginning to change dramatically during the time period the Northups were farming. Self-sufficient family farms were rapidly giving way to larger family farms that specialized in certain products. The recent opening of the Erie Canal meant that grain produced more cheaply elsewhere was flooding New York, and regional farming was shifting from growing grain and general produce to specializing in dairy (whose regional economic advantage was that it could not be shipped over great distances). Northup was in the business of growing grain, whose price was generally falling, and its future was in question. Given the immediate transportation prospects before the railroads, farms in the upper Hudson Valley were less well situated than those in the lower valley to export dairy products to New York City—and really no better situated than the Midwest to ship grain there. It is possible that declining long-term regional farming prospects contributed to Solomon's and Anne's decision to leave farming.[106]

Moreover, Northup did not own the farm. To envision being a farmer for life is to envision owning one's own farm, so that the results of efforts expended on it can accumulate over time to one's benefit. Even a long-term lease will not have the same effect. It may have been that financial circumstances did not permit the North-ups to envision buying a farm, or that there were other barriers to ownership. The price of land rose substantially in the Hudson Valley in the first third of the 19th century, doubling, for example, in Columbia County, between 1799 and 1835, even before the shift to dairy was fully underway.[107] Northup's prospects for owning his farm may have receded as time unfolded. Or his use of the word "prosperous" to describe their circumstances may have been an overstatement (indeed, he was seriously in debt by 1831).[108] Whatever the reason, there was the urge to move on.

THE MOVE TO SARATOGA

According to the account in *Twelve Years*, Solomon and Anne moved to Saratoga Springs in March 1834.[109] They initially occupied a house owned by Daniel O'Brien in the neighborhood of Washington Street, and later lived at the United States Hotel. O'Brien's property was located on Congress Street, near Washington.[110] Anne lived at the Pavilion Hotel during the summer after the kidnapping, and both may have been living there beforehand.[111] With them were daughters Elizabeth and Margaret. Their youngest child, Alonzo, was born in Saratoga around 1836 (Map 2 gives the principal Saratoga Springs locations mentioned in Northup's account).

The seven years the Northups lived in Saratoga followed a quarter-century of municipal growth that saw the community change from a small town servicing the surrounding farm economy to a nationally known resort. Saratoga's life as a famous "watering place" began with the visionary Gideon Putnam, who opened a hotel there in 1802, and who was influential in designing its layout. Others soon followed suit, and hotels sprang up in quick succession: the Columbian in 1809, Congress Hall in 1811, The Pavilion in 1819, and The United States in 1823. Numerous visitors began to arrive for many reasons, but in the early days, health and healing were major draws: curative qualities were attributed to the waters; perhaps more important, fleeing pestilential urban areas in summer was considered prudent.[112] In addition, summers were cooler than in New York City, and much more so than in the South.

By the 1820s, Saratoga Springs had established itself as a desirable destination, and had begun to eclipse its early rival Ballston Spa.[113] The prospects of improving one's health may have been an early draw, but soon the resort added other diversions, including gambling, liquor, and entertainment. Its public spaces were improved appropriately to enhance its attractiveness, and developers not only supported the creation of such spaces, but also developed plats of private lots for sale and lease.[114] Prominent visitors, such as Washington Irving, began to give the resort credibility,[115] and soon the opportunity to mingle socially added another dimension to its desirability. The 1825 opening of the Erie Canal, only a day's drive from the town, made it easier to reach, adding to Saratoga's growth as a tourist site. When the Northups arrived in 1834, Saratoga was well on its way to national fame.

Access was the single biggest drawback, as the town was handicapped by the unpredictable conditions of dirt roads and the discomforts of traveling on them. This problem was addressed by the construction of the Schenectady and Saratoga Railroad, which opened between these two towns in 1833.[116] It was the second railroad built in New York—reflecting the growing prominence of Saratoga and the opportunities for passenger travel that the resort offered. New York's first railroad had been built between Albany and Schenectady not long before.[117] The two railroads together enabled a person to go in relative comfort by steamboat from New York to Albany and then by train to Saratoga in a day.[118] Within a few years, the Schenectady and Saratoga Railroad had 30,000 passengers.[119] The completion of the Rensselaer and Saratoga Railroad (also known as the Troy and Saratoga Railroad) in 1835 shortened the New York–Saratoga trip even further. Not only was travel faster and more comfortable, it was also less expensive than before the days of the iron horse.[120]

Railroads created an enormous instant boom for Saratoga. The chance to participate in the opportunities offered by this dramatic expansion of economic activity undoubtedly attracted the Northup family to Saratoga. They arrived a year after the railroad was built. The growth of Saratoga as a resort in these years was truly impressive. Before the railroad, "Saratoga had probably never hosted more than six thousand guests in any season, but in 1833, the number of visitors at the Springs jumped to eight thousand," and by 1835 they were arriving at the rate of 2000 per week.[121] This surge was accompanied by an influx of celebrities and the town's social reputation was solidified: Martin Van Buren, Henry Clay, John C. Calhoun, and Daniel Webster all visited before 1840, most during the time the Northups were there. Clement Clarke Moore, of "Night Before Christmas" fame, even wrote a poem about Saratoga.[122] Hotels were expanded, and more were built, including the American Hotel in 1840.[123] Not only did Saratoga's economy expand dramatically, its visitor-based prosperity persisted during the depression that began in the late 1830s,[124] although there was apparently a slowdown in construction.[125]

Saratoga's resort-based prosperity, however, was seasonal. It was not until 1868 that the American Hotel became the first to stay open all year around.[126] Permanent residence in the town therefore presented both the opportunity to earn money during the tourist season and the need to maintain an income flow during the winter months. Cyclical work patterns (or job opportunities) were, of course, not unusual in upstate New York—the entire farm economy in which the Northups had participated was seasonal. Even before moving to Saratoga, the Northups were familiar with seasonal work patterns. The move to Saratoga therefore represented a major change in summer activity, at least for Northup, but did not alleviate the need for finding temporary jobs during at least half the year. This, then, was the exciting, but cyclical, economic environment in which the family lived between 1834 and 1841.

African Americans constituted a small, but long-standing portion of the Saratoga community, going back to its founding era.[127] When the Northups arrived, they were one of more than 65 black families in Saratoga and one of nearly 90 by 1840, when blacks constituted 6 percent of Saratoga's population.[128] About 60 percent of blacks were female, presumably reflecting the pattern of job opportunities in this resort town.[129]

Although Northup's roots were in Rhode Island, many free blacks in Saratoga at the time had 18th-century roots in upstate New York and were either recently emancipated slaves or descendants of local slaves.[130] These slaves had worked in the rural upstate economy, as domestics and as farm workers, and when emancipation took hold during the late 18th and early 19th centuries, some continued to work on those farms, but many moved into towns. The Northups' move to Saratoga was therefore part of a general migration of African Americans from rural settings to urban ones. This may partly have been the result of a lack of capital for newly freed slaves to acquire farm property, and it may also, in the case of Saratoga, have been the special attractions of its continually expanding economy.

Theodore Corbett describes this process:

> African-Americans in the eighteenth century had been integrated into the white economy of the Saratoga region. Many moved from slavery to working . . ., black females as domestics and black males as waiters. Yet blacks had additional skills and reasonable opportunities at the spa that made the resort the most attractive place in the area for them to make a living between 1820 and 1850. From the beginning of the nineteenth century, they filled the spa's needs for workers to support the hotels, to develop the green spaces, and to entertain the visitors.[131]

Corbett, however, provides this perspective:

> While it was a living, it was not an opportunity comparable to that which white men and women had in the spa's building trades or in factory communities. Many jobs in the resort business required only domestic skills. The greatest demand was for servants, who were usually women. At the resort they could hold these jobs into middle age, whereas in industrial communities domestic work was a young woman's occupation. And the seasonal nature of work at the spa meant that even the skilled resort workers had to hold several jobs to tide them over during the off season.[132]

Given the disproportionate percentage of black women in Saratoga, and Corbett's vocational explanations of why this was the case, it's possible that the move to Saratoga may have had as much to do with Anne's employment opportunities as Solomon's.

Anne, even before her marriage, "had become somewhat famous as a cook," presumably well known throughout the region for her skills. She had worked at the Eagle Tavern, and "on public occasions" had been "employed at high wages in the kitchen at Sherrill's Coffee House."[133] When the family lived in Saratoga she was employed at the United States Hotel "and other public houses of the place."[134] In the off-season, she "was in charge of the culinary department at Sherrill's Coffee House, during the session of the court."[135] She had substantial experience working as a domestic, and may also have worked as such during the winter months between the periods when the courts were in session.

During the resort season, Solomon worked for two years as a hack driver in the employ of Isaac Taylor who owned Washington Hall, a quiet hotel or boarding house near the north end of Broadway. Taylor sold it in 1836, which may be why Northup went to work elsewhere.[136] From then on, he worked mainly at the United States Hotel, located on Broadway between Washington and Division streets, although at times he, like Anne, also worked at "other public houses."[137] This hotel, the largest public structure in Saratoga at that time, and arguably its most prestigious hostelry, was owned by Judge Thomas Marvin and his brother James. It could accommodate 400 guests; its huge dining room once seated 800 at a dinner honoring Henry Clay, and its salon once entertained President Van Buren.[138] Solomon's duties at the United States Hotel were sufficiently prominent for him to know Judge Marvin well enough to seek his help in getting released from captivity in Louisiana. He could have worked variously as a driver, a waiter, carpenter, and musician.[139]

Black musicians were an important part of the Saratoga scene during this period. One highly recognized musician was Francis Johnson and his Cotillion Band of African Americans, who performed there every season, save one, from 1821 to 1844.[140] The 1850 Census lists musicians among the semiskilled black residents of Saratoga.[141] Northup likely played frequently at the United States Hotel and other hotels during his time in Saratoga.

Solomon and Anne also lived at the United States Hotel for part of their time in Saratoga. This arrangement may have been in partial compensation for their labors. However, as Corbett observes, "blacks in the servant's quarters of hotels were exploited, overworked, and underpaid by hotel proprietors, who tried to minimize wages and maximize the fact that they were giving their workers room and board."[142]

In the off-season, when it was necessary to find other employment, Solomon played his violin to earn extra income.[143] This might have been at dances in Saratoga itself, or back in Kingsbury, Fort Edward, or Sandy Hill, where his fiddling was well known. But he also found other work during the off-season. For example, he labored on the construction of the Troy–Saratoga Railroad during his early days in Saratoga.[144] He possibly cut lumber during this period, because timber sources were not far away and the construction needs of the expanding resort would have created a steady demand. He may have done some carpentry at the hotels during the off-season.

Northup also engaged in rafting on the Champlain Canal while in Saratoga. Because the canal was frozen in the winter, he could have rafted in late fall or early spring, or even during the resort season if it promised more remuneration than jobs in Saratoga. A court case involving Northup gives proof of rafting activity in 1838.[145] On June 8, 1838, he entered into a written contract with Washington Allen of Peru, Clinton County, to use rafts to transport some timber ("dock sticks") from Whitehall to Waterford via the Champlain Canal. As he prepared to depart with a raft at Whitehall—manned by a crew he had hired—a confrontation took place between him and Allen, both of whom were standing along the towpath near the lock. A witness, Louis Shattuck, later testified that Allen told Northup, he "did not want him any longer, and did not want him to have anything to do with it." Northup asked why and was told "because I don't want you." Another witness, Dyer Beckwith (with whom Northup had worked before),[146] said that Allen told Northup, "I do not think you fit and that the hands would not go with him." Allen stated his reason more directly during the June trial after Northup sued him to collect what he was owed: he believed Northup was intoxicated and not able to handle the job.[147]

Northup had indeed had some drinks, according to witnesses. Shattuck testified Northup had been drinking "but that he was not so bad that he could [not] get about or to incapacitate him for business." And James L. Prindle said that he'd been drinking "considerable" but "not so much as to disqualify him for business." Prindle added that Northup was generally industrious and "not in the habit of being intoxicated, though in the habit of drinking some."

The case was presented before a jury on June 25, with both men apparently representing themselves.[148] The jury sided with Northup, but Allen appealed. On June 30, Northup was awarded a judgment of $100, including court costs.

Canal life on both the Erie and the Champlain was a rough one. It was highly competitive, and there were many opportunities for rafters and canal boat captains to come into conflict. The opportunities and incentives for physical combat among rafters and canal boat operators were many, and fights were not infrequent. It is not surprising that men in this business would resort to their fists, often out of necessity. In addition, the work was hard, the hours interminable, and the rewards often not great. It is therefore also not surprising that men engaged in this business found relief in alcohol on their off hours.[149] Northup was no exception in either case. Habits acquired in one context can carry over to others. Records show that he was convicted of assault and battery on three occasions between 1834 and 1839;[150] and the 1838 court case and his own statements in *Twelve Years* attest to the fact that he drank. Although the circumstances of his convictions are not known, he apparently spent no serious time in jail, which suggests that either the offenses were minor or the blame not entirely his. These convictions do, however, attest to a willingness to use his fists, and give serious credibility to several episodes in Louisiana when he says he did just that in order to survive. They also suggest in this context that he was a person accustomed to standing his ground. He was an individual who could take care of himself in a tight circumstance.

Life in Saratoga was a mixed blessing for the Northups: "the flattering anticipations which, seven years before, had seduced us from the quiet farm-house, on the east side of the Hudson, had not been realized. Though always in comfortable circumstances, we had not prospered."[151] Moreover, "the society and associations at that world-renowned watering place, were not calculated to preserve the simple habits of industry and economy to which I had been accustomed, but on the contrary, to substitute others in their stead, tending to shiftlessness and extravagance."[152] Northup may have been unduly harsh with himself in this last judgment, but life in Saratoga would certainly have been different than on the farm.

For one thing, there would have been greater interaction with others and far more daily contact with a wide range of individuals. The Northups "occupied a house" upon arrival,[153] which probably meant that they lived as a unit in their own household. This would not have been unusual for an African American family in Saratoga.[154] Clearly, they established relationships, including with storekeepers William Perry and Cephas Parker, who played an important role in Northup's rescue. Residential patterns were segregated much more on the basis of class and income than of race, and the village was sufficiently small that nothing like a ghetto formed, even on class lines. The opportunity for people of all races to intermingle was real. There are instances where black and white families shared the same living quarters.[155] Even the public spaces were not segregated in the early days, despite the presence of many southern visitors.

This did not mean that racial attitudes were uniformly progressive. In fact, in the early 1820s, legislators representing Saratoga led the opposition to extending suffrage to African Americans, supporting, as a compromise, making it more difficult for blacks to vote than for whites.[156] When politicians take such a visible stand, it can be presumed their views are widely shared throughout their constituency. Nevertheless, the Northups had the opportunity to become acquainted with a wide range of people across the color line. They also could encounter visitors from other parts of the country, and their retinue. Solomon met slaves accompanying southern families to the spa, and had numerous conversations with them.[157]

Saratoga may have been a place that challenged values, as Northup suggests,[158] but it was nevertheless an exciting place to be in the 1830s and early 1840s, with interesting, various, and intense activity and contrasts. On the one hand, it offered parks, quiet vistas, and many opportunities to sit, promenade, relax, and unwind. At the same time, it was a place where one could easily drink, gamble, dally, and depart from convention. The yearly cycle from abandoned backwater in the winter to intense visibility and notoriety in summer may have had a destabilizing effect on its permanent residents. Northup reported that his character changed for the worse in this "watering place." Whether or not the town encouraged "shiftlessness and extravagance,"[159] it certainly would have encouraged a more worldly attitude, receptivity to novelty, and perhaps a willingness to take risks. Had his kidnappers wheeled up to his farm in Kingsbury and suggested that he accompany them to New York, they probably would have received a very different answer than the one they got in Saratoga.

3

Kidnapped

On a morning in late March of 1841, Northup met two men in Saratoga Springs "on the corner of Congress Street and Broadway, near the tavern . . . kept by Mr. Moon," which was located in Montgomery Hall (see Map 2).[1] These were Alexander Merrill and Joseph Russell, two adventurers who had grown up about 30 miles northwest of that town.[2] After interrogating Northup about his musical abilities, the two (using the names Merrill Brown and Abram Hamilton, respectively) proposed that he accompany them to New York City, saying that they worked for a circus then in Washington, D.C. They explained that they had come north "for the purpose of seeing the country" and were financing their journey by presenting "exhibitions" or "entertainments." They had "found much difficulty in procuring music" for these shows, and offered Northup a generous sum to supply that music. They were in a hurry to leave. Northup appears to have accepted the offer promptly and the three left Saratoga that same day.[3] Thus began the elaborate scheme to kidnap Northup.

In *Twelve Years*, Northup recalls that Hamilton and Brown may have been introduced to him "by some one of my acquaintances . . . with the remark that I was an expert player on the violin."[4] This suggests there were witnesses to the meeting (or at least to Northup's decision to leave) and one of these witnesses, according to testimony given 13 years later, was Norman Prindle, a stagecoach driver and acquaintance of Northup's. Prindle testified that he and others had warned Northup about Hamilton and Brown, telling him he "had better not go off with these men, as they would not know him when they got away south." Prindle testified that he informed Northup he'd heard they were from the south. He added that Northup was aware of a kidnapping possibility, and was willing to take that risk.[5]

The kidnappers, in fact, were not from the south. They were from upstate New York and certainly did not speak with a southern accent—with which Northup would have been quite familiar, because Saratoga was a popular resort for southern travelers. Therefore, it is not surprising that Northup would have disbelieved that the men were southerners. That Prindle (or others) might have warned of kidnapping is plausible. Kidnappings of free black citizens did take place, and although the bulk of them were in states along the Mason-Dixon Line and the Ohio River, there *were* examples from New York, where vigilance societies had been formed to protect free blacks. It is unlikely, however, that the Saratoga region had been affected by many episodes of kidnapping, and therefore Northup may have easily dismissed the possibility—especially at a time when his destination was to be New York City. It is interesting to note that the kidnappers mentioned Washington, D.C., as their own destination at this point—suggesting that they had kidnapping in mind from the beginning. The fact that they only asked Northup to go to New York, however, implies that they knew they had to entice him into slave territory by degrees.

Why did Northup agree to go? One reason was that he needed employment "until the busy season should arrive."[6] Since coming to Saratoga, the Northups had relied on odd jobs during winters, and he would have seen this proposal as another such opportunity, albeit a novel one. He was accustomed to earning money with his violin, and clearly met their stated needs, even if the location was distant. Moreover, this late in the off-season, with three children to support, it is probable funds were low, and they were relying principally on Anne's income from Sherrill's Coffee House in Sandy Hill. In addition, Northup was apparently bored with his immediate circumstances, "having at that time no particular business to engage my attention,"[7] and the prospect of a trip may have been exciting. He had an adventuresome spirit and a high level of curiosity about people, places, and practices. He had visited Rochester and Buffalo,[8] and when in Canada he had traveled to several locations, including Montreal and Kingston;[9] New York was less distant than these. He says that he went partly due to "a desire to visit the metropolis."[10] He was a person who was used to standing up for himself and had little fear. He probably felt he could handle whatever he might encounter, either from his companions or circumstances in general. The potential rewards were promising; the downside may have appeared minimal. Finally, the children were either with Anne or her sister, he had no other immediate responsibilities in Saratoga, and expected to be back soon. Little wonder that he drove out of Saratoga with a feeling of elation.[11]

THE JOURNEY TO NEW YORK

The journey to New York was in an elegant, probably expensive, carriage.[12] Northup served as the coachman. They stopped the first night in Albany, where Merrill and Russell put on a sparsely-attended entertainment at the Eagle Hotel,[13] accompanied by Northup on the violin. This was almost certainly a cover to give credence to their story. The trip from Albany to New York would have taken several days, but Northup gives no details. The most-traveled road between these cities was the New York and Albany Post Road, following the east bank of the Hudson. Fast stages made it in two days, passengers spending the night in Fishkill.[14] It is highly unlikely that the trio made the trip that quickly. It probably took at least three days, with one driver, and probably few, if any, changes of horses.

Why did they travel by coach and not by steamboat? One reason may have been financial. Although Merrill and Russell certainly had a good amount of working capital and could have afforded the tickets,[15] buying a carriage in Saratoga and selling it in either New York or, as it proved, Baltimore, would have minimized the cost of the trip. Their cost for transporting Northup would have been negligible—as they could anticipate recovering whatever they paid to him after they'd drugged or seized him. Their only expenses would have been his board and accommodations—even these might have been paid by Northup in advance of his promised compensation. A carriage trip would also have facilitated further entertainments. But perhaps even more importantly, a carriage journey lasting three or more days, with overnights at local inns, would have added to Northup's familiarity with them, allowing them to develop a level of confidence and trust that would be needed to persuade him to continue to Washington. Had they taken a steamboat, it would have been less intimate, with separate quarters and many potential distractions. Their time alone together would have been shorter and of a different quality.

FREE PAPERS

In New York City, they lodged on the West Side. That same evening, in an apparently extended conversation, they convinced Northup to accompany them to Washington.[16] The following morning they suggested that, since he was traveling into slave territory, they should obtain "free papers" at the Custom House that would certify his status as a free man.[17] This they did.[18] The episode is interesting. Why did the kidnappers suggest this? There are at least four possibilities. First, it could have been part of their general confidence-building campaign. Northup certainly viewed it as a very considerate act. It might allay any lingering suspicions he might have had. Though he'd already agreed to go to Washington, the more comfortable he was with them, the less chance that he might change his mind and bolt.[19]

Second, and equally important, by city ordinance free black residents of Washington had to carry papers certifying their free status.[20] This regulation would have applied to black non-residents as well. Presumably, the kidnappers knew that Northup would need free papers. Obviously it would have spoiled their plans had Northup been arrested on the streets of Washington for lack of them.

Third, as Frederick Douglass describes in his autobiography, train conductors regularly checked the free papers of all blacks on board.[21] Since Merrill and Russell planned to take a train into Washington, passing through the slave state of Maryland, it would have been important for Northup to have free papers on him.

It is also possible that the kidnappers had another purpose in mind. Many years later when they were arrested, a story circulated that Northup had been in collusion with them, agreeing to be part of a plot to sell himself, and then share in the proceeds from the sale. Northup's retrieval from slavery would have required free papers. While the theory makes little sense for a variety of reasons (discussed in Chapter 8), it is possible that the kidnappers considered making him such a proposition, and were keeping open their option to do so.

THE TRIP TO WASHINGTON, D.C.

As soon as the papers were secured, the three men departed for Philadelphia. Northup does not say whether they arrived that same day or if the trip took longer. After a night in Philadelphia, they left early the next morning for Baltimore. They left the carriage at Baltimore and took the train ("the cars") for Washington. This train would have been drawn by steam engine to the outskirts of the capital, then by horses the final stage of the journey, as steam engines were outlawed in the District of Columbia at that time.[22] The duration of the journey from New York would have been at least two days, but possibly more, if they stopped overnight on their way to Philadelphia.

IN THE NATION'S CAPITAL

The party arrived in Washington on Tuesday evening, April 6, 1841, and made for Gadsby's Hotel, one of the leading hostelries in the city (Map 3.1 gives the principle locations associated with Northup's time in Washington, D.C.). After supper, Hamilton and Brown paid Northup $43 for his services to date (a sum substantially larger than he was owed) and warned him not to venture forth onto the streets of the city.[23] Shortly thereafter, he retired to a room in the back of the hotel, presumably a section reserved for slaves and free African Americans.[24]

The following day, Northup and his companions witnessed the lengthy funeral ceremonies for William Henry Harrison, the first U.S. President to die in office.[25] The solemn pageantry took place throughout the city, and the three spent the better part of the day observing the many proceedings. Northup mentions the frequent firing of cannon, the tolling of bells, houses shrouded with crepe, and streets black with people. He describes the funeral procession itself as "carriage after carriage, in long succession, while thousands upon thousands followed upon foot—all moving to the sound of melancholy music."[26] His recollections of the ceremonies, recounted 12 years later, were very accurate. A description of the funeral in a Washington newspaper describes a city draped in black, with huge crowds, mournful music, and a funeral procession two miles in length.[27] Cannons were indeed fired frequently, beginning at dawn.[28] Former President John Quincy Adams, who was in the procession, also described the day's events, mentioning the ringing of the city bells, the firing of cannons, and "vast crowds of people" following in the procession.[29] Afterward, Northup and his dubious comrades wandered around as the throng dwindled, viewing the Capitol, the President's House, and doubtless other attractions. By five o'clock, the crowds had departed and they would have had much of the city to themselves.[30]

The Washington they explored was a "City of Magnificent Intentions,"[31] as Charles Dickens described it after a visit in 1842, almost exactly one year after Northup's kidnapping. There were a few elegant edifices in addition to the Capitol and White House,[32] but it was largely a city of brick and wooden buildings, some quite humble, with intermingled public, commercial, and residential usages. The mall had already been set aside, and a canal ran along its northern border. The street grid had been laid out, but it was largely unfilled. Dickens described it as a city with: "Spacious avenues, that begin in nothing, and lead nowhere; streets, mile-long that only want houses and inhabitants; public buildings that need but a public to be complete;

and ornaments of great thoroughfares which lack only thoroughfares to ornament."[33]

KIDNAPPED

When Northup, Merrill, and Russell roamed the city, most shops were closed for the funeral. Taverns, hotels, and other public houses, however, were apparently open for business. "Several times during the afternoon," Merrill and Russell "entered drinking saloons, and called for liquor," each time pouring a glass and handing it to Northup.[34] Toward evening, after consuming one of them, Northup began to feel ill. Upon returning to the hotel, his condition worsened, and his companions suggested he retire, which he did. He spent a restless few hours in agony, at one point getting up in search of water. In the middle of the night, several men arrived and dragged the semiconscious Northup from the room, saying they were taking him to a physician. According to Northup, he was taken out of the hotel and down an alley to Pennsylvania Avenue. He was dragged toward a light which he thought belonged to the doctor, and then he lost consciousness, waking up the next day in Williams' Slave Pen.

Gadsby's Hotel, where the kidnapping took place on the night of Wednesday/Thursday, April 7/8, 1841,[35] was located on the north side of Pennsylvania Avenue, at the east corner of Sixth Street, NW.[36] It was one of the most prominent hotels in the city and the residence of many famous Washingtonians, including at one time Andrew Jackson and later Henry Clay, who may have been in residence when the kidnapping occurred.[37] Just a few weeks earlier, President-Elect Harrison himself had stayed there upon his arrival in Washington.[38] Created in 1826 from a row of houses, the hotel was sold and remodeled extensively in 1844 after Gadsby's death. At that time it was renamed the National Hotel.[39]

Referring to what is almost certainly Gadsby's Hotel, Dickens, who stayed there a year later, described it as "a long row of small houses fronting on the street and opening at the back upon a common yard. . . ."[40] With this physical layout, the hotel would have had many rear entrances, and therefore would have been especially suited for conducting victims unseen out the back, into that yard, and then into an alley along the side of the hotel. Dickens also describes buildings across the street from the hotel. One may have been the source of the light Northup saw as he emerged from the alley.

John Gadsby, the hotel's owner, was a regional hotelier of long standing who at the time lived in the Decatur House on Lafayette Square, where, according to at least one account, he operated a slave market.[41] In the spring of 1841, when Northup was there, the hotel was operated by Gadsby's son, William Gadsby. In 1844, it was sold to the Calvert family, and William opened another "Gadsby's Hotel" on the same side of Pennsylvania Avenue about two blocks east.[42]

Between the sites of the old and new Gadsby Hotels was located the United States Hotel, on the same side of Pennsylvania Avenue.[43] The 1846 City Directory gives this hotel as an address for James H. Birch, the slave dealer who bought Northup from his kidnappers.[44] He may have been an owner or operator of this hotel.[45]

Across Third Street from the second Gadsby's at the corner of Pennsylvania and Third (near the railroad station where Northup and the kidnappers would have debarked)[46] was located the St. Charles Hotel, another famous Washington establishment, which had a slave pen in its basement.[47] These three prominent hotels, therefore, appear to have had a direct or indirect relationship to the slave trade, as certainly did many taverns in the District of Columbia, Alexandria, and Georgetown.[48] A reasonable hypothesis is that many hotels and taverns in Washington (and their owners) played important roles in its slave trade. Indeed, slave dealers—including Birch—often advertised hotels and taverns as their places of business for purchasing slaves.[49]

Map 3.1 gives the direct route between Gadsby's Hotel and Williams' Slave Pen as the probable route of the kidnapping. As can be seen, Gadsby's was conveniently located for the purpose of whisking a kidnapped person directly across the Mall to the pen—suggesting that the kidnappers knew what they were doing when they registered there. It was certainly not the closest hotel to the railroad station where they arrived late in the day.

Moreover, Gadsby's was located just around the corner from a tavern run by Benjamin O. Shekell. This tavern (in the middle of the block on the east side of Seventh Street between Pennsylvania and North B Street, which is now Constitution) figured in testimony given at Birch's trial in 1853. Shekell, a slave trader and one-time partner of Birch,[50] testified that he operated the "Steamboat Hotel" at the time of the kidnapping in 1841,[51] although it was probably called Shekell's Tavern at that time.[52] The Birch and Shekell slave-trading partnership had operated out of this tavern on Seventh Street.

Shekell and Benjamin A. Thorn (another barkeeper turned slave trader)[53] testified that they were witnesses to the sale of Northup at this establishment (whether called the Steamboat Hotel or Shekell's Tavern), that Northup was present, was from Georgia, and did not object to the transaction.[54] Although the testimony about Northup was an obvious fabrication (see Chapter 6), it is quite possible that the deal between Birch and the kidnappers *was* made at Shekell's on their first evening in town after Northup had retired, which may be one reason why they suggested he retire early and not go out.[55] It is also quite possible that Northup was given the drugged drink at this tavern. As noted, he mentions drinking with the kidnappers in several taverns, and becoming ill shortly after returning to the hotel. Shekell's Tavern was very close to the hotel, so it would have been an obvious place to administer the drug if it were not done at the hotel itself. Also, if the kidnappers brought Northup to Shekell's for a drink, it would have given Birch and Shekell the opportunity to look him over discretely and assess his value in advance of the kidnapping and sale.[56]

Further, it should be noted that the tavern was strategically located very close to the probable route for transporting Northup from Gadsby's Hotel to Williams' Slave Pen. It might have been used as a "safe house" where Northup could have been quickly hidden in an emergency. There was no police force operating at night in Washington in 1841, so the kidnappers had little to fear from law enforcement officers.[57] However, had a crisis in the kidnapping operation occurred (for example, had inquisitive citizens taken an interest in the proceedings), it would have been much easier to take Northup into the tavern than return him to the hotel. Even without a crisis, the tavern would have been a convenient place to strip him of his clothes, money, and papers before loading him onto a cart. It is possible that they took him there anyway. Moreover, they might have planned to subdue him there had he not passed out quickly. For any of these reasons or possibilities, Shekell's Tavern probably played a major role in the advance plans for the operation.

The physical layout of Gadsby's (with many rear exits), together with its location—strategically placed with respect to both Shekell's and the Seventh Street bridge across the canal to "The Island" (so-called) and Williams' Slave Pen—strongly suggest it was thoughtfully chosen to facilitate the kidnapping. It may also suggest that this was not the first kidnapping for "Hamilton" and "Brown."[58]

It is not known who undertook the actual kidnapping. According to Northup, several men were involved. Merrill and Russell perhaps were present, although Northup, at the edge of consciousness during the kidnapping, could not later recall if they were. It is very likely that experienced slave handlers, such as Birch and Shekell, did most of the physical work of conveying Northup from the hotel to the tavern or the pen.

Williams' Slave Pen

Williams' Slave Pen, Northup's unwitting destination that night, was probably the most infamous establishment of its kind in the capital. This pen (or "jail," as slave pens were commonly referred to) was operated by William H. Williams. According to tax records and other accounts, it was located in the 433 block of the city's grid (which is faced by South B Street, now Independence Avenue, on its north; Seventh and Eighth Streets on its East and West; and Maryland Avenue on its south). Such pens held slaves awaiting purchase or transportation to other markets, and temporarily boarded (or punished) slaves on behalf of their owners.

Williams was also a slave dealer. He frequently placed advertisements (sometimes appearing near similar ones for Birch) seeking: "Negroes of both sexes, for the Louisiana and Mississippi markets," offering "the highest prices the Southern markets will justify." Some ads also offered to board slaves "at the low price of 25 cents per day."[59] Birch presumably either had leased space or was "boarding" slaves when he held Northup in Williams' Slave Pen.

W. C. Clephane, an authority on Washington, writing around the turn of the 20th century, describes the pen as a "three-story brick house covered with plaster and painted yellow," which was "set back some distance from the street amidst a grove of trees." There was an outbuilding at which "most of the slaves brought to this District for sale or shipment elsewhere were kept," though some slaves were kept in the house in a room next to the kitchen. Though from the outside the facility looked pleasant, the interior revealed its seamy function; a later owner found "staples driven into the walls to which the slaves were shackled."[60] Northup similarly describes a main house and an outbuilding, separated by a yard. From Northup's description, it appears he was held, initially at least, in the house's basement, from which he could see the outbuilding 30 feet or so across the yard.

The precise location of the pen on the block is difficult to pin down, although there is excellent evidence that the front entrance faced Seventh Street. One advertisement by Williams asked sellers to stop by his "jail, on Seventh Street, between Center Market and Long Bridge, at the rough cast house that stands in the large garden surrounded by trees, on the west side of Seventh Street."[61] Another ad describes the establishment as "a yellow rough-cast house, the first on the right hand going from the market house to the steamboat wharf"[62] (fully consistent with a Seventh Street location). In addition, Northup describes the Capitol as looking down on the house, which would put it on the

east side of Seventh, facing the Capitol.[63] Lincoln with disgust refers
to "a sort of negro-livery stable" (probably Williams' Pen), which was
"in full view from the windows of the Capitol."[64] The official public
entrance to the facility, therefore, was probably in the large main house
facing Seventh, with the house itself well back from the street and hidden by foliage. The rest of the complex, behind the house, consisting of
the yard and outbuilding, probably stretched back to the other block
with the outbuilding itself fronting on Eighth Street.[65] Northup, when
taken from the pen at night saw the lights of Pennsylvania Avenue (or
their reflections). All this points to the pen being at the north of the
block on property running from Seventh to Eighth.

One observer noted that when preparations were underway to send
a group of slaves to the southern markets, passersby would see "the
heavy shutters thrown back" and "dark, sweat-begrimed faces, pant-
ing for air" poking through the "substantial iron bars" on the windows. If a group of slaves had just been taken away, the property sat
"silent and gloomy," until new inmates were acquired."[66] Such a perspective would have required more proximity than the view from Seventh, making this a description of the outbuilding fronting on Eighth.
There may have been an exit from this building to Eighth Street, but
primary access to the complex seems to have been from Seventh. Northup describes a "narrow covered passage leading along one side of
the house into the street."[67]

The "jail" was part of a cluster of several slave facilities in this neighborhood. A block east of Williams' was Washington Robey's slave
pen (situated on the east side of Seventh between B and C south),[68]
although it may not have been in operation at the time.[69] On the same
block as Robey's, and to the east, was Neal's slave pen (again there is
uncertainty as to its dates of operation).[70] On the same block also was
slave dealer, William H. Richards, known to be operating in 1836.[71]
There were, therefore, in the 1830s, three pens and at least one other
slave business near the south end of one of the few major thoroughfares across the Mall. The offices and pens in this slave-trading district
were convenient to downtown Washington, yet far enough away to
enjoy privacy and be out of view of many who found such institutions objectionable.[72] All were easily accessible to wharves located a
few blocks away, so the slaves could be quickly moved to and from the
river. A short, direct walk took buyers and sellers across the Mall from
Pennsylvania Avenue (the city's downtown axis) to transact business,
and dealers would have a 15 minute walk south to the docks to ship
or receive slaves. Although there were other slave pens in Washington and in nearby Alexandria (where Birch in later years had a slave
business),[73] it was logical for Birch to use Williams's;[74] in fact, he lived

or had an office only two blocks from it on the same side of Seventh Street.[75]

Incarceration

Northup spent about two weeks in Williams' Slave Pen. After an initial series of severe beatings by Birch to quell his protests that he was a free citizen, he was eventually permitted to mingle in the yard with other slaves. This yard (located between the house and the outbuilding) was, he says, enclosed on two sides by these buildings and on the other two sides by high brick walls. Roofs slanting upward toward the center of the yard from the tops of the walls formed sheds where the inmates could rest on shelves during either bright sunshine or inclement weather. The roofs would be difficult to gain, making escape over the wall much more problematic. The shed feature may have been on at least three sides of the enclosure.

While in this pen, Northup met other slaves placed there by Birch: John Williams, taken for payment of a debt, but redeemed while Northup was still there; Clem Ray, from the Washington, D.C. area; and Eliza Berry with her two children, Randall and Emily. Randall was already in the pen when Northup emerged from seclusion; Eliza and Emily came later, just before they left for the south.[76] Northup's conversations with his fellow detainees introduced him to the realities of his own circumstances and to larger realities regarding the human costs and tragedies engendered by slavery. He soon became familiar with the difficulties of escape, and he soon heard tales (and saw examples) of broken families and shattered lives. With the departure of John Williams, five human beings, claimed by Birch as his property, remained in the pen awaiting shipment.

Thus, Northup's kidnapping transformed his life from one with many challenges—but also many choices—to a life of severely controlled and often brutal circumstances.

4

The Journey South

Around midnight on the night of Sunday, April 25, 1841,[1] James Birch aroused Northup, Clem Ray, Eliza, and her two children. He ordered them to prepare to "board the boat."[2] Birch and Ebenezer Rodbury[3] then marched them through the streets of Washington to the Potomac River. Map 3.2 shows the likely route taken by Northup and his fellow captives from Williams' Slave Pen to the nearby wharf. Northup states that his trip from Washington to Virginia was by steamboat,[4] suggesting the point of embarkation was Steamboat Wharf (located at the bottom end of 11th Street, near G Street,[5] not far from the Long Bridge to Alexandria).[6]

Northup gives a very brief description of his trip from Williams' Slave Pen to the river, mentioning he saw the distant lights of the city (or their reflections) over toward Pennsylvania Avenue.[7] They boarded the boat in darkness.[8] A year later Charles Dickens, with his wife, made this same trip to Virginia, writing that the ship left at four in the morning[9] (possibly the same schedule, perhaps even the same boat, as Northup). Dickens's descriptions of Washington and Virginia supplement those of Northup's and allow us to envision what Northup experienced. The celebrated novelist arrived at the boat the evening previous to departure:

> . . . moonlight, warm, and dull enough. The steamboat (not unlike a child's Noah's ark in form, with the machinery on the top of the roof) is riding lazily up and down, and bumping clumsily against the wooden pier, as the ripple of the river trifles with its unwieldy carcass. The wharf is some distance from the city. There is nobody down

here; one or two dull lamps upon the steamer's decks are the only signs of life remaining when our coach has driven away.[10]

Dickens paced the dock for a while and then returned to the boat, sleeping in the gentlemen's cabin in crowded conditions with many other travelers. Northup, on *his* journey, had been sent below decks with the other slaves. Both arose early. Both noted Mount Vernon in passing. Both breakfasted on the boat, though in different circumstances. Both spent much of the daylight journey on deck—Northup, of course, in handcuffs. Both noted the beauty of the country along the river banks. Both debarked in the morning. Northup says he landed at Aquia Creek, Dickens at Potomac Creek (almost certainly the same place).

Northup's steamboat trip was followed by an overland journey to Fredericksburg by stagecoach, with Birch and his five slaves occupying one coach exclusively.[11] Dickens, too, took the stage from the boat to Fredericksburg. He describes the scene that Northup in all probability saw:

> Seven stage-coaches are preparing to carry us on. Some of them are ready, some of them are not ready. Some of the drivers are blacks, some whites. There are four horses to each coach, and all horses, harnessed or unharnessed, are there. The passengers are getting out of the steamboat, and into the coaches; the luggage is being transferred in noisy wheelbarrows; the horses are frightened and impatient to start. . . . The coaches are something like the French coaches, but not nearly so good. In lieu of springs, they are hung on bands of the strongest leather. . . . They are covered with mud from the roof to the wheel-tire, and have never been cleaned since they were first built.[12]

As Dickens described it, the carriages, led by a mail wagon, proceeded in file to Fredericksburg. Northup does not share the details of this journey, but Dickens does. The first half-mile was over quaint and questionable bridges, the rest through mud and up hills with much difficulty. The whole trip he estimated at 10 miles, and in his case, it took two and a half hours. Northup does not tell us how long his journey was, but he does say they stopped, and implies that they did so more than once.[13]

At Fredericksburg, Birch and his company took the train ("the cars") to Richmond—as did Dickens and his wife.[14] Northup says they arrived "before evening;" Dickens implies that he arrived between six and seven. It is entirely possible that they followed the same train schedule.

Northup gives no details of this leg of the trip either, but again Dickens does, and again his description is illuminating. The train was segregated, with a "negro car," so Solomon and his slave companions were presumably separated from Birch during this part of the journey.[15] In Dickens's words:

> In the negro car belonging to the train in which we made this journey, were a mother and her children who had just been purchased; the husband and father being left behind with their old owner. The children cried the whole way, and the mother was misery's picture. The champion of Life, Liberty, and the Pursuit of Happiness, who had bought them, rode in the same train; and every time we stopped, got down to see that they were safe.[16]

Dickens describes in stark terms the Virginia countryside through which the train traveled:

> The tract of country through which it takes its course was once productive; but the soil has been exhausted by the system of employing a great amount of slave labor in forcing crops without strengthening the land: and it is now little better than a sandy desert overgrown with trees. . . . In this district, as in all others where slavery sits brooding, . . . there is an air of ruin and decay abroad which is inseparable from the system. The barns and outhouses are mouldering away; the sheds are patched and half roofless; the log cabins . . . are squalid in the last degree.[17]

RICHMOND

Upon arrival in Richmond, Northup was taken to a "slave pen, between the railroad depot and the river, kept by a Mr. Goodin" (probably Goodwin).[18] Goodwin's pen, according to an advertisement by Templeman and Goodwin was located on "Valley-street [sic] . . . adjoining Seabrooks' Warehouse," the warehouse being about a block from the "C.R.R. Depot" and four blocks from the river.[19] Northup describes the pen as similar to Williams's, except that it was a bit larger and with two small houses in its yard, standing at opposite corners.[20] These were used to do business with customers or to give customers a chance to inspect slaves privately, as they were often stripped naked for such inspections.

Richmond's slave pens were located close to each other, constituting a district: "In the middle of Richmond—not at the center of the

main commercial strips, mind you, but in slightly marginal spaces, adjoining cooperages, wagon repair establishments, and the basements
of fine hotels—one found the slave trade."[21] Although slave traders operated throughout the city, they were largely concentrated in a
four- or five-block area on either side of Wall Street between Broad
Street and the James River.[22] And like the Washington, D.C., trade,
Richmond's appears to have relied heavily on hotels and taverns:
"Much of the slave-trading activity in Richmond took place in hotels
located in the area of Shockoe Bottom. Venues like the Eagle Tavern,
built in 1787 and located on the south side of Main Street between
Twelfth and Thirteenth streets, the Exchange Hotel, and many others
had special holding pens and showrooms where sales took place."[23] As
historian Jack Trammell describes it:

> Some of Richmond's most famous hotels played a less glamorous role
> as convenient sites for slave traders. Agents and buyers would rent
> upper rooms and utilize "office space" on the first floor. Popular ante-
> bellum venues included the St. Charles Hotel located at the northeast
> corner of Wall Street and Main Street. . . . Other hotels included the
> well-known Exchange Hotel on the southeast corner of Franklin and
> 14th and the Ballard Hotel on the northeast corner. They were eventu-
> ally connected by a walkway over the street. Visitors with windows
> on the east side could look out over Shockoe and the Wall Street slave-
> trading district.[24]

At Goodwin's pen, Northup met (and was handcuffed to) Robert
Jones, a man from Cincinnati, who had been kidnapped under circumstances similar to his own. He also mentions four other slaves sleeping in the same quarters who had been sold from a single plantation:
David, his wife Caroline, Mary, and Lethe. The following morning,
they were told to prepare for a journey, and then that afternoon they
were marched through Richmond, two-by-two, with Northup and
Jones in the lead—probably so that Birch and Goodwin could keep
a close eye on the two kidnapping victims—the slaves most likely to
attempt escape.[25]

ON THE *ORLEANS*

The group of six slaves was placed on board the brig *Orleans*, which
sailed that afternoon for New Orleans, Louisiana. The *Orleans*, com-
manded at this time by William Wickham, with Luther Libby as first
mate, was a relatively new ship, built in Baltimore, Maryland, in

1838. It was a one-deck, two-masted, square stern, billet-head brig, whose dimensions were 104 feet, five inches by 24 feet, one inch by 8 feet, seven inches. Its registered weight was just under 196 tons.[26] In 1841, it was registered at Richmond.[27] Northup describes the ship as "of respectable size, full rigged, and freighted principally with tobacco." The slaves were stowed in the hold at night. The men and women were probably separated by containers of tobacco stacked to form a partition.[28] These ship dimensions show how crowded the conditions in the hold would have been with over 40 slaves and a load of tobacco, for a journey that lasted more than three weeks (and that began in stormy weather, during which "sea-sickness rendered the place of our confinement loathsome and disgusting").[29]

The *Orleans* routinely transported slaves. An invoice dated November 1839, shows a consignment of slaves shipped on her to New Orleans to the same dealer who received Northup. There were 124 slaves in the consignment—nearly triple the number on Northup's voyage. The charge for transporting this consignment, probably also from Richmond, was $20 per slave for 104 of them, and $10 a head for an additional 20 (these were likely children). This voyage carried little other cargo, leaving most of the space for the slaves. A February 1840 bill of lading for the *Orleans* shows five slaves shipped from Birch to Theophilus Freeman. From Richmond to New Orleans, the charge was $20 per slave. This evidence indicates Birch spent about $20 to ship Northup to New Orleans.[30]

The transportation of slaves in American domestic shipping required a slave manifest to be signed by the Port Collectors at both ends of the journey. One reason for this was the Federal ban on importation of slaves from other countries. The United States was also at this time a party to international conventions outlawing the slave trade. It was important that careful records be kept to ensure that ships arriving at American ports carried only slaves that had been embarked at other American ports. Slave manifests provided this necessary documentation.

The slave manifests for the voyage of the *Orleans* that carried Northup to Louisiana exist in the National Archives and provide important information that supplements and confirms Northup's account. There are two manifests, one executed at Richmond, the other at Norfolk, where additional slaves were taken on board.[31]

According to the Richmond manifest, the brig carried 41 slaves when it left that port.[32] It shows 11 consigned from Birch and 30 from a George W. Barnes of Richmond.[33] It appears, however, that the ship actually carried 43 slaves from Richmond, and this correction was made on the Norfolk manifest.[34] Northup is listed on the Richmond manifest as "Plat Hamilton."[35] How Birch arrived at the name Plat is unknown. It is spelled "Platt" in most subsequent documents and by Northup in *Twelve Years*, and was to be Northup's assignation while in slavery, although he did not know about this name change until he arrived in New Orleans. While on the ship, he was called "Steward," the role assigned to him for the voyage. Northup would not have seen the manifest on the trip, nor did he see it in New Orleans after the rescue. If he had, he would have been certain that "Hamilton" had betrayed him.

Eliza was renamed "Drady Cooper" on the Richmond manifest.[36] She was sold under this name in New Orleans. Her daughter is listed as "Emily Cooper," age seven.[37] Her son Randall, although certainly somewhere on the list, is not identifiable.[38] Above the listing for Northup on the Richmond manifest are four slaves in Birch's consignment, who may have been the David, Caroline, Lethe, and Mary he'd met at Goodwin's slave pen.[39] There are also a few more not mentioned by Northup.[40]

The *Orleans* passed down the James River and into Chesapeake Bay. According to Northup, they arrived off Norfolk the next day, where a lighter came alongside and transferred four slaves to the *Orleans*: Frederick, Henry, Maria, and Arthur. The Norfolk slave manifest, however, lists seven new slaves: five that seem to have actually came from Norfolk, and two that boarded at Richmond, but had not been listed on the Richmond manifest.[41] One of the latter was Robert Jones. By the time the ship cleared Hampton Roads, it held 48 slaves.

Once at sea, the handcuffs were removed and the slaves were permitted to go topside during the day, but were locked beneath the hatches at night.[42] The ship's security seems to have been moderate at best. Robert was selected to be the Captain's waiter; Northup was asked to "superintend the cooking department and distribute the food" to the slaves. He had three assistants—Jim, Cuffee, and Jenny.[43]

Arthur, one of the slaves brought aboard off Norfolk, was yet another kidnapping victim. He had been a free black mason living in Norfolk who was seized by a gang late at night in the street on his way home from a job. He resisted strenuously when being taken off the lighter at Norfolk. If Northup had not already realized that his own kidnapping was not an isolated episode, it must now have been clear to him, with three victims on this one small ship. In fact, kidnapping free African Americans and selling them into slavery was a fairly widespread practice, as the early abolitionist Jesse Torrey chronicled in his book *A Portraiture of Domestic Slavery in the United States*.[44] In 1853, Harriet Beecher Stowe wrote:

> Around the [slave] trader are continually passing and repassing men
> and women who would be worth to him thousands of dollars in the way
> of trade—who belong to a class whose rights nobody respects, and who,
> if reduced to slavery, could not easily make their word good against
> him. The probability is that hundreds of free men and women and chil-
> dren are all the time being precipitated into slavery this way.[45]

Although it is difficult to estimate the actual magnitude of kidnapping practices, it was probably extensive, as Stowe suggests. Carol
Wilson, in *Freedom at Risk*,[46] details many cases of known kidnappings.
As described in her book, the practice was sufficiently widespread for
many states to enact legislation to deal with it, such as that enacted by
New York in 1840, by means of which Northup was rescued. Many
vigilance committees were also formed, run largely by African American communities in northern cities, to help combat the practice and
warn potential victims of the dangers.

The appalling injustice of their new circumstances must have been
felt acutely by the three kidnapping victims on the *Orleans*. Northup and Arthur in conversation concluded that their prospects were
grim and even worse than death.[47] As a result, they began carefully
to explore the possibility of mounting a shipboard revolt and to seek
Robert's assistance. This is a very interesting part of Northup's narration. The plan, apparently, was for the three of them to seize the ship
by force (with the help of other slaves, if needed), "dispatch" the captain and first mate, and steer it to New York.

It is fully credible that they might have considered this, given their
desperate circumstances, and having the recent *Amistad* episode as
precedent. The *Amistad* revolt, capture, and trial had been very much
in the news. The ship itself had been seized in American waters in
August of 1839, less than two years before the voyage of the *Orleans*.
Legal proceedings began shortly thereafter, and the case had worked
its way through the appeals process to the U.S. Supreme Court by
February of 1841. The hearing before that body commenced on February 22, with former president John Quincy Adams arguing for the
defendants, beginning on the 24th. Mr. Justice Story rendered the near-
unanimous verdict of the Court on March 9, 1841, almost exactly one
month before Northup and his kidnappers arrived in Washington.[48]
This case attracted enormous national attention. The facts surrounding
it, the trials, and the final verdict were probably all well-known in free
African American communities.

What Northup and his fellow conspirators may not have fath-
omed was that their legal standing would have been very different
from that of the *Amistad* captives had they arrived in an American

port, even a port where they might expect sympathy. The "dispatched" Captain and crew of the *Amistad* were engaged in illegal activity, and as participants in the international slave trade, might theoretically have faced the death penalty had they been captured by British or American warships. Also, those who revolted weren't legally slaves, as the courts ultimately determined. Killing the captain and crew under these conditions was a different proposition from killing the captain and crew of an American ship engaged in the legal activity of transporting slaves from one American port to another. Northup, Robert, and Arthur, given their status as free citizens wrongfully kidnapped, might have had a fighting legal chance,[49] but any other participating slaves would have faced severe, probably capital, penalties. Governor Seward of New York might well have been sympathetic had they landed there,[50] but since the ship seizure would have been on the high seas, the jurisdiction would have been Federal, not state. Those who captured the ship would be subject to arrest by Federal officials anywhere in the United States, including New York. They would have been tried in a Federal court. There was no apparent way Seward could have intervened, and there is no reason to believe that a Federal court in 1841 would have been sympathetic to a ship seizure that included killing an American captain and some of his crew. Arthur, who was freed when the ship reached New Orleans, was certainly lucky that the attempt was not made. And it was lucky for Northup as well, because there is an excellent chance that, had they landed in New York, he would have been arrested by Federal officials, tried, and quite possibly executed.

Had Northup and his companions taken the ship and sailed it to a British-controlled port, however, their chances might have been better. About six months later, on November 7, 1841, the brig *Creole,* similar in design to the *Orleans,* but a bit smaller,[51] carrying over 130 slaves from Richmond to New Orleans (more than three times the number that sailed with Northup on the *Orleans*), was seized by the slaves on board and sailed to the Bahamas, which was British territory. There the local officials freed them.[52] Despite considerable agitation in the United States and an official protest by Secretary of State Daniel Webster to the British government demanding return of the slaves, Britain stuck to its decision, although a claims court eventually awarded compensation to the owners.[53]

Given the success of the *Creole* revolt, largely led by one individual, it is quite possible that an attempt to seize the *Orleans,* with three vigorous cooperating initiators, would have succeeded. Security was certainly no better than on the *Creole,* the crew was no larger,[54] and the officers no more prepared. The plan, however, was frustrated when Robert contracted smallpox and died. Northup and Arthur reluctantly concluded that the two of them alone could not pull it off. They trusted no one else, and they abandoned the plan.[55]

The *Orleans* arrived in New Orleans on May 24, 1841,[56] after a voyage of 23 days from Norfolk, during which it had experienced a severe storm off the Virginia and North Carolina coasts and a three-day calm off the Bahamas. On the eve of their arrival, Northup enlisted the help of an English sailor, John Manning, who agreed to mail a letter written by Northup to attorney Henry B. Northup in Sandy Hill. Manning accomplished his mission and this letter did reach the addressee. There is some evidence that Henry pursued the matter, but with no information as to where Northup was headed, and with the change in his name, nothing came of efforts to locate him (see Chapter 6).

NEW ORLEANS

The *Orleans* docked, and Northup was consigned to Theophilus Freeman, a New Orleans slave trader associated with Birch. Freeman is described by Northup as a "tall thin-faced man, with light complexion, and a little bent."[57] His slave pen at the time of Northup's incarceration there was located on Moreau Street.[58] Northup's description of the pen is brief. It was similar to Goodwin's, but enclosed by vertical planks with sharp tops, instead of by brick walls.[59] Freeman was operating on a large scale, with over 50 slaves there during Northup's brief stay. Forty-three of the 48 slaves on the *Orleans* were consigned to him, 30 from George W. Barnes, and 13 from Birch. This was apparently the off-season, since, according to one estimate, the pen would be filled in winter with as many as 500 slaves.[60] Despite his scale of operation, Freeman was operating on narrow margins, and his business collapsed about a year later.[61]

Northup describes Freeman as a cruel, profane, yet cunning trader, capable of physical and psychological abuse. Another source says: "He was known for his unethical business practices."[62] In this regard, the *Dictionary of Louisiana Biography* states that he "falsified ages of slaves to make them appear younger,[63] separated young children from their mothers (contrary to Louisiana law) and whipped or kicked slaves in his yard."[64] He apparently also engaged recurrently in predatory practices with slave women,[65] giving credence to escaped slave (and former inmate) John Brown's observation that "The slave pen is only another name for a brothel."[66]

And so, for the third time in just over a month, Northup found himself in another slave pen (or jail), now more than a thousand miles from home.[67] Not surprisingly, a strong sense of despair swept over him. But escape remained very much on his mind: he calculated that if he could be bought by someone from New Orleans and not the back country, he might be able to stow away on a ship or otherwise find passage back north.

Upon arrival at Freeman's pen, the slaves were ordered to wash and, where necessary, shave. Northup was immediately fed, clothed in new garments, groomed and made ready for sale. With positive and negative inducements, he was prompted on how to behave while on display. As he describes it, two lines were formed for public inspection—males in one, females in the other—arranged by height.[68] The public was invited to examine Freeman's "new lot" and the slaves were made to stand at length while questioned by prospective buyers, examined physically, and often asked to perform—to run, dance, play the fiddle (in Northup's case). Northup was examined ("like a racehorse," as he put it) and then paraded before prospective owners.[69] The same procedures were applied to the others.[70] There were special rooms where the slaves, male or female, were stripped for inspection by prospective buyers.[71] This was not an auction under the gavel, but a public sale with an asking price established for each slave, as a starting point for bargaining.

Some slaves sold right away. Others, including Northup, did not. Freeman asked the high price of $1,500 for him—after all, he was strong, healthy, deemed intelligent, and could play a violin—but at that price he did not sell.[72] While awaiting sale, Northup witnessed first-hand one of the supreme cruelties of slavery: Eliza's son Randall was sold away from her. She was devastated and completely broke down for a time.

During the night of that first auction day, many of those who had arrived on the *Orleans*—including Northup—became very sick. While the doctors puzzled over the symptoms, Northup told them about Robert dying of smallpox en route and suggested that he and the others may have contracted the disease. The doctors quickly concurred, and Northup, together with a large number of sick slaves in Freeman's pen, was taken to the Charity Hospital on the outskirts of the city.[73] Northup remained there for several days. The hospital records still exist and confirm this.[74] Northup and other slaves he names, including Eliza and daughter Emily, are listed in those records under their newly designated names.

Northup's symptoms worsened: he experienced temporary blindness. He came near to death; he expected to die. Many did. Coffins were manufactured in the rear of the hospital, and as the patients died, a bell was rung and their remains were placed in them. The bell rang often throughout the few days and nights Northup was there, but it did not ring for him.[75] He recovered, as did Eliza and Emily. The recovering slaves were taken back to Freeman's pen and put back on the block. In a few days, Northup was sold to William Prince Ford of Rapides and Avoyelles Parishes in central Louisiana—thus frustrating Northup's hopes to be sold to a New Orleans owner.

Ford also bought Eliza and one other of Birch's slaves, but despite his willingness to buy Eliza's child Emily (and Eliza's repeated pleas), Freeman refused to sell the child to Ford. According to Freeman, "there were heaps of money to be made from her when she was a few years older. There were men enough in New Orleans who would give five thousand dollars for such an extra handsome, fancy piece as Emily would be, rather than not get her."[76] The implication was that this obviously good looking female child would eventually fetch a high price as a concubine (or could be used by Freeman himself for his own pleasure). Whether Freeman retained Emily as an investment, or whether he intended to sell her right away and was just being cruel to Eliza, is unknown. The parting was devastating to Eliza, who had also just been separated from her son. She was never to recover emotionally from these cruel losses that occurred in defiance of the law.

Northup, who originally had been offered for sale at $1500, was bought for $900.[77] Since the kidnappers had been paid about $650, the profit to Birch and Freeman was $250 before expenses, which would have included the $20 for passage on the *Orleans*. The actual profit was probably not much more than $200. If, however, an average $200 profit was achieved for each slave, the total profit on Birch's 13 slaves that shipped on the *Orleans* was probably over $2,000—the price of a respectable house in those days.

It was June 23, 1841. Northup had been in New Orleans almost a month. Ford escorted his new "belongings" to the river where they boarded the steamboat *Rodolph*, which plied the Mississippi regularly between New Orleans and Alexandria. They reached their destination in three days, took a train to the small town of Lamourie, and then walked several miles to Ford's plantation in the "Great Pine Woods." Northup's life as a working slave was about to begin.

5

Survival

Solomon Northup survived his ordeal: many did not. At the end of the experience he was still himself, *Solomon Northup,* not Platt. He survived physical attacks, whippings, humiliations, wretched living conditions, intense labor, inhospitable climate, separation from family and acquaintances, and above all the loss of freedom to get away—the basic American freedom to change one's circumstances. He survived because he had a will to survive and never lost hope of escape. He survived because he had internal resources—physical, intellectual, psychological, and cultural. He also survived because he received help from others, both black and white, slave and free.

THE DIFFICULTY OF ESCAPE

Escape was on Solomon's mind recurrently, if not constantly, but it was a daunting prospect.[1] "I never knew a slave to escape with his life from Bayou Boeuf."[2] Barriers to escape began at the plantation level, where owners and overseers exercised careful supervision over each slave. Slaves leaving without permission for more than a few hours were soon detected. They could sneak into nearby woods at night or visit neighboring plantations briefly, but if not back by daybreak, their absence would be noticed. Owners had a significant economic stake in each slave, which kept them constantly on guard.

Slaves could travel on errands to another plantation or a town, but written passes were required. Any white person could demand to see a slave's pass, and without one, slaves could be legally detained. There were substantial rewards for catching slaves lacking passes, so poor whites had the incentive to demand them frequently and turn in those slaves who lacked them. In this way, the white citizenry became part of the enforcement mechanism. Northup frequently mentions the pass system and his adherence to it.[3]

There were also organized enforcement bodies that patrolled the roads for runaway slaves or those without passes. Northup says these mounted "patrollers" were authorized to stop—and even whip—wayward slaves, and could shoot those attempting to run.[4] Edwin Epps himself served as a patroller.[5]

An important part of the enforcement system was the use of dogs, which could track, catch, wound, and kill.[6] Patrollers used them; many plantations had a pack readily available. Northup himself was chased by hounds after fleeing Tibaut through the swamp.[7] Epps also owned a pack of dogs, but in this case, Northup secretly trained them to fear him, minimizing their threat.[8]

Geography presented a tremendous barrier to escape. The Bayou Boeuf region was located between the relatively wide Red River, the Great Cocodrie Swamp, and the Great Pine Woods. The swamp was difficult to cross, teeming with alligators, poisonous snakes, and other dangerous wildlife. The Pine Woods, more penetrable, was nevertheless a wilderness stretching as far as the Texas border.[9] Most slaves could not swim (though Northup could),[10] and the Red River, bayous, streams, and lakes created natural barriers that runaways were unable to cross. Even if successful in traversing the swamps, woods, or rivers, slaves were subject to apprehension on the other side, as they reentered Louisiana or Texas communities. There were no cities nearby with significant free black populations into which escapees could blend (Map 4 shows the parts of Avoyelles and Rapides Parishes in the Red River Valley where Northup was enslaved).[11]

Northup knew of slaves who had attempted escape. He mentions six instances of escapes or plots to escape, and none was successful. Some managed to live in wilderness areas for various lengths of time,[12] some hid in cabins on other plantations,[13] some planned escapes to Mexico,[14] and some struck out on their own.[15] All were caught; some paid with their lives. One runaway was cornered on a nearby plantation and torn to pieces by dogs. Hearing occasional talk of insurrection, Northup adamantly advised against it.[16]

A high recapture rate meant Louisiana slaves were effectively deterred from fleeing by the near certainty that they would be severely punished for doing so. Although Northup had been physically restrained with chains in Washington, Richmond, and New Orleans, the recapture rate meant that there was no need for such restraint on Louisiana plantations, except in conjunction with punishment. Slaves were free to move about on the plantation when not performing assigned tasks, but met with punishment if away from the plantation without a pass, or if they did not perform as directed while working. This system of deterrence and compulsion effectively controlled behavior and prevented escape.

Northup, held illegally, was in a different situation than most other slaves. However, he risked potentially severe consequences from making a claim of freedom either to a master or to public officials, who would tend to side with the slave owner. Telling Birch in Washington he was free-born led to his being beaten and threatened with severe punishment or death should he repeat this claim to others.[17] In Richmond, inadvertently saying he was from New York brought renewed threats from Birch.[18] Birch might indeed have done away with him, to avoid severe penalties for kidnapping and incarcerating a freeman.

Circumstances were a bit different, but still daunting, after William Prince Ford acquired Northup. Holding a free citizen in slavery did not incur penalties if a "good faith" purchase had been made.[19] Ford, unlike Birch, had not been involved with kidnapping, but he faced the loss of a valuable piece of property if it could be shown that Northup was held illegally. If there was a chance that a slave might be freed, it was customary to hide or quickly resell the slave. Northup apparently calculated that the risks of this happening were too great. He considered revealing his status to Ford (whose decency Northup came to trust), and later wondered if this might have been the best course of action. But when he was sold to Tibaut and then Epps, such a revelation would have been disasterous. Northup concluded that "the slightest knowledge" of his real circumstances "would consign me at once to the remoter depths of slavery. I was too costly a chattel to be lost, and was well aware that I would be taken farther on, into some by-place, over the Texas border, perhaps, and sold."[20] This assessment was not unfounded. Epps, informed by Henry Northup of Solomon's real status years later, said that "if he had only had an hour's notice . . . he would have run me into the swamps, or some other place out of the way, where all the sheriffs on earth couldn't have found me."[21] This possibility was certainly foreseen by lawyer John P. Waddill, who rushed proceedings to prevent advance word of Northup's impending rescue from reaching Epps.

Would Northup's chances of escape have been lessened if he'd been moved further "up-country" or into Texas? Probably. Northup mentions only two methods of escape that he seriously contemplated: communicating his plight by letter, or sneaking onto a boat headed for free soil.[22] The latter was on his mind from the beginning. While in New Orleans, he'd hoped to be sold to someone there because the city's location would facilitate such a stratagem. Years later, when he was returning from the sugar plantations in southern Louisiana, he unsuccessfully approached a steamboat captain, asking for help in stowing him away.[23] He may have believed that the further he moved away from the Mississippi-based navigation system, the less chance he'd have to escape by boat. He may also have felt that the further he was from New Orleans generally, the colder the trail would be for potential rescuers to follow. After the possibility of approaching Ford receded, Northup decided to rely on ". . . Providence and my own shrewdness for deliverance."[24]

Escape, however, always remained his hope. Northup, unlike most other slaves, had a home to which he could have escaped, and believed there were individuals who would help him escape if he could communicate with them. He had a safe haven, if only he could get there. But the whole force of the society he was in was ranged against him— at least until he could get proof of his status. That was only possible through the agency of others, and those who might help did not know where he was.

Although he had tried to contact home, this was very difficult after he left the boat in New Orleans. Slaves were not allowed to post letters without written permission from their masters.[25] Obtaining paper and ink excited suspicion. These were small towns, postmasters knew their communities, and posting anonymously was nearly impossible. Northup was once able to obtain paper, make ink, fashion a quill, and write a letter home, but he could not post it on his own. In seeking help he misjudged a man's character, was almost caught, and had to destroy the letter for fear of discovery.[26] This lesson left an indelible mark. His luck eventually turned when he correctly deduced that Bass could be trusted to communicate for him,[27] but the opportunity was a long time coming.

Perhaps even more importantly, Northup resisted the temptation to share his story until the circumstances clearly warranted it. He kept his secret from everyone. Even telling fellow slaves was avoided, because no slave could help him, but any slave could expose him.[28] This showed an enormous amount of self-discipline, self-control, and commitment to survive.

THE CONTROLLED ENVIRONMENT

If escape was truly a remote possibility, then Northup was faced with the reality of survival in often brutal conditions of enormous constraint and control. Slave owners and "supervisors" varied greatly in their social and economic circumstances, as well as in their temperament and general approach to the institution of slavery—and they used a wide range of incentives, positive and negative. The mechanisms of control could vary with the work circumstances, as well as from owner to owner. The system was shaped primarily by two factors: 1) the enormous personal discretion owners had when it came to their slaves, and 2) the reality that escape attempts would inevitably mean return to their owners to face even harsher treatment. Owner control was nearly absolute. To be sure, there were economic, social, religious, and occasionally legal factors influencing owner conduct toward their slaves, but these often failed to encourage decency or restraint. Economic pressures on planters operating near the margin forced them to extract the maximum from their slaves, balancing positive against negative incentives, and in the case of the latter, weighing the deterrent value of brutal punishment against the commercial interest in not degrading the physical capacity of the slave.

Social pressures also cut both ways: Ford, for example, averred that it was in the interest of planters to treat slaves humanely, and that all planters should frown on those who didn't.[29] Others set a high value on the willingness of slave-owners to employ harsh treatment, claiming those who didn't do so were unfit to own slaves.[30] Slave owners' judgments about neighbors' practices were part of the culture, and the desire for approval shaped values and behavior. On small plantations, slaves provided immediate opportunities for owners to take out their frustrations, while on large plantations they might undergo the rigors and humiliations of impersonal treatment. Slaves could suffer from both proximity *and* distance from the owner.

The resulting system operated in a peculiarly arbitrary fashion when it came to the circumstances of individual slaves. For instance, the luck of the draw often determined whom the slave would work for (conditions could instantly deteriorate when a slave was sold to another owner). Individual owners could and did behave capriciously when it came to their slaves. Thus, slaves worked in a system characterized by unpredictability and therefore enormous operational and psychological insecurity. Northup faced many different circumstances and had to forge a serious working relationship with more than a dozen people, including three different owners of very different temperaments.[31]

FORD AND TIBAUT

William Prince Ford, Northup's first owner, apparently believed in positive incentives to motivate his slaves—at least this was how he handled Northup, who was never beaten while owned by Ford.[32] He performed heavy tasks ably, and received interesting duties as well.

Most were lumber-related tasks he could accomplish, given his skills and work experience in the north. Laboring under overseer Adam Taydem at Ford's mills, Northup describes no serious issues with him, despite a rivalry between them, as evidenced by the rafting incident (with Taydem predicting Northup would fail and Northup determined to prove he could succeed). However, the relationship appears to have been a productive one.

Ford's incentives included praise for a job well done: "It was a source of pleasure to surprise Master Ford with a greater day's work than was required. . . . It was the desire of Ford's approving voice that suggested to me an idea [the rafting project] that resulted to his profit."[33] Northup, through his own efforts, could at least earn praise and the accompanying satisfaction. Such praise was also a subtle recognition of Northup's own superiority over Ford's other slaves—and that recognition was likely valuable to Northup in his early months of slavery. It seems Northup was handled in such a way that he became proactive in his work—as the rafting and loom experiences show. As a slave owner, Ford no doubt could use negative incentives if needed (although Northup provides no examples of such), but he clearly made effective use of the proverbial carrot as well.

Northup portrays Ford as a decent human being, paternalistic, religious, and caring. Northup probably first noticed his decency when Ford offered to buy Emily, Eliza's child, from Freeman in New Orleans. These qualities were very important to Northup in his chain of survival. Not only did Ford and his agent Chafin literally save Northup's life on at least one occasion, but Ford's home on the Texas road was an oasis, occasionally providing Northup with a sense of security and respite from the constant challenges and dangers of his circumstances.[34] Northup even stated, remarkably, that were it not for the absence of his family, he might have borne Ford's "gentle servitude, without murmuring all my days."[35]

John Tibaut, Northup's second owner, was the polar opposite of Ford. He was an insecure lower-middle-class white man, living at the economic and social margins, who apparently slid below those margins shortly after selling Northup. As Northup described him, he was a "small crabbed, quick-tempered, spiteful man."[36] Northup was his most valuable property, but Tibaut's personal problems and resentments trumped economic calculation, and he seemed incapable of using this asset well or even caring about his financial stake in it. The nature and full extent of Tibaut's personal and psychological problems remain unknown, but whatever they were he took them out on Northup—the most proximate person and one under his complete control. Northup was smarter, and probably a better carpenter. Instead of recognizing and taking full advantage of Northup's talents, Tibaut resented them. His usual method of dealing with Northup involved constant criticism. He complained about everything Northup did, cursed, and gave contradictory directions. He would not listen to suggestions, nor recognize a job well done. He used no carrots, and the stick was applied constantly, not selectively, whether tasks were well or poorly carried out.

It was not just the hostility, but the capriciousness that became unbearable. If one's quality of life depends on successfully doing the bidding of others, perhaps the worst circumstance to be faced is never knowing what's expected. This is what Northup encountered—the full inability to satisfy his master's wishes because they were inherently and structurally unsatisfiable. Yet failure to satisfy them meant escalating belligerence. Little wonder that when Tibaut reached for the whip, Northup, angry and at his wit's end, rebelled and fought back. This was not unheard-of behavior for a slave in Northup's situation.[37] Though nearly costing him his life, it may have been a major psychological turning point in his fight for survival. He defied and he survived.

DEALING WITH EPPS

Edwin Epps, Northup's third owner (and for 10 of his 12 years in slavery), exercised control in yet another way. A former driver and overseer, he was well-practiced in the use of the lash. In fact, he was proud of his skill with it, using it frequently. He was a small planter with less than 12 slaves, but a hard worker and a hard taskmaster. He was known throughout the region as one who "broke" slaves and subdued their spirits like a jockey breaking a horse.[38] His efforts, calculated to squeeze the maximum out of his chattels, were both ruthless and efficient. He was not, however, an automaton—he dealt with his slaves in very personalized ways.

Like Tibaut, Epps had little education, but unlike Tibaut, he was smart, shrewd, and cunning—an ambitious and driven businessman operating in an agricultural economy fraught with challenges and the constant potential for disaster. A profitable and sustained cotton operation depended on careful navigation through the recurrent dangers of market fluctuations and crop failure. The margins were narrow. Larger operators, and especially those like Ford who had a lumber mill on the side (its business was less imperiled by weather and disease), had more wiggle room, but small planters like Epps constantly faced failure. They themselves had to scramble and supervise all the plantation's details. The "Great House" they lived in was often not much larger than a cottage. It was a hard life, and frustrations were often taken out on spouses, and especially slaves. In this connection, Epps was addicted to alcohol and engaged in drinking bouts during the first few years Northup was with him, although he later kicked the habit. Despite his own tough circumstances, however, Epps managed to stay above water during the time Northup knew him. By using efficient agricultural practices, being quick to take advantage of market opportunities, and extracting maximum performance from his slaves— driving them to the limit of their endurance (while supporting them at a subsistence level)—he managed to succeed, save enough money to buy his own plantation, and raise a family.

But life under Epps' control was extremely difficult, especially in harvest time, when Epps never hesitated to use the lash. He severely punished slaves who were not in the field when the workday began, or whose rate of labor fell short of his standards. When crops were being harvested, the hours were very long, and life an intense daily cycle of constant demands.

The important difference between Epps's severity and that of Tibaut was its level of calculation. Epps used no carrots, but his stick was carefully tailored to produce an intended effect. Slaves were punished frequently, but usually for specific reasons. If they were late, if they left the plantation without a pass, if they slacked off on their work, or if their work quota fell short, they could expect a whipping. Otherwise, they were left alone. Two important exceptions to this rule occurred when Epps was drunk or when he perceived a challenge to his mastery. In the former case, his skill with the whip was diminished and his actions therefore could be dealt with. In the latter case, however, the consequences could be dire. When he learned Northup was trying to post a letter, when he heard he wanted to be sold, when he saw him giving instructions to another slave, and when he thought his own unwilling concubine, Patsey, was cheating on him, the challenge to his authority or to his manhood could produce severe recrimination. It was then that his insecurities surfaced and the disciplinary or punitive relationship between master and slave became highly personal. Northup talked his way out of the first of these, but not out of the second and third, and the hapless Patsey was lashed mercilessly. Epps, however, by and large, made it clear to his chattels what was expected of them. His constant supervision was not arbitrary, but consistently designed to intensify their efforts at predictable and understandable tasks. This made life under Epps, though far inferior to that under Ford, at least better than it had been with Tibaut.

Epps often used his slaves for entertainment to take his mind off of his severe circumstances. When in a foul mood after a drinking bout, he would chase them around with his whip, often playing a sort of hide-and-seek game. Once, he drunkenly chased Northup about with a knife, a potentially dangerous situation, but one which Northup was able to handle. When in a merrier mood, also after a drinking bout, Epps made his slaves dance. Tibaut had told him that Northup could play the violin, and Mary Epps prevailed on her husband to purchase one in New Orleans for Northup to play. Northup sometimes played for just the both of them and their family, but Epps got special pleasure from dances where his slaves performed briskly for him. These revelries were occasions of intense and frenetic activity, with the forced merriment proceeding at a hot pace to the quick-stepping tune of Northup's fiddle. Epps, boisterous and merry, often with whip in hand, danced along with them well into the night. Although there was always variety in Epps's drunken revelries, his diminished capacities on most occasions lowered the risk of serious injury to his slaves, and the certainty that he would revert to type when sober again, meant that they could discount the threats he made while drunk. For all his foibles and idiosyncrasies, he was predictable, which helped Northup navigate through the minefields created by Epps's colossal insecurities.

These insecurities were extensive and important in defining his conduct. He was both economically and socially insecure. He responded rationally to the first insecurity with his severe plantation practices. Less rationally, his drinking may have been another means of escaping those harsh economic realities. With respect to his social insecurities, his being white and the need to assert the superiority of whiteness were very important to this lower-middle-class person who was at some distance from the top of his community's social hierarchy: he may have been economically challenged, but at least he was white. He therefore found it necessary to emphasize what he perceived as a chasm between himself as a white person and the blacks surrounding him. This stereotypical behavior was manifested in his constant use of the standard "n. . . . r" appellation, in his generally derogatory language when referring to blacks in his conversations with Bass (when he referred to them as monkeys and baboons),[39] and in the way he contemptuously made them dance.[40] Most of all, perhaps, was his frequent use of the whip, which not only sent the message that he regarded his slaves as animals,[41] but which was also a chance to demonstrate superior physical dexterity, to remind his chattels of their inferior status, and to reassure himself constantly with respect to his own status.[42]

Northup's narrative conveys just how freely the whip was employed.[43] The threat of corporal punishment was a constant fact of life in the slave culture, and Northup gives many incidents, especially involving Epps, and especially at cotton time: Epps unsuccessfully tried to whip Northup into picking cotton faster, and "It was rarely that a day passed by without one or more whippings" when the cotton was weighed. "It is the literal unvarnished truth that the crash of the lash and the shrieking of the slaves, can be heard from dark to bedtime, on Epps' plantation, any day almost during the entire period of the cotton-picking season."[44] He describes the whipping of fellow-slave Wiley by patrollers and again by Epps after he was caught returning from a nocturnal visit to a nearby plantation, and a second whipping by Epps after he ran away following this episode.[45] Northup also describes the brutal and vindictive whipping of Patsey whom Epps suspected of cheating on him.[46]

For his last eight years in slavery, Northup was entrusted by Epps to be a driver in charge of the other slaves and was tasked to use the whip on them to ensure performance in the field. Drivers were typically appointed for "their strength, intelligence, loyalty, and managerial ability."[47] Northup conspired with the others to make Epps think he was whipping them severely, when he was not really doing so. He is careful to distinguish his behavior from that of the typical overseer, who used his instruments of punishment relentlessly.[48] He could not, however, fool Epps when the latter was close by, and if Epps concluded that Northup was not vigorous enough when inflicting punishment, he himself was subject to the lash.[49]

It is possible that Epps and Northup reached a sort of unstated accommodation somewhere along the way because by the time he was rescued it appears that Northup was not subject to frequent whippings. His references to his next-to-last whipping and to his last whipping suggest that a substantial amount of time had passed between them.[50] Interestingly, none of the last three punishments (or attempted punishments) Northup describes was for underperformance of a task assigned to him or to discipline him in the narrow sense of the word; rather all three seemed to be reassertions of Epps' superiority—reminders of who was boss: one was for telling Patsey to avoid Epps's lecherous invitations (causing Epps to come after Northup with a knife, though nothing serious ensued), one was a whipping as punishment for Northup's expressing a desire to be sold to someone else, and the last immediately followed Northup being acclaimed for a successful series of musical performances at Christmas time. The common denominator was the need for Epps to maintain his status of unquestioned superiority when Northup appeared to defy him, was anxious to escape his control, or received acclaim in the community.

Fear of punishment therefore constituted a central motivating force on many plantations, including Epps's, and fear as a control mechanism was pervasive: the slave ". . . fears he will be caught lagging through the day; he fears to approach the gin-house with his basket-load of cotton at night; he fears that when he lies down he will oversleep himself in the morning."[51] This condition "broke many slaves psychologically as well as physically."[52] But Northup says punishment became truly unbearable when inflicted for failure to perform tasks that were beyond a slave's capacity or in an unpredictable or capricious manner. By contrast, when Northup worked for Randall Eldred in the Big Cane Brake, he labored very hard, often to the point of fatigue, yet he "could lie down at night in peace, and arise in the morning without fear."[53] Christmas was also portrayed as a "brief deliverance from fear."[54] The possibility of such respites was an important factor in Northup's survival.

Northup recognized that slaves had no legal recourse for barbarous punishment inflicted on them. The system provided no effective means of resistance or remonstrance.[55] Even worse, the system could not even guarantee slaves would be punished according to the law. Northup was almost lynched by Tibaut, and he describes mass lynchings in nearby Alexandria, which had occurred before his arrival, in response to citizen panic and hysteria over rumors of a slave revolt (actually a planned escape).

In addition to facing unremitting instruments of control, Northup also endured a daily life in primitive living conditions. Epps was not lavish in his expenditures on maintenance. Northup's rations were at subsistence level, his living conditions spartan. He could supplement his rations and improve his abode on his own time and with his own resources. At times he did so, but foraging for those extra rations added another challenge to his daily existence, and, given Epps's temperament, it was probably not prudent to improve one's cabin too much or too visibly.

These, then, were the conditions under which Northup labored. Faced with the near-impossibility of escape, with the instruments of plantation and community control, and sparse living conditions, how did Northup survive 11 years and six months in Rapides and Avoyelles Parishes?

RESOURCES FOR SURVIVAL

First, he was in good physical condition. He could run, swim, and fight. His experience as a farmer, rafter, and lumberman had certainly kept him in good shape. He survived smallpox contracted on the *Or-leans,* and also a serious illness that incapacitated him for weeks not long after his purchase by Epps. His physical strength and fighting skills saved him from being killed by Tibaut in their two encounters—and his running and swimming skills enabled him to escape the dogs during his flight through the swamp. Physical strength produced en-durance and was a very important factor in his survival.

Second, Northup was smart and competent. In his book, he dis-creetly indicates he did not feel intellectually challenged by his com-panions—black or white. The book itself attests to his intellectual abilities: although Wilson was Northup's amanuensis, the story line is obviously Northup's and his level of recall is enormous. Northup's memory was extraordinary and the details he provides check out in almost all instances where there is evidence to test them.[56] This is proof not only of his intelligence but also of a high level of engagement with his environment, including an ability to observe accurately and assess carefully his surroundings and circumstances. He could read situations and correctly weigh their potential. He confronted harsh circumstances with a sober and careful realism and understood con-straints. He exhibited neither wishful thinking, nor a willingness to gamble against the odds, nor a heroic romanticism—and he certainly was not suicidal. As noted above, he understood the risks of revealing his past history (even to Ford). Knowing the odds against escape, he didn't attempt it, and advised fellow slaves against an uprising. In the Armsby episode, he knew when to cut his losses and burn his letter. He recognized potential dangers around him and took precautions—for example, training Epps's dogs to fear him so they wouldn't track and injure him. He also knew where to seek help when in trouble. In each of these cases, if he had not acted prudently the story's ending might have been very different.

At first glance, the two fights with Tibaut seem to be an exception to his rule of caution—and the first fight, born of intense frustration, was certainly uncalculated. But in some ways, these two fights dem-onstrated both a strong survival instinct and a sense of self-control. Even at the height of passion in the first fight, Northup knew enough to hold back and not kill Tibaut. In the second fight, he was attacked by Tibaut, perhaps with murderous intent, and fought back preven-tively, fully consistent with a posture of minimizing potential losses. He seemed to keep his head during the flight through the swamp fol-lowing the second fight, strategically aiming toward water and cross-ing it to hide his scent, halting (to avoid the dangers of the swamp) when the hounds had abandoned the chase, getting his bearings as soon as nightfall revealed the stars, and then heading immediately for the protection of Ford so as to avoid becoming a fugitive in the eyes of the law.

During his earlier life as farmer, rafter, and lumberman, Northup developed the economic and social survival skills of a small business-man. One of these skills was the ability to read people. He gives us shrewd and thoroughly convincing descriptions of many people in *Twelve Years*—their physical appearance, level of intellect, experiences, motivations, and patterns of conduct.[57] His record was not perfect—he misread Armsby,[58] not to mention Merrill and Russell—but generally speaking, it was excellent.

The ability to read people accurately is certainly an intellectual sur-vival skill that would aid anyone in Northup's circumstances. Walter Johnson, in his extraordinary study, *Soul by Soul*, comments extensively on the importance of slaves being able to read people, both black and white, and to assess accurately whom they could trust. One example he gives is Northup's careful approach to Arthur to feel him out before they hatched the plot to seize the *Orleans*.[59] Northup knew how to read Ford and serve him well to earn recognition and approval. He also learned how best to handle both the sober and the drunken Epps; in the Armsby episode, Northup deftly redirected the target of Epps's insecurities from himself to Armsby; when a drunken Epps chased him with a knife, Northup knew how, indirectly, to bring Mary Epps into the picture to provide him with cover until Epps sobered up. He finally convinced Epps to use him for tasks other than picking cotton; despite Epps's disappointment over that, he still selected Northup to be a driver. The relationship was never a calm one (impossible, given Epps's need for bluster and to show repeatedly that he was boss), but it became manageable from both sides.

Third, Northup had vocational skills that were of importance to his owners and to himself. They contributed to his ability to survive. They made him a valuable slave. Ford knew it; even Epps knew it. And these were not skills in the narrow sense of the word. Throughout *Twelve Years*, Northup demonstrates a marvelous curiosity about how things are done and how things work—and a desire to convey that to his reading audience—especially for those practices his northern read-ers would be unfamiliar with. Knowing how and why things work is very valuable not only for maintenance and repair work, but also for finding substitutions in emergencies and for developing improved techniques to accomplish old tasks.[60]

As described in Chapter 2, Northup could raft, lumber, and farm. He was therefore handy with axe, hammer, and saw. He had handled farm machinery and farm animals. He'd prepared soil for cultivation; he had planted and harvested and could build and fix things. To be sure, he had to learn new skills in this different agricultural environment, but he approached this from the position of one who understood their importance and who already knew related skills. Hence, for Ford he could immediately fill the role of artisan slave, handling just about any task at his lumber mill.[61] He could raft Ford's lumber to market (apparently never attempted by anyone else);[62] he could build looms, having inspected one at a nearby plantation;[63] he worked on a cotton press;[64] he did carpentry work for Ford,[65] Tibaut[66] and Epps;[67] he made tools, plow beams, and wagon tongues for Epps, and repaired furniture for Mary Epps;[68] he built cabins, repaired a sugar house, and helped Bass build the Epps "Great House."[69] Artisan slaves had the highest status and value, and Northup stood out in this category. He had obviously earned Ford's respect before the rafting episode (or Ford wouldn't have let him attempt it), but Northup's success in this enterprise augmented his relationship with Ford, paving the way for his experiment in looms—and the relationship with Ford enabled Northup to survive his stormy passages with Tibaut. Hence, his skills as an artisan and Ford's recognition of them became a decisive factor in his chain of survival.

Northup's acquaintance with tools and farm machinery probably made it easy for him to acquire the skills needed to work in a sugar factory, first for William Turner, later for a Mr. Hawkins. He does not describe the details of what he did in these mills, but at Turner's he was a driver in charge of a gang of a hundred slaves—suggesting he had the opportunity to educate himself well about the process. He may have been similarly employed at Hawkins's mill, or he may have worked in maintenance, but he does not say. His detailed description of Hawkins's operation[70] suggests that at some point he worked on the machinery. His factory work also gave him the opportunity to get away from Epps for sustained spells, which helped with his morale.

With respect to his work in the field, both on Epps's plantation and in the cane fields, his skills from the north again stood him in good stead in terms of planting, cultivation, and corn harvesting, though he was not prepared for cotton picking or sugar cane cutting. He describes the planting and the "scraping" (cultivating) of cotton, a process involving both ox- or mule-drawn plows and hoe-wielding slaves.[71] He later describes the planting and cultivation of sugar cane.[72] Although the specifics were obviously different from planting and cultivating corn, the processes were similar and the machinery and tools largely the same. He mentions no difficulties in participating in both processes. Northup quickly became highly proficient using a cane knife to cut sugar cane, earning the position of lead cutter.[73] Cotton picking was a different story. He was terrible at it. He describes the ability to pick cotton as a gift, a natural dexterity of the hand possessed by some slaves and not others. Northup lacked it. Much practice went to no avail, and whippings did little to improve his technique. It was apparently not unusual for a slave to lack this skill, and Epps, realizing that Northup would never be able to pick his minimum quota of 200 pounds a day, assigned other tasks to him.[74] Had Northup not been a valuable slave in other respects, Epps might have disposed of him and condemned him to labor in much worse circumstances.

Northup also used his skills and ingenuity to improve his own living circumstances. Some of these skills could earn him money for work done on Sundays, which added to his resources. He hunted possums and raccoons to supplement his diet (and apparently easily learned how to do so without firearms).[75] He invented a trap to catch fish so precious time would not be wasted fishing with a rod and line.[76] This invention, of which he was quite proud, produced a decent supply of fresh food when the plantation bacon was putrid and full of worms.

Another skill that helped him survive was his proficiency on the violin. Performing earned him money for adding amenities and conveniences to his cabin.[77] Fiddling gave him access to the region's Great Houses and thereby augmented his ability to read and understand many important details of the white social structure. His musical skill set him apart and increased his value to Epps.[78] All these added to Northup's resources and hence his chances for survival.

Fourth, Northup received help from others, white and black. Without Ford and Chafin, Tibaut probably would have killed or severely maimed him. Without Manning and Bass, he couldn't have communicated with acquaintances in Saratoga. Kindnesses extended by Randal Eldred and Mary McCoy made life a bit more tolerable. Even Epps sent for Dr. Windes (whose name Northup gives as Wines) to protect his property when Northup became sick, although it is uncertain the good doctor's prescription of cutting back on Northup's food aided his recovery. And in his rescue, Northup certainly received the assistance of many people in New York and Louisiana.

He was also helped and supported by many of his companion slaves. Fellow inmates of the Washington, Richmond, and New Orleans slave pens were sources of encouragement and valuable information. There were kindnesses when Northup was in duress: Rachel bringing him a cup of water when he was tied up by Tibaut,[79] the kindnesses extended by fellow slaves the evening after Ford saved him,[80] and again upon his return from his flight through the swamp.[81] He also provides snippets of conversations on the job at Epps's plantation where the slaves kept an eye on Epps ("Old Hog Jaw") for their mutual protection.[82] Northup is describing a support system here, and although he does not elaborate with many examples, it is safe to assume that this network of people he lived and labored with was an important resource for him.

Finally, Northup kept himself well-informed. His book reveals the extent of his knowledge of the region and its inhabitants, white and black, and their relationships to each other.[83] Despite some misspellings, he seldom leaves a knowledgeable reader puzzled about whom he is referring to. He supplies brief biographies of fellow slaves and mentions how stories spread via their communications network. He was certainly a recognized and trusted part of that network.[84] His celebrity status (starting with the rafting episode) grew after the widely publicized fights with Tibaut. Augmented by his frequent musical appearances, his notoriety also helped to extend his network of associates, as others would have sought to make his acquaintance. He understood the strategic value of good information, and seems to have known, either directly or by reputation, most of the key actors in the immediate region.

These resources reinforced each other: strength and endurance; intelligence, shrewdness, and judgment; skills as a carpenter, mechanic, farmer, and musician; assistance from others; and information. Coming together they enabled him to deal with people, establish a reputation, become valuable, earn money, cope with changing adversity, maintain a vital interest in his surroundings, and keep alive the hope of escape.

THE WILL TO SURVIVE

Northup also survived because he had a will to survive. He didn't let the system overwhelm him. He didn't lose his own identity, despite four changes in his name.[85] He never forgot who he was and that he had a home in the north. His recurrent thoughts about home[86] could come at moments of despair, but the existence of a home offered hope of rescue to counterbalance that despair. Most important, he used his resources to carve out a small sphere that he could control. He played a role in defining his relationships with his masters—relationships that were not always one-sided. He had victories, many small, some fairly large. He became a leader of sorts among the slaves. He became a celebrity. He became valuable, and he knew it. His narrative contains anguish, resentment, frustration, and occasionally despair, but seldom self-pity and never a loss of self-esteem. He was always in active engagement with his physical and social environment, fighting it, shaping it, and taking advantage of it—and he never gave up hope of escaping it. He had the rare capacity to regard adversity as adventure.

He encountered many examples of people overwhelmed and destroyed by the system. Eliza, who never survived her fall from status and especially the separation from her children, was one whose decline he observed from its beginning. A cultured woman[87] and long-time mistress of a wealthy man who treated her like his wife, she was betrayed, deceived, and sold with her children to Birch. Shipped to New Orleans with Northup, Ford purchased her, but both her children were sold to other buyers and she never saw either again. Crushed by the deception and loss of her children, she obsessed continually about her circumstances, "being more occupied in brooding over her sorrows than attending to her business."[88] Unable to cope with her severely altered circumstances, she was dismissed from household duties, sent into the fields, and declined even more. She quickly aged, lost weight, and couldn't do her work. Traded to another master, she was whipped savagely and finally left to die.[89] Although he does not put it in these terms, she was a stark example to Northup of what could happen if new realities were not recognized and dealt with resolutely.

Uncle Abram on Epps's plantation was another person, originally of great physical strength and "keen" of mind, who was bowed and bent by slavery. He retained some physical ability, but his obsessions about General Jackson and philosophical ramblings belied a weakening and "enfeebled" grasp on reality as the result of "unremitting toil."[90] It would not be difficult for Northup to see Uncle Abram, once regarded as exceptional, as a possible harbinger of his own future.

Patsey was a third example. She was a slave of Epps and his unwilling concubine. Northup's descriptions of her when he first knew her were lyrical. She was young, athletic, vibrant, accomplished in the field and in handling animals, the queen of cotton-picking—"a joyous creature, a laughing light-hearted girl, rejoicing in the mere sense of existence."[91] Unfortunately, she was caught in a triangle with Epps and his wife, suffering at the hands of both individuals, a victim of both lust and jealousy. Apparently near the end of his bondage,[92] Northup witnessed and participated in a cruel scene in which Epps ordered him to whip Patsey, and, when Northup could do it no more, Epps continued himself. Done in brutal and humiliating fashion in front of the whole household, it broke her spirit. The joy of life left her, replaced by "deep melancholy," despondency, and silence. Weeping replaced rejoicing. She, too, had been broken.[93] The effect on Northup seems great. Shortly afterward he rolls the dice and shares his background with Bass.

All three of these examples (and there were surely others) would have provided Northup with strong incentives to differentiate and hence to survive—because they showed the consequences of not doing so.

Northup *does* survive and he remains Northup. He may have been beaten into submission and temporary silence by Birch—but a month later he plots to seize a ship. He may have adopted the language of submission and deference, but apparently he is soon talking on equal terms with Taydem when developing his rafting scheme. He whips the stuffing out of Tibaut. He manipulates Epps (especially a drunken Epps), and maintains a sense of justice and injustice when living under him. He deals with several temporary supervisors pragmatically and in an almost business-like manner, earning their respect. His outward appearances, with calculation, embrace the customs and expectations needed for survival, but his inner self remains psychologically healthy and autonomous.

What were the main components of his psychological health that contributed so importantly to his survival? First, he maintained a high level of self-esteem. Second, he drew support and reinforcement from a network of associates. Third, and very consequential, was his music. He does not present himself as an especially religious man, though he appealed to God during moments of crisis.[94]

There were several important sources and contributors to Northup's high level of self-esteem. One of the most important was the work he performed. He came from a culture that not only had a strong work ethic but also valued work and skills intrinsically as a source of pride and respect. A hard worker was highly regarded. Those who worked hard created an aristocracy of their own—in sharp contrast, for example, to those in a society where leisure exemplified aristocracy. Work provided a sense of mastery and of control, as skills were honed and quality products and services emerged that could be a source of pride. His early background therefore reinforced a very human tendency to find pride and even joy in accomplishment, a tendency he admired in his fellow slaves, such as Patsey. In this regard, Northup describes with approval the hard and skilled work of many female slaves, including the four wood choppers in the Big Cane Brake,[95] and notes that women "plough, drag, drive team, clear wild lands, work on the highway, and so forth."[96] In these and other instances, hard and skillful work earns his respect.

Northup, bringing skills with him and acquiring new ones, could therefore recognize his own accomplishments, even in slavery, irrespective of whether others also recognized them.[97] But others did recognize them. Ford allowed him to raft; Hawkins made him a lead cutter; even Epps made him a driver—all forms of recognition. These accomplishments and recognition under conditions of slavery had to reinforce his level of self-esteem. It is interesting that the one circumstance in which he openly revolts is when Tibaut, obviously an inferior carpenter, interferes with Northup's work, and simultaneously fails to recognize his skills.[98] Northup's sense of self-esteem was also reinforced by a quiet sense of superiority—or at least non-inferiority. He was not overly boastful, but there are hints in his narrative suggesting he did not feel at an intellectual disadvantage when it came to most of his acquaintances, including many of the slaves he met.

It must be remembered that Northup did not embrace his fellow slaves blindly. He was enough of a realist to differentiate between them. As Ira Berlin puts it, "Northup's descriptions of his fellow slaves are . . . textured. Slaves are sensible or shallow, generous or selfish, vain or self-effacing, honest or deceitful. Some are brave and others are cowardly."[99] He "never allow[s] their shared condition or his deep sympathy to affect his judgment."[100]

Walter Johnson comments more critically on this quality of Northup's, asserting that he "was a deeply prejudiced person, certain of his own rectitude, suspicious and disdainful of most of his fellow slaves. He had grown to adulthood as a free person of color in New York. . . . His estimates of the difference between his own origins and those of his fellow slaves are inscribed on every page of the narrative: he comments on their table manners and intelligence, on their obsequity and illiteracy."[101] Johnson is correct in observing Northup's sense of superiority and its possible source in regional culture, but prejudice may be too strong a word. Northup's sense of disdain was not limited to slaves. He speaks of Tibaut and even Epps at times in equally disdainful terms, and he praises other slaves for attaining his own standards of accomplishment, as noted above. Johnson looks upon this characteristic as a sign of Northup's need to read accurately the qualities of those with whom he must deal; it also can be a sign of the important psychological survival mechanisms of maintaining identity, distance, and self-esteem.

Another source of pride and respect is the possession of knowledge—especially knowledge upon which skills are based, knowledge of what makes things work. Demonstrating this knowledge would be a point of pride; sharing it (because his audience might find it interesting and useful) would earn vicarious approval.[102] In slavery, Northup's ability to acquire knowledge of such techniques and master them would have added to his self-esteem. The variety of his experiences in this regard would also have made his life more interesting and even adventuresome.

A second probable component of Northup's psychological well-being was his ability to draw support and reinforcement from a network of companions. He does not give many details of his relationships to other slaves, but there are hints and suggestions indicating that his circle of acquaintances was a source of reassurance, companionship, and psychological strength. Many slaves on Epps's plantations had originally come from the same plantation in South Carolina and had known each other for years.[103] Northup was an outsider to the group, but he describes each of them in some detail and says they often "recalled the memories of other days," which suggests he conversed with them frequently. All lived in close proximity, and Northup sometimes shared his cabin with Uncle Abram. There was, therefore, a comradeship of shared experiences based on similar living and work conditions. As Northup put it (in a slightly different context): "I had dwelt among them, in the field and in the cabin, borne the same hardships, partaken the same fare, mingled my griefs with theirs, participated in the same scanty joys . . ."[104] Moreover, the fact that Northup, as a driver, conspired with them to fake whippings suggests a high level of mutual understanding and trust—as does their common use of the appellation "Old Hog Jaw" for Epps. When Northup was rescued, it was certainly a momentous occasion for the others, suggesting that he had become very much part of their group. Northup describes his departure as an emotional moment for all of them.

It was especially emotional for Patsey. Clearly Northup admired her. His description of her, both her physical attributes and her spirit, is poetic. He obviously had a great amount of sympathy for her plight. The extent of their relationship is not known, but a romantic involvement would have been extremely dangerous for both of them, given Epps's possessiveness. It is likely that they were just close friends sharing a strong and affectionate companionship based on mutual respect and admiration—and the shared challenges of circumstance. It is safe to conclude, however, that Patsey was an important person to Northup, originally a much-needed ray of light; later on, the object of deep empathy. It is entirely possible that the second thoughts Northup had regarding his rescue were occasioned by a sense of guilt at leaving Patsey to her fate.[105]

Northup also knew many slaves in addition to those at Epps's plantation. Whether he forged lasting friendships is not known, but he seemed willing to help others who needed it. For an entire summer, at some risk to himself, he fed Celeste, a refugee from a nearby plantation.[106] He and his companions on Epps's plantation also hid Nellie, another runaway, for several days.[107] He was continually trying to help Patsey. He shows genuine sympathy for Uncle Abram. It seems there was considerable sociability among the Epps plantation group and in several cases, a degree of dependence on Northup. Both can be psychologically important to a person. Northup could draw on his companions for support when needed, and their dependence on him gave Northup a feeling of purpose.

Third, a very consequential component of Northup's psychological well-being was his music. The violin had always been very important to him: "the ruling passion of my youth."[108] In slavery, it was a source of money, pride, reputation, and good will. It got Northup off the plantation and away from Epps, if only for brief spells, and it introduced Northup to people, black and white, throughout the region. More than a useful resource, the violin was also part of Northup's identity and his survival: "Alas! had it not been for my beloved violin, I scarcely can conceive how I could have endured the long years of bondage."[109]

His musical ability enabled him to provide pleasure to others, and it was a great source of consolation, reassurance, and solace to Northup himself: "beguiling my own thoughts for many hours from the painful contemplation of my fate."[110] It was a "constant companion and soother of my sorrows during years of servitude."[111] It was apparently Northup's habit during occasional free moments of solitude to fiddle in his cabin or on the banks of the Bayou. His music expressed "joy when I was joyful" and "soft melodious consolation when I was sad." When mournful of his condition, the violin would "sing me a song of peace." On a Sabbath, the violin would "discourse kindly and pleasantly. . . ." in the open air.[112] Much more than simply a diversion, music was a source of emotional stability. The ability to express in music his deepest thoughts and feelings—would have acted as a valuable form of therapy, emotional release, and catharsis.

Of course he played for others as well and sometimes spontaneously for a small crowd on his way to a large event.[113] This, too, brought some joy into his existence. It also gave him a chance to connect with his African cultural roots. Northup had grown up in a predominately white society. He'd had some opportunity to interact with northern and southern African Americans in Saratoga, including some who were musicians, but the music of the African American south and the style of dance that went with it would have been a new experience for him. Like the Native American music he also encountered and described, it was fascinating, but much more understandable and inspiring to him:

> Oh, ye pleasure-seeking sons and daughters of idleness, who move with measured step, listless and snail-like, through the slow winding cotillion, if ye wish to look upon the celerity, if not the "poetry of motion"—upon

genuine happiness, rampant and unrestrained—go down to Louisiana
and see the slaves dancing in the starlight of a Christmas night.[114]

Although he was the most acclaimed performer at dances in his
region, Northup noted the musical talents of other slave instrumental-
ists and vocalists, and the intensity and richness of the musical and
dance culture he witnessed. He describes in some detail the dances
and the accompanying songs, and even printed a tune called *Roaring River* in his book. As he describes them, the dances and singing
expressed pure unrestrained emotions of fearless joy. They were part
of the slaves' culture of survival, and they became part of his.

6

Rescue

Northup's rescue after 12 years in slavery was an extraordinary accomplishment. It involved his own efforts at communicating his circumstances to friends back home, Henry B. Northup's exertions to marshal community resources on Solomon's behalf, and Henry's month-long expedition to locate Northup and free him through the legal process. The rescue took the better part of five months.

COMMUNICATIONS FROM LOUISIANA

According to *Twelve Years,* Northup's family received information about him on only three occasions between his kidnapping and his rescue. The first was a letter from Northup himself to Henry Northup mailed by the sailor John Manning upon the arrival of the *Orleans* in New Orleans on May 24, 1841. It would likely have arrived in Sandy Hill in June.[1]

The second communication regarding Solomon occurred when Clem Ray (whom Northup had met in Williams' Slave Pen) visited Saratoga, staying with Northup's brother-in-law on his way to freedom in Canada. This visit probably occurred within the first year of Northup's absence, when Northup's wife and children were staying in New York City at the residence of Madame Eliza Jumel (see Appendix B). If Ray had passed through the Saratoga area while they were away, it would explain why he stayed with Northup's brother-in-law, and not his immediate family. Ray could have identified Birch and described Northup's incarceration in the Washington slave pen, his trip to Richmond, the slave pen in Richmond, and perhaps Northup's being put aboard the *Orleans,* but he obviously could give no account of Northup's whereabouts thereafter.[2]

Despite at least one other attempt by Northup to send a letter, it was not until the fall of 1852 that he succeeded in getting word to Saratoga again. This was the set of letters drafted by Samuel Bass and mailed from Marksville on August 15, 1852. It was in response to one of these, the letter to Cephas Parker and William Perry, forwarded by Anne Northup to Henry Northup, that events were set in motion leading to Solomon's liberation.

EARLY ATTEMPTS AT RESCUE

What attempts at rescue, if any, were made after receipt of the 1841 letter to Henry Northup and after Clem Ray's visit?

Northup's account tells us that upon Henry's receipt of this letter, "Mr. Northup visited Albany and laid it before Governor Seward, but inasmuch as it gave no definite information as to any probable locality, it was not, at that time, deemed advisable to institute measures for my liberation. It was concluded to delay, trusting that a knowledge of where I was might eventually be obtained."[3]

Henry went to Seward because recent legislation, signed by Seward, enabled a governor to appoint an agent to rescue New York citizens who'd been kidnapped and sold into slavery. It had long been illegal to kidnap New York citizens, but even if the kidnappers were caught and punished, the victim might still languish in slavery. The law was intended to "more effectually" help enslaved citizens.

Why didn't Seward appoint Henry at that time as an agent to rescue Northup? The stated reason (lack of information as to his whereabouts) may have been the actual reason, but when Henry successfully approached Governor Washington Hunt 11 years later asking to be appointed as an agent, little more was known about his specific whereabouts than was known in 1841, and had Henry been appointed agent, presumably he could have traveled to Louisiana on a search mission in 1841 just as easily as he did in 1852. Clearly, Henry wanted to attempt a rescue—the fact that he went to Seward confirms this.

Why did Seward demur? After all, he was a committed abolitionist, even this early in his career. He had just decided not to run for reelection, so there were no immediate inhibiting electoral considerations. Moreover, he was willing to take risks on behalf of principles he believed in, despite political consequences. After leaving the governorship he represented, on two different occasions, two allegedly insane African Americans accused of murder, and was vilified by his townspeople for doing so.[4] Most importantly, Seward supported the very legislation under which Henry would be appointed an agent—and this law, which had passed the Whig-controlled legislature in 1840, bore his signature.[5] The Northup kidnapping would have been a perfect test case for the legislation.

To be sure, when Henry approached Seward, he was not as prominent as he was more than a decade later when he approached Hunt. Still, he was a recent Town Justice in Kingsbury,[6] Clerk of the Board of Supervisors of Washington County,[7] a member of the bar of the state Supreme Court,[8] and a committed Whig. Like Seward, he began in politics as an activist member of the Anti-Masonic Party. It is highly likely that Seward knew Henry before this meeting, and would have taken the matter seriously.

What may actually explain Seward's reluctance was the fact that he was deeply engaged in a highly publicized controversy with Virginia over his refusal to extradite free African Americans being held in New York, who were wanted for helping slaves escape.[9] Seward had argued that since slavery was not legal in New York, the actions of these people were not a crime there, and therefore he was not obligated to comply with the extradition requests. His position had led to a spirited correspondence with governors and other officials in southern states, to a retaliatory act by the Virginia legislature, to a temporary refusal by Virginia to extradite an accused forger wanted in New York, and ultimately to legislative resolutions condemning Seward's action in Virginia, Georgia, and Mississippi. He may indeed have concluded that it was an inappropriate time to send an agent south holding a commission bearing his signature.

Moreover, Seward at the time was at odds with the administration in Washington, he was facing a personal financial crisis, and may not have fully recovered from a "period of severe depression" he'd suffered during the previous winter.[10] Combining all these factors, Seward may simply have told Henry to return when he had better information on Northup's whereabouts.

Henry may have tried to locate Northup at this time. In his 1852 affidavit, he states (referring to the letter of 1841), "That deponent has since endeavored to find where said Northup was, but could get no farther [sic] trace of him until September last." What efforts he made are not described. Presumably he did not travel to Louisiana—this surely would have been mentioned at some point in the accounts of the rescue. He may have employed agents there, or written to officials in New Orleans seeking information. The full contents of Solomon's 1841 letter are not known. Therefore, it is unclear how much information Henry had. The only clues it contained for certain were the date (or approximate date) of Northup's arrival there and the ship's name. Thus, there was scant information for anyone in New Orleans to conduct a search for Northup, especially since his name had been changed by the slave dealers. It would not be surprising if inquiries to New Orleans authorities would have been fruitless.

Henry may have made a second effort after Ray's visit. His affidavit does not say when he endeavored to discover where Northup was. Some time may have passed between Henry's receipt of the letter and the search, and it is possible that information from Ray prompted the inquiries. When Ray passed through Saratoga, however, Seward may no longer have been governor, and his successor, Governor William C. Bouck, a Democrat,[11] might not have been at all sympathetic to this sort of mission. Without further information regarding Northup's whereabouts, the matter lapsed.

Given Seward's unwillingness to act, the only realistic way of find-ing Solomon (absent further communication) was for Henry to go to Louisiana on his own. But such a visit would have been financially daunting and probably unproductive unless Henry was acting as an agent of the State of New York. So for the time being, his hands were tied. Under these circumstances, he may have hoped for further com-munication from Northup, enabling him to make a renewed appeal to the governor, but it was more than a decade before such a communi-cation arrived.

THE LETTERS FROM BASS

According to *Twelve Years*, three letters were drafted by Bass on Nor-thup's behalf in August 1852: one was sent to the Collector of Customs at New York; one to Judge Thomas J. Marvin, who had employed Nor-thup at the United States Hotel; and the third to William Perry and Cephas Parker, storekeepers with whom Northup had done business.[12]

Solomon did not ask Bass to address a letter to Henry, perhaps because his first letter had seemingly produced no results. He did not know that Henry had made an effort on his behalf. The fact that Anne turned to Henry, however, suggests that she was aware that such an effort had been made.

The fate of the letter to the Customs Collector remains unknown. Apparently, no response reached Marksville before the rescue. As far as the second letter is concerned, approaching Judge Marvin would have made sense to Northup. He was one of the leading citizens of Saratoga, a joint proprietor of its largest hotel, and a judge of Common Pleas from 1836 to 1847. His biography in *The History of Saratoga County* states "no man would go further or do more to aid a friend in distress, while his heart and hand were ever open to the needy, and he seemed to take as much delight in making others comfortable and happy as to be so himself."[13] Making allowances for the laudatory style of Victorian-era biographical sketches, it still appears Marvin was a decent and generous human being who might be expected to help a person in distress. Marvin, however, probably never received Bass's letter, as he died on December 29, 1852, in Havana, Cuba, where he had gone to improve his health. It is likely that he was in Havana and a sick man when the letter reached Saratoga; by the time it could have been forwarded to him, he was probably in no condition to respond or to act.

Parker and Perry did receive their letter. They were storekeepers Northup had dealt with, and their store was located near where Northup and Anne had lived when they first moved to Saratoga Springs.[14] They forwarded the letter to Anne. The family hastened to Sandy Hill to consult with Henry, who enthusiastically agreed to help.[15]

HENRY B. NORTHUP

Attorney Henry Bliss Northup's willingness to make a major effort to rescue Solomon Northup likely stemmed from a strong commitment to see that justice was done, combined with a life-long acquaintance with Solomon. Henry's willingness to go to Louisiana might also have stemmed from a sense of adventure—as a young man he ran away from home and went to sea before returning to settle down, get an education, and study law.[16] Henry was also compensated for the time he spent on the rescue—he received $300 from the State of New York for this purpose[17]—but this would not have been an especially attractive emolument for nearly two months' work (he paid the Louisiana attorney he hired $50 for four days' work).

His motives may also have stemmed, more deeply, from the Quaker influence in his family. By the end of the 18th century, Quakers were among the leading advocates for abolishing slavery—one of the earliest religious denominations to do so. Clarke and Mary Northup, for whom Mintus Northup worked, were not the only Quakers in the Northup family. Records show that a Henry Northup, great-great-grandfather of Henry B., contributed to the building of a Quaker meeting house;[18] Carr Northup, his grandfather, married a Quaker. After Carr died, his Quaker wife, Sarah Clark Northup, lived at times with her son John Holmes Northup, Henry B. Northup's father, while Henry B. was growing up. Therefore, Henry B. Northup was almost certainly exposed to Quaker values as a young man from both his grandmother and his aunt and uncle, although his adult church affiliation was Methodist.

PREPARATION

The Bass letter reached Saratoga in "early September." It likely reached Anne in Glens Falls no more than a week later, sometime in the middle of the month. It may have taken Anne a few days before she could visit Sandy Hill, so Henry Northup may not have received it until late September 1852. However, he did not leave for Louisiana until December 14, 1852. Why the delay? Northup's account gives Henry's "professional and political engagements" as the reasons. At this time, Henry was heavily involved in politics. He was about to be nominated for Congress by the Whig Party, and thereafter he no doubt expended time and effort conducting a campaign. For several days after the election, the outcome was in doubt; he lost by only 295 votes out of 19,681 cast. It is also possible that Henry waited purposely until the election was over, expecting to win it and thereby hoping to have more clout when carrying out his mission. Finally, it is possible that the governor, who came from the western part of the state, was not in Albany until after the election.

As soon as the election outcome was final, Henry proceeded with dispatch. He decided once again to approach the governor and ask to be appointed an agent of the State of New York to rescue his friend. Such an appointment would give him the credibility, the resources, the immunities, and ultimately, if necessary, the protection of the state when he ventured into territory that might prove hostile to the purpose of his mission, advantages that he might lack should he simply proceed south on his own.

Not surprisingly, given his experience with Governor Seward, Henry decided to approach Governor Hunt with a persuasive dossier. His strategy was to assemble evidence that Solomon was indeed a free citizen of the state by obtaining affidavits, not just from people who knew this to be the case, but from politically prominent people who knew it—including leading citizens from Sandy Hill and Fort Edward who were active in both political parties. Drawing upon a network of personal associations, Henry assembled an impressive body of legal documentation on Solomon's behalf, some of which he probably drafted himself:

- A Memorial (or affidavit) from Anne Northup stating that Solomon was her husband; that he was a free citizen of New York; that she had received word from him in 1841 that he had been kidnapped in Washington, D.C.; that a recent letter said he was being held in slavery at or near Marksville, Louisiana; and that he had been born free to a father who died in Fort Edward, New York, and to a mother who had never been a slave. She asked the governor to appoint an Agent of the State of New York to achieve this objective, pursuant to a state law enacted on May 14, 1840.

- A petition to the governor referencing Anne Northup's affidavit asking that Henry Northup be appointed an agent of New York to rescue Solomon, signed by nine prominent citizens of Sandy Hill and Fort Edward.
- An Affidavit from Henry B. Northup, attesting to the fact that he had known Solomon Northup since childhood; that he had known both of Solomon's parents (who were free citizens of New York); that Solomon was literate; that he, Henry, had received a letter in 1841 from Northup stating that he had been kidnapped and was being held as a slave; that Henry had tried unsuccessfully to locate him; that he had now received information as to his probable whereabouts; and that he was wrongfully being held in slavery near Marksville, Louisiana.
- Five other affidavits from prominent citizens of Sandy Hill and Fort Edward, which variously attested to the status of Mintus and his wife as free citizens; to having known them well for many years; to the fact that Solomon's mother had never been a slave; to the esteemed status in the community of Solomon's and Anne's fathers, and that they both could vote; to Solomon's free citizenship; to his long-standing residence in the area; to his marriage to Anne; to his having a family; to the belief that Solomon was being held in slavery in or near Marksville, Louisiana; to Anne's good character; and to the fact that her memorial should be given credit.

These documents were designed to establish two important facts: that Solomon Northup was a free citizen of New York, and that he was currently being held in slavery.[19]

It is important to remember that Northup went to outgoing Governor Washington Hunt on this occasion not as a single person holding a victim's letter in his hand, but as a recognized political figure[20] and a member of the governor's own political party, supported by an impressive array of politically prominent people from his area. His ability to mobilize such support at that time may also have been aided by the hardening of antislavery sentiment in the North: Henry Northup visited Governor Hunt about six months after the publication of *Uncle Tom's Cabin*.

THE PETITIONERS AND AFFIDAVIT SIGNERS

The account in *Twelve Years* says that the petition to the governor was signed by "several well-known individuals." The nine men who signed it certainly fit that description. They were: 1) Elisha D. Baker, editor of the *Sandy Hill Herald*, and a strong partisan Democrat, who "enjoyed the acquaintance of the leading Democrats of the state . . . [and] held responsible offices in the Legislature when his party was in power;"[21] 2) Josiah Brown, town physician and ordained Methodist Minister;[22] 3) Almon Clark, a founder of the local Masonic Lodge;[23] 4) Orville Clark, a contractor and real estate developer, general in the state militia, state senator, and a prominent Democrat;[24] 5) Benjamin Ferris, a Whig, former Sheriff of Washington County, Champlain Canal Superintendent, textile manufacturer, paper manufacturer, and a founder of the Glens Falls Bank;[25] 6) B.F. Hoag, who served with Orville Clark and Henry Northup on the executive committee for the Sandy Hill and Fort Edward Union Cemetery (organized in 1847);[26] 7) Peter Holbrook, owner of a meat market, Justice of the Peace, and long-time Inspector of Elections;[27] 8) Charles Hughes, a trial lawyer who apprenticed with Henry Northup, a law partner of Henry Northup's brother Lyman, a former Town Justice, and the newly elected Democratic Congressman from Washington and Saratoga counties (having just defeated Henry Northup himself for that office);[28] and 9) Daniel Sweet, one of Sandy Hill's wealthiest property owners.[29]

The six "prominent citizens" of Sandy Hill and Fort Edward who signed affidavits were Josiah Hand, N.C. Northup, Orville Clark, Benjamin Ferris, Henry Northup (all from Sandy Hill), and Timothy Eddy (from Fort Edward). Both Orville Clark and Benjamin Ferris signed the petition *and* provided an affidavit.

The three affidavit signers who did not sign the petition (excluding Henry Northup) were also well-known figures in the area and active in civic affairs: 1) Josiah Hand, a tanner and shoemaker by trade, Supervisor of the Town of Kingsbury (which included Sandy Hill) for 14 years in the 1830s and 1840s, and Whig Presidential elector in the election of 1840;[30] 2) Nicholas Carr Northup, Henry's older brother, a blacksmith, a partner in a firm that prepared hemp for ropewalks, Town Constable, and Town Jailer;[31] and 3) Timothy Eddy, owner of a clothing mill, and at various times Town Supervisor for the Town of Fort Edward, Justice of the Peace, member of the New York State Assembly, Inspector of Common Schools, and one-time Chairman of the Democrat–Republican County Convention (Map 5, based on an 1853 Sandy Hill map, shows the homes and businesses of many petition and affidavit signers).[32]

Of the 12 people (in addition to Anne and Henry) who provided support for the effort, at least eight held public office at some point during their lives. It is also important to note their political affiliations. Henry B. Northup was a Whig. Of the other six whose party affiliation can be determined, four were Democrats (Baker, Orville Clark, Eddy, and Hughes), and two, like Henry, were Whigs (Ferris and Hand). This was a bipartisan list, including the two opposing congressional candidates in the most recent election. See Table 6.1.

There are several good reasons why Henry Northup might have assembled such a bipartisan collection of notables. First, believing that

Table 6.1
Petition and Affidavit Signers on Behalf of Solomon Northup

Name	Party	Occupation	Public Office
Elisha Baker[+]	Democrat	Editor	Postmaster
Josiah Brown[+]	Unknown	Doctor	
Almon Clark[+]	Unknown	Unknown	
Orville Clark[+*]	Democrat	Contractor, Attorney	State Senator
Timothy Eddy[*]	Democrat	Manufacturer	Town Supervisor, State Assembly Justice of Peace
Benjamin Ferris[+*]	Whig	Manufacturer	Sheriff
Josiah Hand[*]	Whig	Tanner, Shoemaker	Town Supervisor, Presidential elector
Charles Hughes[+]	Democrat	Attorney	Town Justice, Congressman-elect
B.F. Hoag[+]	Unknown	Unknown	
Peter Holbrook[+]	Unknown	Butcher	Town Supervisor, Town Justice, Inspector of Elections
Anne Northup[*]	Unknown	Chief cook	
Henry Northup[*]	Whig	Attorney	District Attorney, Congressional candidate, Justice of the Peace
N.C. Northup[*]	Unknown	Blacksmith, Foundry owner	Town Constable
Daniel Sweet[+]	Unknown	Unknown	

[+] Petition signer.
[*] Affidavit signer.

his primary obligation was to his client, he may have decided that it would be unhelpful to make a partisan political statement out of the rescue attempt: he was not going to use Solomon Northup's plight as a *cause celebre* for the Whig Party—or to support his own future political ambitions. A strongly bipartisan list would also impress the governor. Moreover, had Governor Hunt not been willing to appoint Henry as agent, the presence of leading Democrats on this list would have provided entree to the newly elected Democratic Governor Seymour with at least some chance of success. Finally, a bipartisan list of signatories would make it easier to approach Louisiana politicians of both parties in Washington, D.C., and in Louisiana itself. No matter what political figure Henry encountered, he could point to members of that person's own political party who supported the rescue.

Why were these individuals willing to sign? People sign such petitions because they know and are concerned about the injured parties, because they are asked to sign by people they know and respect, and because they feel they will be in good company, given the list of those who signed before them.

Many signers knew Solomon personally: all six affidavit signers knew Anne, Solomon, and Mintus; four knew Solomon's mother; and four knew Solomon's brother, Joseph. One attests to knowing Anne's family as well as Solomon's. Anne herself would have been very well known in Sandy Hill and Fort Edward, and it is highly likely that she knew most or all of the petition signers.[33]

Sandy Hill and Fort Edward were relatively small towns. What evidence we have regarding familial, social, political, or religious connections between these people suggests that, as is the case in small towns, there were many associations between them. Many were close neighbors. Eddy was the only one from Fort Edward, and he would have been an obvious choice because he could attest that Anne was, in fact, Solomon's wife—he had married them.

Henry Northup himself had an identifiable familial, social, economic, or church connection to 10 of the 13 other individuals who supported the rescue, while Orville Clark had an identifiable social, political, or church connection to nine individuals. These patterns of association suggest that Orville Clark may have played a larger role than simply signing the petition and an affidavit. Clark's interest in the case was clearly more than casual. He even went to Washington after Solomon's rescue to take part in the trial of James H. Birch, the slave dealer. Moreover, David Wilson (who was later approached to help write *Twelve Years*) had been Clark's law clerk. Clark is one of two people to sign both an affidavit and the petition. It is even possible that Clark circulated the petition urging Henry's appointment (signing it last) to save Henry from circulating it on his own behalf.[34] Sweet and Hand are the only persons on the entire list who do not have an identifiable familial, political, or social connection to either Henry Northup or Orville Clark, but Sweet had business relations with Henry, and Hand, long-time town supervisor and fellow-Whig, probably knew him well. Given the network of connections in this small town, it is not surprising that many leading figures were willing to sign the affidavits and the petition. In a sense, under the leadership of Henry, and likely assisted by Clark, the rescue effort became a town effort.

THE APPOINTMENT

Armed with this impressive set of documents, Henry Northup approached New York's Governor Washington Hunt. Hunt had been elected in 1850 over Horatio Seymour by a margin of only 262 votes, and Seymour had returned to defeat him in the election of 1852. The lame-duck Hunt was probably well disposed to appoint his fellow-defeated Whig as an agent, not only in response to the appeals from Sandy Hill and Fort Edward, but also because he was (although a political moderate) an opponent of slavery. While in Congress, Hunt had criticized President Tyler for supporting the extension of slavery into the southwest, and during his term as Governor he had spoken sympathetically about the plight of New York State African Americans in his Annual Message of 1851 (quoted in Chapter 2). Apparently without hesitation, the governor signed the necessary papers appointing Henry as agent.

With Hunt's commission, Northup was now prepared to embark on his journey. He had indeed moved quickly as soon as the November 1852 election was over. The affidavits and the petition were all signed on November 19 and 20. The governor's commission was signed a week and a half later on November 30, and Northup left on his mission to Louisiana two weeks afterward on December 14, 1852.

THE STOP IN WASHINGTON

After receiving the governor's commission, Henry Northup did not travel directly to Louisiana, but first went to Washington, D.C. The account in *Twelve Years* is silent on his reasons for doing so, but there are two strong possibilities. First, the Bass letter mentions Washington as the city where Solomon was sold into slavery, and Henry might have wanted to investigate the territory to see if his inquiries could turn up leads on who might have been involved. Inquiries about long-established slave dealers could at least have produced some names.

Second, since he was journeying to Louisiana, which was unfamiliar territory to him, it may have seemed prudent (and was probably customary in those days) to obtain letters of introduction and support to lend credibility to his mission and provide friendly entrees. Given his unsuccessful attempts to obtain information about Solomon's whereabouts after receiving the first letter (and possibly after the Clem Ray visit as well), Henry appears to have been determined to arrive in Louisiana well equipped with credentials that would convince local officials to take his inquiries seriously. Moreover, he was heading for potentially hostile territory, seeking to locate a slave and take legal possession of him. Competent and willing local counsel would be needed to handle such a proceeding, and Henry knew it would be useful to find sources to identify such an attorney and write letters of introduction for him. Washington was a logical place to find people from Louisiana important enough to be impressive references.

By a happy coincidence, Henry himself had a well-connected contact in Washington who could be of help. Samuel Nelson, Associate Justice of the U.S. Supreme Court and former Chief Justice of New York's highest court, had grown up in North Hebron, about a mile from where Henry was born and raised (Map 1).[35] Nelson was 13 years older than Henry, but only two years older than Nicholas Carr Northup, Henry's older brother, who had signed one of the petitions. Nelson, a close neighbor by rural standards, had probably known Nicholas as a young man. It is entirely possible that Nelson had known Mintus Northup and his family; Nelson certainly would have heard of them. So when Henry called on Justice Nelson to talk about Solomon, he could personalize the story in a way that might quickly earn a sympathetic ear, despite the fact that Nelson was a relatively conservative justice, concurring four years later in the Dred Scott decision (though not with the more extreme language of Chief Justice Taney in that infamous case). Henry could also have reminisced with Nelson not only about Hebron (which Nelson had left at age 15), but also about Granville Academy and Middlebury College, which both had attended, although more than a decade apart. According to *Twelve Years,* Nelson wrote at least one letter of introduction for Northup, which he carried with him to Louisiana.

It is not known to whom Nelson addressed his letter. It could have been a general letter of introduction and attestation regarding Henry's character, which, coming from a Supreme Court Justice, would have helped credential Henry to any attorney or public official. It is also possible that Nelson had contacts in Louisiana, although none of his brethren on the court at that time was from there. Nelson's specialty was maritime and admiralty law. He would have known professionally many of the leading maritime attorneys in the country—which would have included some from New Orleans, one of the nation's largest ports. It is more than likely that he had heard many cases argued before the court by Louisiana attorneys arising from maritime controversies.[36] It would not have been improper by 19th century standards for him to have written to such attorneys on Henry's behalf.

Twelve Years also records that Northup brought letters of introduction to Louisiana from two other individuals: the Hon. Pierre Soule, Louisiana's senior senator; and Mr. Charles Magill Conrad, a former Congressman and U.S. Senator, and the current Secretary of War in the outgoing cabinet of Whig President Millard Fillmore.[37] It is quite possible that Nelson introduced Henry to them. Washington was a small town in 1853; Supreme Court justices would know senators and cabinet members socially; both Conrad and Soule were lawyers, and both may have appeared before Nelson.

It seems that Henry approached others from Louisiana as well. The account of the rescue in the *New York Daily Times,* January 20, 1853, mentions Nelson, Soule, Conrad, and "other gentlemen" as having written "open letters to gentlemen in Louisiana strongly urging their assistance" in securing Solomon's freedom. Regardless of who else may have written in addition to these three, Soule and Conrad would have been good choices. Soule, like Nelson, was a Democrat; Conrad, like Henry, was a Whig. Henry, thus, continued his practice of soliciting help from members of each political party. Both Soule and Conrad had wide experience in Louisiana politics. Soule had served in the Louisiana state senate for one year, and had been a delegate to a state constitutional convention in 1844—so he'd had contact, if only briefly, with a wide range of political figures across the state. He was elected to the U.S. Senate in 1846.

Conrad had even more state-wide experience than Soule. He had been a member of the state legislature for several terms and had also served in the same state constitutional convention as Soule. Conrad had been appointed U.S. Senator from Louisiana to fill an unexpired term in 1842 but had not been reelected. His time in the senate would have overlapped Washington Hunt's time in the House, so these men had probably met. In 1848, Conrad was elected to Congress from the 2nd District of Louisiana, serving until 1850, when he was appointed by Fillmore to the Cabinet. His wife, M.W. Angela Lewis, was the grand-daughter of George Washington's sister Elizabeth; thus, Conrad was very well connected, both politically and socially in Washington.

Both Conrad and Soule had lived and practiced law in New Orleans, providing them with extensive connections to the political and legal communities of that city. Soule wrote Henry a letter of introduction to Thomas Genois, New Orleans City Recorder, who was helpful to Henry when he visited there with Solomon after leaving Marksville. Both Soule and Conrad may have written letters of introduction to other relevant people in New Orleans, since Henry had intended to go directly there, probably to trace the records of slave transactions in his search for Solomon's ownership and precise location.

As far as Marksville is concerned, it is very likely that either Conrad or Soule, given their state-wide political experiences and their present positions, either knew lawyer John Pamplin Waddill directly or had at least heard of him. Attorney Waddill, whom Henry employed when he reached Marksville, was himself an experienced politician; he was elected to the Louisiana State Senate in 1848 and to a state constitutional convention in 1852. Because the legislatures in those days elected the U.S. Senators, he would have had the opportunity to vote in the legislative election contest that sent Pierre Soule to the Senate in 1849, and it is very likely Soule at least knew of him.

Failing such knowledge, Soule and Conrad would have had enough contacts among their fellow-Louisianans in Washington to get information about the availability of legal counsel in Marksville. Henry, therefore, probably knew about Waddill before he set foot in Marksville, and may have had a direct letter of introduction to him from either Conrad or Soule.[38]

As to the willingness of both Soule and Conrad to assist Henry, Soule may have been especially sympathetic for personal reasons. In his youth, he had been a political prisoner in France, where he was exiled, pardoned, and then later jailed due to his opposition to the monarchy and his support for republican institutions. Soule also seems to have been politically a moderate: he opposed secession in 1860, although he supported the Confederacy when the Civil War began.[39] Henry could have reminded him that one of the petition signers was a newly elected congressman from Soule's own party who, incidentally, had been born in New Orleans. Finally, Soule had remarked emphatically to Henry that, "it was the duty and interest of every planter in his state to aid in restoring [Solomon Northup] to his freedom."[40] Although it is not stated in *Twelve Years* why Soule believed this, certainly one factor might have been the Fugitive Slave Law, passed in 1850, which required northern officials to cooperate in returning escaped slaves to the south. The precedent of southern officials cooperating in returning a kidnapped free citizen could be used as an example to urge reciprocal cooperation on the part of reluctant northern officials—and therefore would be in the interest of "every planter." This is not to impeach Soule's apparently genuine support for Solomon's rescue, but it certainly could have been an argument he might have employed to help effect that rescue.

Conrad, though described by one source as personally belligerent (he killed a New Orleans physician in a duel), may also have been a political moderate. Originally a Jacksonian Democrat, he split with the party over the re-chartering of the Second Bank of the U.S., and joined the Whigs. In the divisive election of 1860, Conrad, like many southern Whigs, supported the Constitutional Union Party and not the party of the more extreme Democrat, John C. Breckinridge. Like Soule, he supported the Confederacy after the war began, serving in its Congress.[41] As a leading Louisiana Whig in Washington, D.C., serving in the cabinet of a New York Whig President, it would not be surprising to find him sympathetic to the ministrations of Henry Northup, the just-narrowly-defeated Whig candidate for Congress from Sandy Hill, New York.

THE TRIP TO LOUISIANA

Armed with Anne's affidavit, the petition to the governor, the affidavits from Sandy Hill and Fort Edward citizens, the governor's commission, probably the name of Attorney Waddill and other officials to contact in Louisiana, and at least three letters of introduction, Henry left Washington for the south. He almost certainly took the Baltimore and Ohio Railroad to Pittsburgh, and then a steamboat down the Ohio and Mississippi Rivers.[42]

When he left Washington, it was his intention to go to New Orleans. On impulse, he cut short his journey and took a boat up the Red River to Marksville, where Bass's letter had been mailed. He went directly to Attorney Waddill, laid his case before him, and asked for help. Waddill, a prominent Marksville attorney, plantation owner, and large slaveholder, was presumably impressed by the letters of introduction (at least one of which may have been written to him personally) and by the prospects of appropriate compensation. He agreed to take the case and proceeded with enthusiasm to the task at hand.

LOCATING SOLOMON

Bass's letter to Parker and Perry, sent in Solomon's name, had "Bayou Boeuf" as an inside address. It gave a few bits of biographical information about Solomon, so that its recipients might remember who he was; it also asked them to obtain "free papers" for him and forward them to him at the Marksville Post Office. A postscript added that he had been taken into slavery in Washington, mentioned that someone else had written the letter for him, and stated that this person was in danger for having done so. This last comment may have discouraged Henry from responding to the letter (which would have saved Solomon several months' anxiety), or he may have wished to wait until he had had some success with the governor.

What Bass's letter did not say is even more interesting. Consistent with Solomon's long-standing caution and fear that Epps would discover his true identity (as well as Bass's own fear of retaliation), Bass does not give Northup's slave name, his own name, nor the name of the owner of the plantation where Solomon was held—or even the community nearest to that plantation. The letter mentions neither Birch, Freeman, the *Orleans*, nor New Orleans. In short, had the letter become public, it would not have been immediately obvious who had written it or who "Solomon Northup" was. Interestingly, his real name was now serving as a "pseudonym" hiding "Platt's" identity as the person mentioned in the letter.

The problem was that Bass's understandable caution meant that the letter did not contain much information useful for locating Solomon. It contained few clues as to where he was held and no suggestion that he was held under a different name. What it did contain was enough information for a person familiar with the region to make some successful deductions.

Henry arrived in Marksville on a Saturday morning, and after an initial conversation, he and Waddill turned immediately to the task of finding Solomon. Because the letter had been postmarked in Marksville, Waddill immediately sent for one of his own slaves to see if he had heard of any slave named Solomon Northup in the vicinity of Marksville. The slave, though well networked in the area, had not heard the name. Concluding that there was no Solomon Northup in the vicinity of Marksville, Waddill and Henry then began to focus on the region surrounding the Bayou Boeuf, the location named in the inside address of the letter. The problem was that the bayou, 23 miles distant from Marksville, lent its name to a considerable piece of territory, stretching for scores of miles on either side. Going from plantation to plantation up and down the bayou, searching among the thousands of slaves in the region, would have been an enormous task, paralleling that of Joseph Cochrane, who in 1856 embarked on a similar rescue mission and intensively sought another reportedly kidnapped New York citizen.[43] Although Henry and Waddill did not yet know it, this task would have been made even more complicated by Solomon's name change. Nevertheless, they resolved to launch such a search first thing Monday morning. Waddill volunteered the use of his carriage and enlisted the help of his younger brother, a law student, to accompany Henry on the mission. They planned to travel systematically up and down each side of the sinuous stream.

By this time, it was Saturday afternoon, and because there was nothing else they could do before Monday morning, Waddill and Northup fell into conversation. Both were active and experienced politicians, and the conversation naturally turned to politics. Newspapers in those days carried considerable coverage of political events in other states, and Waddill had heard quite a lot about New York politics and its many factions. According to the account in *Twelve Years,* he asked for further enlightenment, and Henry proceeded to give him a sketch of the New York political landscape. In due course, he came to the Free Soilers and abolitionists, and Henry jokingly remarked that there were probably not a lot of them in Louisiana. Waddill laughed, and responded by saying that they actually did have one in the area by the name of Bass, a harmless fellow with strange opinions and a fondness for argument. The thought of Bass, however, gave Waddill pause. Asking to see the letter again, he re-read it and reflected on the Marksville postmark and the dated reference to the Bayou Boeuf. Bass lived in Marksville, but frequently worked out of town in various locations. Turning to his brother, Waddill asked him where Bass had worked the previous August. His brother found out that it had been on the Bayou Boeuf, and Waddill instantly put two and two together. Pounding the table for emphasis, he exclaimed "He is the man who can tell us about Solomon Northup."[44]

Inquiries were made immediately as to Bass's whereabouts, and it was determined that he was currently at a landing on the Red River about to depart for a couple of weeks. Henry rushed there with Waddill's brother and located him just as he was about to embark. Henry drew him aside and asked if he had written the letter. Bass, on his guard, refused to answer, but when Henry explained the purpose of his questions—and his mission—Bass admitted that he was, indeed, the author of the letter and gave the details of Solomon's whereabouts and current name. Waddill now had the necessary information to initiate legal proceedings. That evening he drew up the papers needed to free Solomon from Epps's possession. The legal strategy was to seek a writ ordering the Sheriff of Avoyelles Parish to take immediate possession of Solomon and sequester him in protective custody until a hearing could be held and a court could rule on the issue of his right to freedom. By the time the legal papers had been drawn up, it was

Saturday evening and too late to proceed until Monday. Henry retired to his hotel.

THE TRIP TO BAYOU BOEUF

The next afternoon Waddill called on Henry in a state of apprehension. The story was leaking out in Marksville. Bass had confided in someone, and that person was spreading the news of the mission to free one of Epps's slaves. Waddill feared that if the story reached Epps, he would hide Solomon so he could not be easily found. Both attorneys sprang into action. No papers could be signed on Sunday, so three local officials were asked to be in readiness immediately after midnight. When the hour struck, Waddill got the necessary signatures from Judge Ralph Cushman, posted a $500 bond with parish clerk Ade Barbin, and took the papers immediately to Sheriff G.P. Voorhies, who was expecting them. Documents in hand, the Sheriff and Henry Northup rolled out of Marksville in the middle of the night on their way to the Bayou Boeuf.

Although Henry could have identified Solomon, he felt the need for unimpeachable evidence as to Solomon's identity—evidence from another party that would stand up in a Louisiana court. On the carriage ride he therefore suggested to Sheriff Voorhies that he ask "Platt" several questions to prove conclusively that he was Solomon Northup—questions that asked for Solomon's real name, Henry's name and residence, the maiden name of Solomon's wife, the names of their children, the person who married them, and so forth. Since there had been no communication between Henry and Solomon, correct answers to these questions (most of which appeared in the affidavits Henry had brought with him) would determine beyond a reasonable doubt that Platt was Solomon.

Henry and the Sheriff arrived at Epps's plantation early in the morning. Stepping down from the carriage, the Sheriff spotted some slaves picking cotton in the field and proceeded toward them, with Henry following at a distance. The Sheriff walked up to a slave and asked for Platt. The slave pointed to Solomon. The Sheriff then approached Solomon, pointed to Henry, and asked, "Do you know that man?" Standing at a distance of a few rods, Henry would have heard Solomon's exclamation of recognition. The Sheriff then began to ask Solomon some of the questions Henry had suggested, but before he was finished, Solomon rushed up to Henry and seized him by both hands. The emotion was overpowering, and Solomon for a moment could find no words. Henry himself was silent also, his months of efforts reaching a successful culmination. "Sol," he said at length, in the deliberate manner of his region, "I'm glad to see you." The two upstate New Yorkers stood together, in silence. "Throw down that sack," Henry finally said, "Your cotton-picking days are over. Come with us to the man you live with."[45]

The party proceeded to the house where Henry and the Sheriff met Epps and revealed their purpose. Epps fussed and fumed and swore, saying if he'd had an hour's notice, they never would have found "Platt," but the Sheriff had his orders and his papers. After some formalities, he took possession of Solomon. There were brief, but heartfelt, partings between Solomon and his slave companions, who were as shocked by his rescue as were Epps and his wife. Then the Sheriff and the two Northups proceeded to the carriage, and Solomon was on his way to freedom.

On January 4, 1853, the day after Solomon's recovery from the plantation, a hearing was held in Marksville where Epps and his attorney were formally confronted by Waddill and Henry Northup before Judge Cushman. Henry presented his commission and his affidavits; the Sheriff described the scene in the cotton field where Solomon had answered the questions put to him; Solomon himself was cross-examined at length. Northup's identity having been established, Epps's attorney advised his client that it would be futile to contest the matter further. Epps signed Northup over to Henry's custody as representative of the State of New York, the papers were recorded, and Northup was once more a free man. The proceedings over, the two northerners immediately departed Marksville for the Red River, and were soon on their way downstream. Attorney Waddill and the Louisiana officials had cooperated fully and honorably in the rescue, and matters had proceeded strictly according to the law.

IN NEW ORLEANS AND WASHINGTON

Two days later, Solomon and Henry were in New Orleans. By this time, they had probably decided to file charges against Birch, and Henry needed evidence of Birch's role in the kidnapping. The City Recorder had the bill of sale for Ford's purchase of Solomon from Freeman, and presumably he provided a certified copy to Henry along with a pass permitting Solomon to cross slave territory. In New Orleans, Henry and Solomon may have been able to establish that Freeman had been partners with Birch. These things accomplished, they headed north, initially by train, passing through Mobile to Charleston. There they boarded a boat to Wilmington, North Carolina, arriving on January 15,

1853, and staying in the Carolina Hotel.[46] From there, they would have taken a train to Richmond, where Solomon spotted Goodwin's slave pen near the depot, as they changed for Washington. They arrived in D.C. on January 17, where Henry, and presumably Solomon, stayed at the National Hotel (as Gadsby's Hotel had been renamed).[47] It is likely that they passed by Williams' Slave Pen—which was right on the route from Steamboat Wharf to their hotel. By now, the slave trade was outlawed in the District of Columbia, and the slave pen was no longer in business.[48] Solomon must have felt intense emotions as he retraced backward his route of sorrows from 12 years before, but he did not have a lot of time to dwell on them. He and Henry were determined to bring James H. Birch immediately to justice.

THE TRIAL OF BIRCH

Henry had probably wired to Orville Clark, his most active Sandy Hill confederate in the rescue effort, outlining his intention to institute proceedings against Birch. By the time Henry and Solomon had reached Washington, Clark was already there. The two wasted no time in proceeding. On the same day as his arrival, Henry obtained approval to practice before the D.C. courts,[49] but, as in Louisiana, he also had local help. Justice Nelson, given his position on the bench, could not have provided such help (at least not directly). But the notoriety now surrounding the story had become so great that Henry received an offer from Salmon P. Chase, then a U.S. Senator from Ohio, later Lincoln's Secretary of the Treasury, and afterward Chief Justice of the U.S. Supreme Court. An abolitionist, Senator Chase joined Solomon's legal team and participated with Henry and Orville Clark in the proceeding against Birch.

Also on January 17, Henry and his team located Ebenezer Rodbury, the former keeper of Williams' Slave Pen, and the lackey who assisted Birch in beating Northup. Rodbury identified Northup and confirmed that he had been placed in the pen by Birch. Members of the legal team then ascertained that Birch was still in Washington and filed a suit against him. Birch was promptly arrested and charged with kidnapping Solomon and selling him into slavery. Bail of $3,000 was made by another slave dealer, Benjamin Shekell, a former partner of Birch's. Justice B.K. Morsell presided over a hearing held the following day, January 18.[50] Joseph H. Bradley, a prominent long-time Washington lawyer, represented Birch.[51]

A newspaper account states that a Mr. Townshend of Ohio (probably Norton Strange Townshend, a member of Congress at that time) and "many others" observed the proceedings and were much interested.[52] The story of the rescue spread rapidly into the press, with a long front page article in the January 20, 1853 issue of the *New York Daily Times* (now the *New York Times),* a newspaper then less than a year old.

Orville Clark testified that he had known Solomon from childhood and that Solomon was a free man like his father before him. Radburn testified for the prosecution that Birch had placed Northup in the slave pen; the defense stipulated that Birch had indeed done so. The prosecution then rested, having established that Northup had been a free man and that Birch had placed him in the slave pen.

Birch's ally Shekell then testified for the defense. Before doing so, he had heard Solomon's account of the kidnapping. Having posted Birch's bail, he also had time before the proceedings to consult with him and fabricate a story. Shekell, who had run a tavern near Gadsby's Hotel, stated that he remembered Solomon and his two companions coming to the tavern, that he recalled Solomon playing the violin, that he had witnessed Solomon's sale to Birch, and had seen the bill of sale. He claimed that Solomon had acquiesced in the purchase, saying that he had been born in Georgia, that he wanted to return south, and that his master needed to sell him because he had lost his money on a gambling spree.

Another slave dealer, Benjamin Thorn, also testified on behalf of Birch, stating that he remembered a "colored boy" playing a violin in Shekell's tavern in the spring of 1841, but could not positively identify Northup. The prosecution called Northup to testify in rebuttal, but he was not allowed to do so because he was black, despite the fact that he'd been proven to be a free citizen of New York.

Since Shekell had mentioned a bill of sale, the prosecution demanded Birch produce it, as it would corroborate the testimony of Shekell and Thorn. Birch's counsel conceded the point, and Birch was asked to testify as to its whereabouts. After objections were raised about the propriety of his giving testimony, he was allowed to take the stand, saying there *had* been a bill of sale, but that he had lost it. The judge was thereupon asked to dispatch officers to Birch's place of business and seize his records to see if they contained any notation of the sale. He issued such an order, and Birch's books for 1841 were brought to the court, but they showed no record of Northup's sale and purchase under any name.

Judge Morsell then ruled in Birch's favor, Birch being, like Morsell, a sitting Justice of the Peace in Washington.[53] Despite the preponderance of evidence, and with no more than unverifiable claims in defense of Birch, the testimony of the three slave dealers—backing each other up—prevailed. Birch's story, corroborated by Shekell and Thorn, however, is full of holes. For example, it is absurd that Birch could not tell the difference between a New York and a Georgia accent. Testimony at this hearing that Northup had played the violin for an hour is also highly questionable—it would not take that long to convince a seller that he could play. More decisively, Birch's failure to have any record of the transaction among his papers for 1841 weighs heavily against him— and strongly suggests that the transaction was a clandestine one.

After the case against him was dismissed, Birch filed suit against Solomon, charging he had conspired with Hamilton and Brown to defraud him.[54] Northup was arrested and brought before Justice Goddard, another Justice of the Peace. Henry Northup appeared on behalf of Solomon and demanded that the trial proceed immediately. Birch and Shekell thereupon asked that the charge be withdrawn and after some legal maneuvering, it was. Had the charge been prosecuted, Northup in this case would almost certainly have been able to testify on his own behalf, and he could have exposed under oath the Birch and Shekell perjury. It was probably for this reason that the charges were dropped.

HOME AT LAST

Henry and Solomon soon departed for New York.[55] During the 12 years that Solomon was in slavery, the national railroad network had grown enormously, and the two-day trip was a smooth one. He and Henry almost certainly traveled the entire distance from Washington to Albany by train.[56] Another train would have then carried them from Albany (or Troy) to Saratoga, from whence a stagecoach would have carried them to Sandy Hill. They arrived there late in the evening on January 20, 1853.[57] Solomon stayed overnight with Henry and his family, and then proceeded the next day to Glens Falls for a long-awaited reunion with Anne and their children.

1. In this affidavit, signed with an "X" by Mintus Northup, he says he "had acted and continued as a free man." (Photographer: David Fiske. Courtesy Fort Edward, NY, Town Clerk)

2. This document, signed by Judge John Baker, declared that, in light of evidence presented to him, Mintus Northup was indeed free under the laws of New York State. (Photographer: David Fiske. Courtesy Fort Edward, NY, Town Clerk)

3. The broken gravestone of Mintus Northup, at Baker Cemetery, Hudson Falls, New York. (Photographer: Heath Fradkoff, Courtesy Mandeville Gallery, Union College)

4. Solomon Northup lived in this house, which is today the Old Fort House Museum, in Fort Edward, New York. (Photographer: Heath Fradkoff. Courtesy Mandeville Gallery, Union College)

KIDNAPPING.

Designed and Published by J.Torrey Jr. Philad.a 1817.

5. An illustration depicting the kidnapping of free blacks, an all too common practice in the 1800s. (In *American Slave Trade*, by Jesse Torrey, London: J. M. Cobbett, 1822. Courtesy Mandeville Gallery, Union College)

6. This photo, taken inside a slave pen, in Alexandria, Virginia (probably the Price and Birch pen, though not identified as such), shows a cell similar to the one Northup was kept in at Williams' Slave Pen. (Library of Congress)

7. This portion of the Slave Manifest for the Brig *Orleans* shows Northup listed as Platt Hamilton. (National Archives and Records Administration)

SCHEDULE 2.—Slave Inhabitants in *the Parish of Argyle* in the County of _____ State of *Louisiana*, enumerated by me, on the *3rd* day of *October*, 1850. *Sam. Burdelon* Ass't Marshal.

NAMES OF SLAVE OWNERS	Number of Slaves	Age	Sex	Colour	Fugitive from the State	Number manumitted	Deaf & dumb, blind, insane, or idiotic		NAMES OF SLAVE OWNERS	Number of Slaves	Age	Sex	Colour	Fugitive from the State	Number manumitted	Deaf & dumb, blind, insane, or idiotic
1								1								

8. This listing of Epps's slaves, from the 1850 Federal Slave Census, includes Northup. He is probably the first slave listed, a male aged 40. (Names of slaves were not recorded by the census enumerators.) (National Archives and Records Administration, microfilm #432, Population Schedules of the Seventh Census of the United States, 1850. Roll 242, Louisiana)

ROARING RIVER.

A REFRAIN OF THE RED RIVER PLANTATION.

9. This is the score of a musical piece that was printed in *Twelve Years a Slave* and was undoubtedly performed by Northup in Louisiana. (Scanned by David Fiske)

10. A portrait of Henry Bliss Northup, who traveled to Louisiana to locate and rescue Northup. (Courtesy of the Frick Art Reference Library)

11. A portrait of David Wilson, Northup's collaborator on *Twelve Years a Slave*. (From *Life in Whitehall During The Ship Fever Times*, by David Wilson, Whitehall, NY: Inglee &Tefft, 1900, Courtesy Mandeville Gallery, Union College)

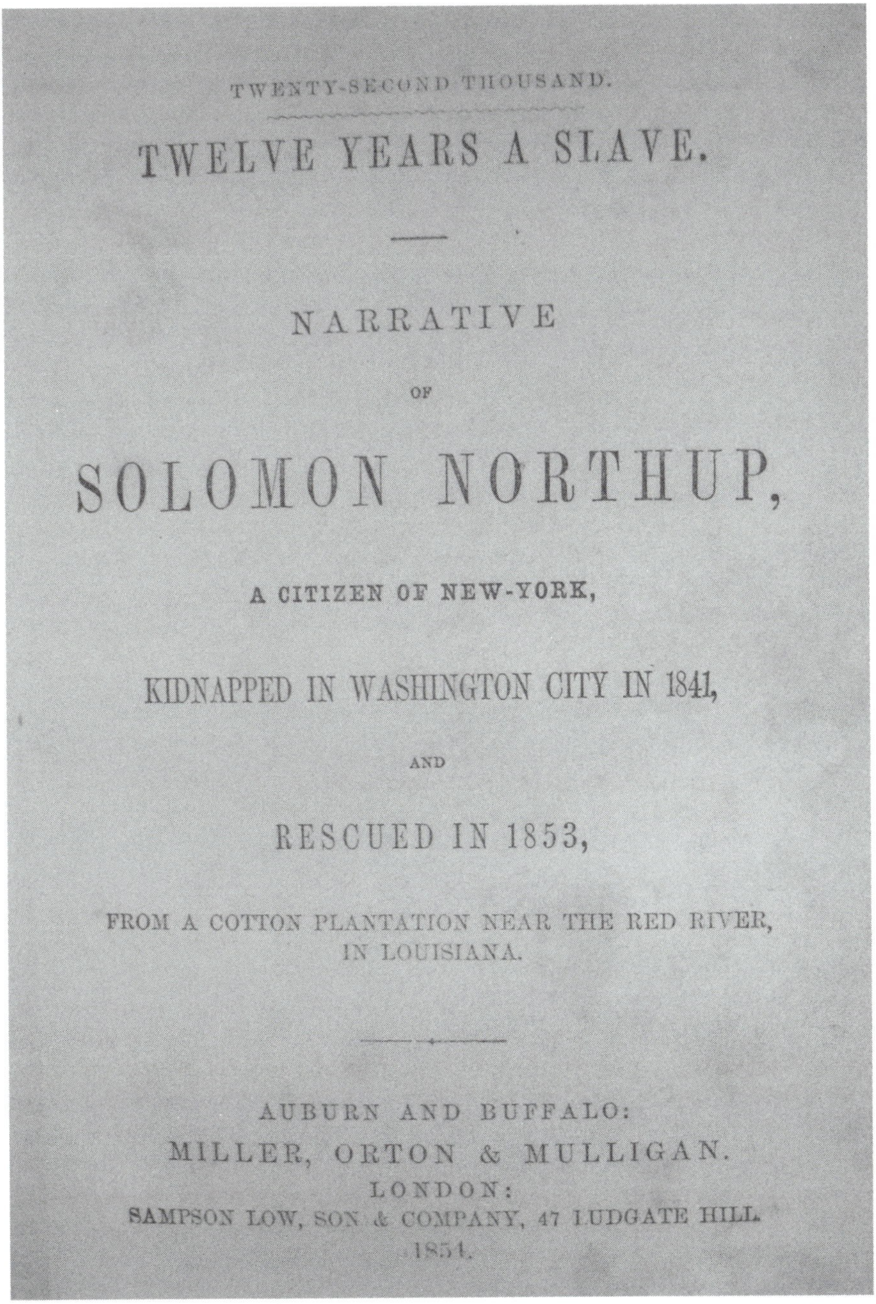

TWENTY-SECOND THOUSAND.

TWELVE YEARS A SLAVE.

NARRATIVE

OF

SOLOMON NORTHUP,

A CITIZEN OF NEW-YORK,

KIDNAPPED IN WASHINGTON CITY IN 1841,

AND

RESCUED IN 1853,

FROM A COTTON PLANTATION NEAR THE RED RIVER,
IN LOUISIANA.

AUBURN AND BUFFALO:

MILLER, ORTON & MULLIGAN.

LONDON:

SAMPSON LOW, SON & COMPANY, 47 LUDGATE HILL.

1854.

12. The title page from the 1854 edition of Northup's book. (Scanned by David Fiske)

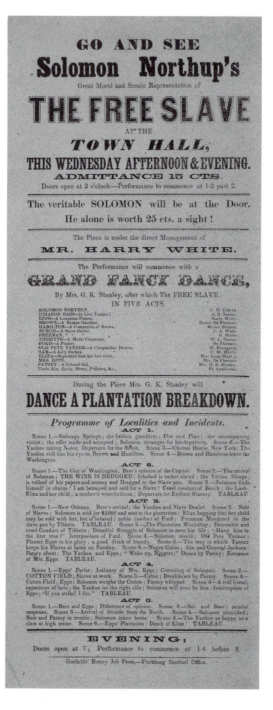

13. A poster promoting *The Free Slave*, a play about Northup's life, at which Northup greeted theater-goers. (Courtesy American Antiquarian Society)

14. A document, signed by Northup, instigating a civil suit against his kidnappers, Alexander Merrill and Joseph Russell. (Courtesy Saratoga County, NY, Historian's Office)

15. One of the letters from John R. Smith mentioning Tabbs Gross and Solomon "Northrup" as having assisted his father on the Underground Railroad in Vermont. (MS Am 2420 (41), Houghton Library, Harvard University)

16. A photograph of Madame Jumel's mansion in New York City, where Anne Northup and her children lived not long after Northup's kidnapping. (Library of Congress)

Sharing the Story

The story of Northup's rescue created a national sensation. The *New York Daily Times* ran a huge page-one story; other newspapers followed suit. The Whig press was more positive than the Democratic press, but coverage by both was extensive. The *Albany Evening Journal* reported his return to his family.[1]

Northup, barely taking time to recover from his ordeal, began making appearances at nearby antislavery rallies. On February 1, 1853, he appeared in Troy with major abolitionists like Frederick Douglass, Jermain Loguen, and Stephen Myers. Northup's description of his captivity, told "with child-like simplicity," elicited "sympathy from the audience." Afterward, Douglass asked the audience for donations for Northup, and over $18 was raised.[2] Northup appeared with Douglass again on February 4 in Albany and "stated some of the wrongs he had received." Henry Northup was there (as he had been at the Troy meeting) and spoke about his southern trip.[3]

In the course of a month, Solomon Northup had gone from living the life of a slave to being a recognized national figure. Although a publicly performing musician for most of his life, he had never experienced anything like the outpouring of attention he now received. For the next few years, he was to live the life of a celebrity while recounting, and in a sense, reliving, the extraordinary story of his kidnapping, enslavement, and rescue.

Numerous speaking engagements quickly provided a vehicle for doing so. More importantly, Northup (with the collaboration of local writer David Wilson) rapidly produced a book that told his story in a much more complete fashion than could be done on the lecture circuit. After the book was published, Northup again went on tour. He then took his story to the stage, producing two plays. Meanwhile, the book's publication led to the arrest of the kidnappers, creating a new round of publicity. His efforts throughout were designed both to help him financially and to further the antislavery cause.

THE WRITING OF *TWELVE YEARS A SLAVE*

The positive press coverage of Northup's tale may have provided the impetus for putting it into print. Just weeks after his early appearances, a newspaper reported that "a local gentleman in this county is engaged in writing the life of Sol. Northup."[4] This item was the first to compare Northup's book to *Uncle Tom's Cabin*, saying sarcastically "we suppose the work will be entitled 'Uncle Sol.'"

Though David Wilson was not mentioned in this early report, he doubtless was the author referred to. Wilson may have been chosen because both Henry Northup and Orville Clark had familial and professional ties to him. Though trained as an attorney (having studied in Clark's law office in Sandy Hill), Wilson's employment in that profession was short. Instead, he turned to literature, a pursuit which had perhaps interested him for some time, as he had served as the "poet" for the Kappa Alpha Society while a student at Union College. His health reportedly did not suit him for the legal profession, and was likely another factor in his decision to author books.[5]

His first book, *Life in Whitehall During the Ship Fever Times*, was published in 1850. Through the years, he wrote or edited several other books, *Life of Jane McCrea; Life of Henrietta Robinson, the Veiled Murderess* (for which he was criticized for appealing to the public's "morbid curiosity");[6] and *Narrative of Nelson Lee, a Captive among the Comanches.* However, the work which achieved the most success was *Twelve Years a Slave.* In the late 1850s, his political affiliation was with the nativist American Party[7] (called the "Know-Nothings"), which had no strong stance concerning slavery, and after the Northup book came out, one writer said of Wilson: "I believe he never was suspected of being an Abolitionist—he may be anti-slavery—somewhat conservative."[8] A few years following publication of *Twelve Years,* he moved to Albany, taking a position with the state government, and serving as Clerk of the Assembly. For the last five years of his life, Wilson adopted an entirely different line of work: he operated a brewery in Albany known as "Wilson & Company." He continued this business until his death, on June 9, 1870.[9]

Once the idea of a book had been hatched, the project came together very quickly. Over the years, readers have wondered whether Northup or Wilson did the actual writing. There is, of course, no way to tell precisely. In the "Editor's Preface" to *Twelve Years,* Wilson refers to himself as the "editor" and mentions that due to "all the facts which have been communicated to him," the completed book was longer than originally anticipated. His object was to give a faithful portrayal of Northup's life "as he received it from his lips." The *New York Times* described the production of the book in this way: "Some curious but no doubt competent person, has . . . been at the pains to elicit from the rescued negro a full story of his life and sufferings . . . and they fill a stout volume."[10]

Another newspaper article admitted that Northup was not the literal author, but had "dictated" the content and that "another acted as his amanuensis."[11] A letter from a relative of Henry Northup agrees with this, because he wrote that "by questions" Wilson "got enough to write a book."[12] Even if not the actual person who put pen to paper, Northup was very involved in its content. Northup, Wilson says, "invariably repeated the same story without deviating in the slightest particular, and has also carefully perused the manuscript, dictating an alteration whenever the most trivial inaccuracy has appeared." Over time— except for some extremely minor errors—Northup's account has held up to all verification efforts directed to it, indicating that the material came from a person who had actually experienced the events related.

The following elements in the book are clearly Northup's: the story line itself; the descriptions of his physical surroundings (e.g., the Great Cocodrie Swamp); the descriptions of his social surroundings; the descriptions of the agricultural and manufacturing processes in which he participated (Northup does not attempt to describe those in which he did not participate, such as the ginning of cotton); the descriptions of daily living on the plantation; and the descriptions and assessments of individual people. Northup was in a position to observe or experience all of these; Wilson was not.

Northup might be called a literalist—an author principally intent on exact narration, with little metaphor or imagery, focused on strict accuracy. The heart of Northup's story lies in the narration of facts and events, articulated by descriptive content. Much of the material is consistent with reports about his straight-forward speaking style. Details such as how a sugar mill works are recorded because Northup found them interesting, given his farming and artisan background, and he expects a worthy audience to find them interesting also. Most details included in the narrative seem to reflect his interests and thinking. But there is also a poetic voice present that can be attributed to Northup. The lyrical descriptions of both Patsey and Mary McCoy; Northup's brief but intense descriptions of the dancing at Christmas balls; and his description of Mrs. Ford's garden, where he sought emotional release following his flight through the swamp, reveal strong romantic streaks in the narrator. Finally, there is the clear human voice of a man terribly wronged, longing for home, witnessing enormities, and seeking justice. At times the syntax and word choices likely come from Wilson's initiatives, but this is Northup's book. Wilson's self-given title of "Editor" is fully appropriate and not unduly modest.

Regardless of the method of Wilson's and Northup's collaboration, the book was prepared amazingly quickly. Its publication was advertised as early as April 15, 1853.[13] Though seeking advance orders ("copies sent by mail, soon as ready"), the ad says the book is "now in Press" and would contain more than 300 pages. The volume was near enough to completion that a lengthy excerpt appeared in *Frederick Douglass' Paper* in late April.[14] Bookstores began advertising its availability in July. So, in less than five months the book had gone from concept to print, certainly quite an accomplishment. The book was published simultaneously by three firms in which three brothers were active (see Appendix C). One brother, James C. Derby of Auburn, was a life-long friend of William Seward. He specialized in printing respectable didactic and patriotic works, which would have added credibility to Northup's narrative. The illustrations were drawn by Frederick M. Coffin and engraved by Nathaniel Orr. They include the frontispiece (depicting Northup in his "plantation suit") and six other illustrations depicting dramatic moments in the tale. Coffin, a frequent illustrator of books published by the Derbys, also drew for *Harper's Magazine*. Orr was one of the country's leading wood engravers.

REVIEWS OF *TWELVE YEARS A SLAVE*

Press reviews were very positive. A literary notice prepared by the publisher contained excerpts from reviews printed by numerous newspapers, including the *Buffalo Courier, New York Tribune, New York Evangelist, Detroit Tribune, Buffalo Express, Cincinnati Journal, Syracuse Evening Chronicle, Syracuse Daily Journal, Cayuga Chief, Frederick Douglass' Paper, Pittsburgh Dispatch, Buffalo Commercial Advertiser,* and *New York Independent.*[15] In an item that included an extract from the book, Frederick Douglass wrote: "We think it will be difficult for any one who takes up the book in a candid and impartial spirit to lay it down until finished . . . ."[16]

William Lloyd Garrison's newspaper called the book a "deeply interesting and thrilling Narrative."[17] Though packed with exciting adventures, it was also perceived to be factual and impartial. Some reviewers were impressed by how equitable Northup's account was: "Its tone is much milder than we expected to see exhibited . . . but, while he seems to fully realize the magnitude of his sufferings, he does not condemn all."[18] "He tells apparently an honest tale, without exaggeration."[19] "NORTHUP will be believed, because, instead of indiscriminate accusations, he gives you the good and evil of Slavery just as he found it. All kindnesses are remembered with gratitude. Masters and Overseers who treated Slaves humanely are commended; for there, as here, were good and bad men. If 'Tibeats' and 'Epps' were coarse, cruel and brutal, 'Master FORD' and 'Madam McCOY' were so just, considerate, humane as to be obeyed, honored and beloved."[20]

Comparisons were of course made to the previous year's *Uncle Tom's Cabin.* That sensational book covered very similar ground, but was admittedly a work of fiction. One reader recommended Northup's book to "those persons who are so conscientious that they will not read '*Uncle Tom's Cabin*' because they say it is a Novel," but noted that Northup's narrative fully supported the degradations portrayed by Harriet Beecher Stowe.[21] Another paper observed, "Let them buy the narrative of Solomon Northup, and when they have read it, we will guarantee that they acquit Mrs. Stowe of all exaggeration."[22]

PROMOTING THE BOOK

Apparently hopeful of duplicating the success of Stowe's work, an advertisement run by the publisher indicated that over 10,000 copies of Northup's book (published on July 15, 1853) had been ordered.[23] At about the same time, bookstores advertised the title's availability,[24] at a cost of $1. James C. Derby, one of the publishers, later wrote that it "caused quite a sensation among the reading community, the book meeting with a rapid and large sale."[25]

Sales were indeed strong. By mid-August 11,000 copies had been sold, even without much advertising.[26] The publisher began promoting the book, promising a free copy to any newspaper that would run their publication announcement.[27] An additional 6,000 copies flew off the shelves over the following three months,[28] and the publisher sought 1,000 agents to handle the book, promising an annual income between $500 and $1,000.[29] A Syracuse newspaper even offered free copies of the book (for use as Christmas gifts) to individuals who recruited four new subscribers to its paper (*Uncle Tom's Cabin* could be obtained by hooking just one subscriber!).[30] Though sales fell short of the phenomenal level reached by *Uncle Tom's Cabin, Twelve Years* was at par with other best-sellers of the day. Publisher Miller, Orton & Mulligan announced that over 27,000 books had been sold by January 1855.[31]

Northup stood to benefit financially from the book. While it was still being prepared, there were reports that "an extensive publishing house in this State has offered Northup . . . $3,000 for the copyright of his book."[32] Notices from the publisher that appeared in newspapers mentioned that some (or all) of the profits from book sales would go to Northup. A Syracuse newspaper, offering copies for sale, added that "Northup gets a profit on all the books sold, and by helping yourselves and neighbors to some of them you will help him at the same time."[33] John Thompson, of Peru, New York, who claimed personal familiarity with Henry Northup, wrote "I understand the profits of the entire sale of the book is to be for the benefit of 'Uncle Sol,' and his family."[34]

Northup certainly saw some monetary gain. Prior to the release of his narrative, he was able to purchase real estate in Glens Falls. On May 16, 1853, he purchased property near the intersection of South and School Streets for $275.[35] This was near the property owned by his son-in-law, Philip Stanton.

The dedication in Northup's book alludes to Stowe's *A Key to Uncle Tom's Cabin*, which had come out not long before his. Stowe's book provided supporting documentation for the types of situations depicted in her blockbuster novel. Though her book referred to Northup, a direct quote from it was apparently not available for the first edition of *Twelve Years*. In 1854, however, another edition was issued, which included a short excerpt relating to Northup.

Northup's clever title was mimicked by other ex-slaves. A book which came out in 1854, just a year after his, used the long-winded title: *Experience and Personal Narrative of Uncle Tom Jones: Who Was for Forty Years a Slave. Also the Surprising Adventures of Wild Tom of the Island Retreat, a Fugitive Negro from South Carolina.* Other titles published in subsequent years included: *Twenty-two Years a Slave and Forty Years a Freeman,* by Austin Steward, in 1857, and *New Man: Twenty-Nine Years a Slave, Twenty-Nine Years a Free Man: Recollections of H. C. Bruce,* in 1859.

One indication of how widely *Twelve Years* was read can be had by noting instances where northern soldiers, on their deployment during the Civil War, described visits to locations mentioned in the book. One recalled visiting "the old slave-pen . . . where was confined . . . Solomon Northrop."[36] Others found the Epps plantation in Louisiana: "Old Mr. Epps yet lives, and told us that a greater part of the book was truth, and that many old Negroes remembered Northrup," whom Epps called "smart."[37] Another soldier who visited the plantation located some blacks who "knew Platt well and have danced to the music of his fiddle often. Some . . . remember when he was taken out of the lot by the 'Northern gemman.'"[38]

Northup's narrative benefited from the antislavery movement, and first-hand stories of people who had lived under the American system of slavery became a rage, whether told in print or orally.

A LECTURE TOUR

The lecture circuit was a lucrative pursuit for former slaves. Speakers appeared before antislavery meetings, abolitionist conventions, and the general public at lecture halls. Soon after the publication of *Twelve Years*, Northup began an extended series of lectures in New York and New England. From the beginning, the book had received substantial coverage in the newspaper published by Frederick Douglass, and Douglass suggested, after hearing Henry Northup relate Northup's story to a teary-eyed crowd at Port Byron, New York, in July 1853, that he travel around the state and spread the word, and that "he should take Solomon with him."[39]

Whether Douglass's comment was the impetus or not, Northup *did* begin traveling to promote and sell his book in the second half of 1853. A surviving copy of the 1853 edition bears the inscription "Purchased on NYCRR [New York Central Railroad] Train of Solomon Northrup himself 1853."[40] A newspaper reported that Northup had lost his pocketbook while in Syracuse in October,[41] probably when he was there for an appearance on October 1, 1853.[42] On that day, celebrations took place commemorating the Jerry Rescue, when antislavery advocates in Syracuse had successfully released a man who'd been arrested under the Fugitive Slave Law. Northup was introduced by Gerrit Smith, the famous abolitionist. The speaker who followed Northup was none other than Frederick Douglass. A newspaper account, unfortunately, gave no details of Northup's remarks.[43]

Though announcements of appearances made by Northup in 1854 were made in newspapers (see Appendix A), many accounts are brief (or even speculative): "In this lecture, we understand, he tells his own story, in his own way; and as he is a plain, uneducated man, it will probably be all the more interesting";[44] "We happen to be somewhat acquainted with 'Sol.' He is a man—every inch of him";[45] and "He will recount in his own simple and unvarnished way, the particulars of his kidnapping and twelve years' subsequent servitude in the South."[46]

A more substantial account of a lecture in Buffalo was reported by one of Douglass's correspondents: "Last night I had the pleasure of hearing Solomon Northup . . . His story is full of romantic interest and painful adventures, and gives as clear an insight to the practical workings and beauties of American Slavery . . . . Northup tells his story in plain and candid language, and intermingles it with flashes of genuine wit. It is a sure treat to hear him give some hazardous adventure, with so much sans [sic] froid that the audience is completely enraptured and the 'house brought down.'"[47]

A brief description of Northup's appearance at the courthouse in St. Albans, Vermont, similarly mentioned "his unaffected simplicity, directness and gentlemanly bearing" and, as some had said of his book, his straightforward presentation was more impressive "than many fervid appeals to which we have listened."[48]

It was speculated that Northup might go to England, probably to lecture, although it's unlikely that he did because at the time of these speculations he was in Syracuse organizing a theatrical production based on his book.[49] After the close of this dramatization, Northup resumed giving talks around the northeast, including ones at Montpelier, Vermont;[50] Concord, New Hampshire;[51] and in several Massachusetts cities.[52] Northup, along with a young fugitive slave called "Ida May," was presented to the Massachusetts Legislature on March 10, 1855.[53]

Henry C. Wright, the noted abolitionist, witnessed several appearances in Boston:

[Though *Twelve Years a Slave* relates Solomon's story] it is far more potent to see the man, and hear him, in his clear, manly straight-forward way, speak of slavery as he experienced it, and as he saw it in others. Those who have read his Narrative can scarce fail to desire to see the man, thus kidnapped and tortured in body and soul, for twelve years, and to hear his story from his own lips.

I heard him relate his experience in the Melonaon, on the evening of the 15th, and last evening, in a private social circle. To-Morrow evening he is to lecture in the Bethel on Commercial Street. But he should have an opportunity to tell his experience in the country towns and villages. I understand that he intends to be at Worcester, at the Non-Resistance Convention. Cannot arrangements be made for him to relate what he has felt, seen and heard in the land of whips and chains, in the towns and villages of Massachusetts?[54]

PRODUCING TWO PLAYS

It is not surprising, given Northup's experiences as a musical performer, that he decided to tell his story using the stage. He produced two plays, one in the spring of 1854, the other in the fall of 1855. Again, he was following the precedent set by *Uncle Tom's Cabin*, which was adapted for theatrical production and was being performed in Troy at the time of Solomon's rescue. His first play opened in Syracuse:

"Solomon Northup . . . is present at Syracuse. We learn that his history is to be dramatized and brought out on the stage, and that he is to take one of the characters."[55] Northup apparently played himself: "The history of Solomon Northup has been dramatized, and is now being enacted at Syracuse—Northup taking the principal character."[56] The play, presented at the National Theater, was especially noticed by the local papers, and Northup spent several weeks in Syracuse, overseeing the play's development.[57]

The opening night was reported to have gone "tolerably well," but there were some problems. The presentation was very short (surprising, given the amount of dramatic material available from *Twelve Years*), and the playwright, a Mr. Kemble, apologized to the audience, promising additional dramatic pieces would follow the Northup play in future performances. Viewers unfamiliar with the book would likely have had trouble following the play, and "some of the characters were well performed, while others were poorly done."[58] The play was presented several times in late April and early May in 1854, and a farce was indeed added to follow it. [59]

The production also took to the road, at least briefly. "Solomon Northrup and his troupe have gone to Auburn, where they intend to perform the new drama of his history for a short season. Solomon is bound to make his fortune out of the new enterprise, if possible."[60]

This, however, was not to be. The production was ultimately a flop. Though acknowledging Northup's cleverness, one writer noted "we think theatrical management rather out of his line."[61] Responding to charges that they had not been sufficiently supportive of the production, local abolitionists said: "The enterprise was entered into by Solomon, without counseling them, and in fact, contrary to their advice . . ."[62] One editor wrote that "Solomon is an excellent fellow . . . We regret his adoption of this new line of business . . . . We hope Northup will not suffer pecuniarily by his operation."[63] In fact, as related in Chapter 9, it may indeed have caused Northup financial stress and embarrassment.

Two years later, the production was recalled as having been unsuccessful "owing to adverse circumstances."[64] Nevertheless, the project is characteristic of Northup's willingness to use initiative and run risks.

There was another theatrical production based on Northup's book in the fall of 1855. More is known about this play's content than the first one. A poster advertising an October 4 presentation of "A Free Slave" at Worcester's Brinley Hall[65] shows that the cast included characters from *Twelve Years* (though Northup's character is played by a "C.H. Edwyn," and not Northup himself). The production consisted of five acts—apparently the earlier mistake of having too brief a play was not repeated, as the poster notes "owing to the length of the piece no Farce will be presented."

The scenes listed on the poster provide some idea of how Northup's book was adapted for the stage. Some liberties were taken,[66] but the plot follows the story fairly well. The following shows the general content of the drama:

Act 1

Scene 1.—Saratoga Springs; the broken gamblers; Plot and Plan; the unsuspecting victim; the offer made and accepted; Solomon arranges for his departure.

Scene 2.—The Yankee taking Notes; Departure for the South.

Scene 3.—Custom House, New York; The Yankee still has his eye on Brown and Hamilton.

Scene 4.—Brown and Hamilton leave for Washington.

Act 2

Scene 1.—The City of Washington; Bass's opinion of the Capitol.

Scene 2.—The arrival of Solomon; THE WINE IS DRUGGED; Ichabod is rather elated; the Victim Sleeps; is robbed of his papers and money and Dragged to the Slave pen.

Scene 3.—Solomon finds himself in chains! I am betrayed and sold for a Slave! Cruel conduct of Birch; the Lash; Eliza and her child; a mother's wretchedness; Departure for Endless Slaver. TABLEAU.

Act 3

Scene 1.—New Orleans. Bass's arrival; the Yankee and Slave Dealer.

Scene 2.—Sale of Slaves; Solomon is sold for $1000 and sent to the plantation; Eliza begging that her child may be sold with her, but is refused; noble conduct of Ford; Freeman Murdered in the slave pen by Tibbets. TABLEAU

Scene 3.—The Plantation Workshop; Detestable and cruel Conduct of Tibbets; Dreadful Struggle of Solomon to save his life; 'Hang him to the first tree!' Interposition of Ford.

Scene 4.—Solomon resold; Old Pete Tanner; Planter Epps in his glory; a good drink of brandy.

Scene 5.—The way in which Tanner keeps his Slaves at home on Sunday.

Scene 6.—Negro Cabin; Abe and General Jackson; Patsey about; The Yankee and Epps; 'Wake up, Niggers;' Dance by Patsey; Entrance of Mrs. Epps. TABLEAU.

Act 4

Scene 1.—Epps' Parlor; Jealousy of Mrs. Epps; Consoling of Solomon.

Scene 2.—COTTON FIELD; Slaves at work.

Scene 3.—Cabin; Breakdown by Patsey.

Scene 4.—Cotton Field; Epps; Solomon weighs the Cotton; Patsey is whipped.

Scene 5.—A real friend; exposition of facts; the Yankee on the right side; Solomon will soon be free; Interruption of Epps. 'If you strike, I fire.' TABLEAU.

Act 5

Scene 1.—Bass and Epps; Difference of opinion.

Scene 2.—Sol. and Bass; painful suspense.

Scene 3.—Arrival of friends from the North.

Scene 4.—Solomon identified; Sam and Patsey in trouble; Solomon taken home.

Scene 5.—The Yankee as happy as a clam at high water.

Scene 6.—Epps' Plantation; Death of Eliza! TABLEAU.

The play was presented on another occasion, most likely in Fitchburg, Massachusetts. An undated poster, printed by a press in Fitchburg, advertises its performance at the "Town Hall." Though undated, the performance probably took place around the same time as the one in Worcester, since the cast list is virtually identical. An extremely notable feature of the latter performance (and an indication of Northup's involvement) is that the poster promises "the veritable Solomon will be at the Door. He alone is worth 25 cts. a sight!"[67]

As the poster showed, the plot generally follows the book's outline. Eliza and Patsey are featured, although the former appears in widely separated (though dramatic) scenes. Patsey's story is given more extensive treatment, although much of this may have been musical performance. Bass's role is greatly expanded. He, not Henry Northup, is the "Yankee" supporting hero. The use of multiple rescuers may have showcased the community support of the rescue.

The scene titles show that the play was full of melodrama, with the use of tableaus and clearly delineated heroes and villains. There is an unvarnished appeal to regional pride and prejudice, with the Canadian Bass turned into a shrewd "Yankee" hero who overcomes the southern villains. But the play is not designed to be simply an entertaining melodrama, as the plays based on *Uncle Tom's Cabin* eventually became. Portraying slavery remains a central focus. This is evident not just from the roles of villains with their lashes and chains, but from the scenes illustrating slave life that do not contribute directly to Northup's own drama.

The play was apparently not a success. The many episodes and story lines, often interrupted by other material, may have given it a fragmented quality. Also, play-going audiences may not have been ready to confront the topics of slavery and race in a performance designed, in part, to entertain. Moreover, Northup's story, both in *Twelve Years* and as presented by him in simple direct language on the lecture circuit, made powerful impressions because the factual narrations came across as authentic, and their compelling immediacy resonated with audiences. The playwrights may have failed to preserve this quality when they tried to dramatize the story and thereby force both interpretation and emotion on the playgoer.

The only evidence of this play's financial fortunes comes from newspaper advisories about the acting troupe leaving towns with unpaid bills. One paper warned printers about a "strolling band of theatrical performers under the charge of a black man calling himself Solomon Northrup," who had left Greenfield and Northampton, Massachusetts without settling their bills.[68] Another paper referenced the "Free Slave" production, warning merchants about the acting group, as "we learn that they have left several places at the north in debt to landlords and printers."[69] This second theatrical failure must have been a severe blow to Northup, and apparently he did not handle it well, because this same newspaper account stated "Solomon Northrup, ('the free slave') is said to have been quite profane and insulting, besides openly repudiating his debts. Solomon does the business, while someone else claims to own the property."

In December 1856, a Vermont newspaper could not recommend Northup's "moral exhibition" (likely some version of "The Free Slave," which the posters had billed the previous year as a "great moral and scenic representation"). While in St. Albans, Northup and some of the performers became intoxicated and fisticuffs had broken out.[70] These reports suggest that he continued to try to show the play, but had little success, instead generating negative personal publicity.

SPEAKING ENGAGEMENTS DECLINE—AND END

Newspaper accounts of appearances by Northup taper off in 1856 and 1857. The story of his enslavement and rescue was becoming stale and the dramatizations were obviously attracting little positive attention. He may have had speaking engagements in other regions of the country, but accounts of these have not surfaced. If Northup ever went to England in search of fresh audiences, this may have been the time it happened, even though the one reference to that possibility, as mentioned, was two years earlier.

He *did* go to Canada, and the result was a disaster. In fact, the last newspaper notice of an appearance by him that the authors could locate related to a planned lecture in Streetsville, Ontario. Accounts vary somewhat, but one states that he was "prevented from lecturing . . . by a mob."[71] As Northup prepared to speak, "he was interrupted by cries of 'down with the bloody negro,' 'brain the blasted Sambo,' etc. The noise and confusion was so great and so universal on the part of the crowd that Northup was forced to leave the hall under an escort of friends."[72] It was also reported that "such a row was kicked up that he ran and locked himself into a room in fear of personal violence."[73] Northup was rescued by the local Quarter–Master.[74] Northup's reception may have been the result of racial tension following years of fugitive slaves moving to Canada.

This traumatic episode appears to be the end of Northup's public speaking career. It came at almost exactly the same time that the Saratoga County District Attorney dropped the charges against the kidnappers, as discussed in Chapter 8. Northup was now 50 years old. It was time to refocus his life.

8

The Kidnappers:
Arrest and Trial

As a result of the publication and wide distribution of *Twelve Years*, many citizens, including potential witnesses, became aware of the remarkable series of events surrounding the kidnapping. To one reader, Thaddeus St. John from Fonda, New York,[1] part of Northup's narrative sounded very familiar, reminding him of some incidents from a trip to Washington, D.C., about the time of the kidnapping. He immediately suspected that the kidnappers were Alexander Merrill and Joseph Russell, whom he had known for many years, and whom he had seen in Washington with a black companion. Press reports at the time declared: "The accused were discovered from the descriptions and incidents given in Northrup's book."[2]

THE ARREST OF THE KIDNAPPERS

St. John arranged to meet Northup in a Fonda hotel.[3] They recognized each other, compared recollections, and St. John's suspicions became certainties in his mind.[4] Henry Northup, recently returned from Europe, was contacted,[5] and plans were made to arrest Merrill and Russell.

Although the apprehension of Alexander Merrill was noted in numerous newspapers (sometimes with misstated facts), a highly detailed account was provided by Rev. Stephen Parks (pastor at the Methodist Episcopal Church in Gloversville, New York, at the time).[6] His account not only relates the dramatic events of Merrill's arrest, but also captures the degree to which it created a local sensation:

> On the morning of Friday [July 7, 1854], while quietly pursuing my pastoral work, a boy rushed into the house where I was visiting, and in

great excitement exclaimed, "Ma, they have caught a fugitive slave, and have got him in Squire Jones' office now." "What," said I to myself, "is brother Jones engaged in that nefarious business?" On repairing to the spot, I found a fugitive slave there, sure enough, but not exactly as the boy had stated. There was Solomon Northup, with his tried friend, H. B. Northup, Esq., and there set in irons Alexander Merrill, one of the two fiends in human form, who, thirteen years ago, decoyed Solomon from Saratoga to Washington, and sold him into slavery . . . [7]

Rev. Parks's account states that Merrill had recently returned from California, and "was traced to his native place," just north of Gloversville. This was Woods Hollow, a village near the current town of Broadalbin.[8] In the picturesque account, Henry, who had been seeking out the kidnappers, is given credit, along with H. Jones and E. N. Spencer, "for the adroitness and success with which they conducted this arrest." The article continues:

A warrant was issued by H. Jones, and as it was uncertain at which of his friend's houses he [Merrill] might be found, very early on the morning in question, a man who was engaged in buying up chickens for the market, was seen going from house to house inquiring for chickens and incidentally for returned Californians. Just at the break of day, not having as yet his full complement of chickens, he called at the residence of Merrill's father. They had no chickens to sell—wanted them to kill for their son who had just returned from California.

The legal process then unfolded, apparently according to a well-conceived plan. Jones and his associates believed in moving with adequate force when facing potentially desperate adversaries:

The chicken merchant disappeared, and in a few minutes two chosen officers, E. N. Spencer, and _____ Rigsby, followed by Solomon, H. B. Northup, and H. Jones, entered the house; expecting a bloody conflict, they were prepared for the worst. They inquired of his father for Alexander. "He is in bed, I will call him," was the reply. Declining to put him to that trouble, they instantly passed up to his room. There he lay, with a splendid revolver and bowie knife on the floor by his side. He was asleep. Solomon and the officers surrounded his bed. The scene had changed since Solomon was in Merrill's power, and was dragged from his bed at Gadsby's hotel to the slave pen.

It is difficult to imagine what Northup must have been feeling as he finally confronted one of the men responsible for his 12 years of suffering. Parks's account continues:

Solomon recognized him in a moment, and awakening him asked, "Do you know me?" He was answered in the negative. "My name," said he, "is Solomon Northup. I know you." The man trembled from head to foot. The officers, after serving the warrant, and searching his clothes for weapons, directed him to dress, when they hand-cuffed, and brought him to Gloversville.

Supporting this account, another newspaper credited the local officers for their actions: "H. C. Jones, Esq., and Deputy-Sheriff Spencer of Gloversville, Fulton County, and Constables Wendell and Harlow of Ballston Spa, are entitled to great praise for their successful and unwearied efforts in tracing out and securing the prisoners."[9]

Northup was apparently sufficiently well known in the region for the arrest to create an instant sensation. Parks observed: "Such was the excitement, and intense anxiety that prevailed, that business was to a great extent suspended, and the examination previous to the commitment was adjourned from the Justices' office to the large room of our public school, which was crowded with anxious spectators." That evening, Parks reported, "as many as could crowd into the M. E. [Methodist Episcopal] church, paid a small admission fee for the privilege of hearing Solomon tell his tale of woe."

As described by Parks, Merrill quickly obtained legal representation:

S. Sammons, Esq., of Fonda, and W. Wait, Esq., of Fonda's Bush, appeared as counsel for the prisoner, and H. B. Northup, and M. S. Adams, Esq.'s., in behalf of the people. After a determined effort by his counsel to procure his discharge on the ground of illegality in the proceedings, he was committed to Johnstown jail, and subsequently to Saratoga county for further examination. In addition to Solomon's positive oath, there is said to be other reliable, overwhelming evidence against him.

The additional evidence included the testimony of Thaddeus St. John. It is clear from this account, written a few days after the events, that Merrill was moved from the Johnstown jail to that of Saratoga County (in Ballston Spa) almost immediately after his Gloversville hearing.

Joseph Russell's capture was not nearly so dramatic: "An officer from Saratoga county, accompanied by officer Brazier, arrested Thursday morning a canal boat captain named J. L. Russell, of the boat J. F. Crain, of the Rochester City Line, charged with being Merrill's associate in the kidnapping. He was handcuffed and taken to Ballston. On his way to the cars he admitted that he was in Washington at the Inauguration, in 1841."[10] It is not clear how Russell was traced. Merrill may have known his occupation and revealed it during questioning. Since he came from the area, his whereabouts may easily have been ascertained.[11]

INITIAL HEARING

On July 11, 1854, a hearing was held in Ballston Spa, the county seat of Saratoga County, presided over by Justices of the Peace Abel Meeker and David W. Maxwell. Its purpose was to establish whether there was probable cause that a crime had been committed, and if so, whether the case should be sent to a grand jury for possible indictment. The prosecution was headed by District Attorney William Odell, assisted by Henry Northup and George Scott.[12]

Solomon was the first witness called. He identified the defendants as the two men he had met in Saratoga in 1841, testifying Merrill had called himself Merrill Brown, and Russell had called himself Abraham Hamilton at that time. He then repeated the story of their offer of employment, the trip to New York, their request that he accompany them to Washington, the events of his kidnapping, and of his enslavement in Louisiana. He testified regarding Merrill's arrest. In the course of being cross-examined he said that he'd seen St. John in Washington, and that Russell or Merrill had poured the drink for him that preceded his sickness and unconsciousness.[13]

St. John then testified that he had known Merrill and Russell since they were children, and had encountered them in Baltimore in 1841, when they were with a black man. They had cautioned him not to use their real names in front of Northup. In Washington, he had spent some time with them at Gadsby's, though he didn't drink with them. On his journey home, he had met them again on a ferry at Havre de Grace, Maryland, and rode with them by train to New York. Both were sporting new clothes and fresh haircuts. Russell even had an ivory cane and a gold watch and chain. St. John remarked to them that they seemed to have come into some money, and told Russell, "Jo, you have made a victim somewhere," jesting that he had sold the Negro or something worse, and that he would watch the newspapers for reports of robberies or killings. Russell showed off some gold coins, and three bank notes, one of which was for $1,000, implying that they were gambling winnings. St. John, again presumably in jest, had asked Russell and Merrill if they had received $500 for the Negro, and Merrill replied that figure was $150 too low. St. John also testified that Russell had moved to Fonda around 1850 and kept a butcher shop near his home, and that he often joked with Russell about his southern trip.[14]

Another witness, Norman Prindle, who had been a stagecoach driver in 1841, testified that he had seen Merrill in Saratoga at Montgomery Hall, and a few days later he saw him and another man leaving Saratoga in a coach with Northup. He remembered Merrill distinctly, but was not certain about Russell. He had first seen the men a day or two before that. In a conversation he had with Northup before they left Saratoga, he claimed that he and others warned Northup about going away with the men, but Northup had said "he would risk the prisoners selling him."[15]

Fulton County district Attorney John Enos testified briefly that he knew Merrill, that he had interviewed him in the Fulton County jail after his arrest, and that Merrill had told him that he had spent three years in California and south on the Mississippi.[16]

Defense counsel called no witnesses, but did cross-examine the prosecution witnesses. They advanced the argument that the statute of limitations was past, so that their clients were no longer liable to prosecution. District Attorney Odell responded that because the crime had continued during all the time Northup was a slave, the three-year limitation had not begun until Northup was freed in January 1853. This question, he said, was for another court to decide, since the current judges sat only to determine if it was probable that a crime had been committed. He also argued that the justices of the peace lacked authority to set bail for a crime of this magnitude. They apparently agreed with these points since they bound the defendants over and refused to set bail. Merrill and Russell were returned to the jail.

In this first hearing, three witnesses (Northup, St. John, and Prindle) established that Merrill was one of the two men who had been seen with Northup; two witnesses (Northup and St. John) established the same with regard to Russell. St. John confirmed Northup's testimony placing the defendants in Washington with him, and also testified as to their use of aliases on that journey. He further presented evidence about their improved financial circumstances on the trip home, and reported the conversation about Northup's sale price. All this testimony was subject to cross–examination. At a minimum, Merrill and Russell had been identified beyond a reasonable doubt as actors in the drama.

The newspapers expressed enthusiasm that, with the kidnappers identified and apprehended, they would be held accountable for their misdeeds. As one paper put it, the kidnappers were finally "in the hands of justice."[17] In early August 1854, Frederick Douglass speculated that the kidnappers would "'do the State some services.' The evidence against them appears to be conclusive. . . . "[18]

At the time of the Ballston Spa hearing, Northup also filed a civil suit against both kidnappers, holding them to bail of $5,000 apiece against damages he had incurred as a consequence of their actions.[19]

THE INDICTMENT

On August 28, 1854, a Court of General Sessions was held in Ballston Spa before a three-judge bench.[20] It empanelled a grand jury to consider the evidence. The grand jury, presumably meeting in secret,[21] brought in a four-count indictment on September 1.[22] The counts are drawn in complex legal terminology, but can be summarized as follows. The first count charged that Merrill and Russell "unlawfully and feloniously" inveigled and kidnapped Northup against his will and without his consent, for the purpose of selling him as a slave. This is the only count containing the word "kidnapping," and was based on a law "declaring it a felony to inveigle or kidnap a person, with the intent to cause such person to be sold as a slave."[23]

The second count charged that Merrill and Russell unlawfully and feloniously inveigled Northup to accompany them to Washington intending to sell him as a slave (with such a sale resulting). The third count charged (as in the previous one) that they had inveigled Northup, and then sold and "transferred his services" without his consent. The final count of the indictment charged that Merrill and Russell inveigled Northup to Washington and sold him as a slave to an unknown person or persons. The last three charges were brought under a law "making it a felony to sell the services or labor of a person of color, who shall have been forcibly taken, inveigled, or kidnapped from this state to any other state, place, or country."[24]

POSTPONEMENT

The trial opened on October 4, 1854, "before a crowded and excited courtroom in Ballston Spa,"[25] but when the proceedings began, Merrill and Russell requested a postponement until the next term of the court. They argued that they had not been able to prepare their case for a number of reasons: their incarceration ("under close confinement"); the amount of time that had passed since the alleged kidnapping; the distance between the locations involved; the absence of their attorney, William Wait, who needed to attend to matters in Fulton County; and the absence of material and necessary witnesses (which included James H. Birch and Benjamin O. Shekell from Washington).[26] The motion for postponement was granted, and trial was set over to February 1855. Merrill and Russell remained in jail. Newspapers at the time reported that Merrill and Russell "have been endeavoring to get Solomon out of the way or make some compromise," that is, a plea bargain.[27]

In December 1854, a request was forwarded to Washington, D.C., asking that James H. Birch, Benjamin O. Shekell, and Benjamin A. Thorn provide responses to seven written questions (interrogatories). No response seems to have been received from Thorn,[28] but those from Birch and Shekell are in the records for the case. Their responses parallel their contentions presented in the January 1853 trial in Washington, D.C.

The interrogatories asked both if they knew Merrill and Russell (and under what circumstances) and if they recalled details about the sale of "Platt," including who had bought him and if he had consented to the sale. They also asked for details about Northup's charges against Birch in 1853. Cross-interrogatories by the District Attorney asked for details about their slave business and Birch's partnership with Theophilus Freeman.

The responses of the two men relative to the alleged purchase of Northup are quite similar—in some cases using identical wording to describe the transaction.[29] Both said that the persons they presumed to be Merrill and Russell had come to Shekell's establishment. According to both Birch and Shekell, one was "a small & well-dressed man, the other a large and taller man calling himself Brown. Said Brown proposed to sell a negro man." It is important to note for reasons discussed below that Birch and Shekell confirmed that two sellers, one tall, one short, were involved in this transaction, and that the name of one was Brown. Interestingly, their account and Northup's in *Twelve Years*,[30] disagree as to who was tall and who was short.

Birch stated that after he expressed interest in making a purchase, should a price be agreed upon, the two men returned with Northup, later identified as "the same man that made charges against me on the 17th day of January 1853 in the City of Washington." Birch stated further:

> Wm. Brown then proposed the sale of the Negro under a name that I do not recollect. He recommended him as a good fiddler and a good bricklayer. A fiddle was procured and he played, at least, an hour.[31]

Birch testified that he had been told that Northup, like Brown, was from Georgia and had been brought up in Brown's family. Brown (Merrill) had lost money gambling, and had no means to get home other than by selling his slave. "In order to find if all was as represented,"

Birch continued, "I told him [Northup] if I purchased him I should send him to the Cotton fields where he would be severely punished and that I intended to whip him for a Sample of what he would get." Northup's response, according to Birch, was, "My Master has a right to sell me and I must submit." This testimony is similar to that given by Shekell at the Washington trial in 1853. The obvious reasons for the fabrication in the earlier case were to undermine the kidnapping charge and also to establish that Northup was a willing party to the sale so that he could be charged with conspiring to defraud Birch. In the later testimony, Birch stuck to this story, which would have been of use to the defendants had they tried to implicate Northup in the kidnapping plot as a defense strategy.

Birch said he'd agreed to pay Brown $625 for Northup (roughly confirming St. John's testimony as to the selling price). "After the sale of the negro to me by Brown," Birch said, "both appeared to be very much affected at parting, so much as to shed tears." The tears were also mentioned in Shekell's responses. Northup was to be delivered to Birch's office at "Union Street near King Street" in Alexandria, Virginia.[32] When Northup arrived there, Birch testified, he handcuffed him (Northup) and "informed him that I had purchased him and was going to take him to jail and give him One Hundred lashes. He answered by saying that I cannot help it." This testimony, again, could have been used to support a charge of complicity on Northup's part.

Shekell, who had seen Northup at Birch's trial in Washington, also alleged in his response to the interrogatory that "The said negro is much marked by the Small Pox. He confessed that he was the same man sold by Brown in 1841 and that he could play the fiddle and that his name was Solomon Northup in the office of the magistrate when Birch was arrested in Jany [sic] 1853."

Cutting through all the nonsense and fabrications, one piece of evidence does emerge: Birch and Shekell confirm that "Brown" and one other (unnamed) individual were involved in selling Northup. The fact that "Platt Hamilton" is the name used on the *Orleans* manifest confirms that Russell, using that surname, was the other party—and that Birch knew his alias at the time of the sale. In short, two men were present at the sale, and Birch knew the correct aliases of each.

Responding to the cross-interrogatories, Birch sought to limit his perceived association with the slave trade, testifying that he had not both bought *and* sold slaves in Washington, D.C. since 1842, that he had dealt with Freeman only in 1841 and 1842, and that he had never sold a slave to a third party in Washington.[33] Both Birch and Shekell claimed that as slave traders they had allowed slaves to purchase their own freedom. Shekell even boasted, "I think I have been the means of getting more [slaves] free than any man in Washington." They appear to have been attempting to portray themselves in as positive a light as possible. Their testimony, had it been used, would have helped the defense build a claim that Northup was involved in his kidnapping. However, it would also have supported the District Attorney's claim that both Merrill and Russell were involved with a transaction to sell Northup.

THE TRIAL

The postponed trial opened on February 8, 1855, in Ballston Spa before the Court of Oyer and Terminer. The four-count indictment was read. Merrill and Russell pleaded "not guilty" to the first count, and contended the other counts were "not sufficient in law," challenging the legal grounds on which the grand jury had presented them. The lawyers then engaged in legal wrangling, mainly over whether a court in New York had jurisdiction over an offense committed in Washington. The defense argued that the accused could only be prosecuted for the first count (inveigling and kidnapping without reference to place), and not for inveigling Northup to accompany them to Washington, nor for theft of services, nor for his actual sale as a slave, all of which took place outside the state.

The defense demanded a ruling from the court as to the legality of proceeding to trial on the last three counts of the indictment. The trial judge ruled they had no basis in law, and rendered a judgment for the defendants, dismissing those three counts, without proceeding to trial on the first one.[34]

At a session a few days later, presided over by Judge August Bockes, bail was set at $800 for Merrill and at a minimal amount for Russell. Both made bail and were released from custody.[35] They had been in jail about seven months. As things turned out, this was the only jail time they were to serve for the kidnapping of Solomon Northup.

THE SUPREME COURT RULING

District Attorney Odell appealed the court's decision to dismiss the three counts to the Supreme Court, the first appellate level in the state.[36] A Supreme Court bench, consisting of Justices James, Bockes, and Cornelius L. Allen, decided (in a two to one decision) at its July 1855 session in Essex County, to uphold the judgment of the Oyer and Terminer court that the kidnappers could not be tried on the last three of the indictment's four counts. The one count whose legality the court upheld was the charge that Merrill and Russell had inveigled Northup out of the state with *intent* to sell him. The inveigling—and their intent to sell him—had taken place within the jurisdiction of New York courts. The Supreme Court held, in the decision written by Allen, that the other counts were *not* valid, and, in fact, the statutes under which they were brought were unconstitutional. The court argued that the U.S. Constitution provides that an accused person should be tried in the locality in which the offense was committed. The counts in question dealt with the actual *sale* of Northup, which occurred in Washington, D.C. In normal practice, fugitives are extradited to the jurisdiction where their offenses occurred, and tried there. That, of course had not happened in this case.[37]

In their decision, the judges used examples of thieves who had stolen items in other states, but who were caught in New York. According to earlier court decisions, they could not be prosecuted in New York. Consequently, state law was changed, making it a crime to *possess* property stolen in another state. Writing "the penal acts of one state can have no operation in another state," the court upheld the trial judge's decision on the three charges in contention.[38] Odell appealed this decision to the Court of Appeals, New York's highest court.

THE DECISION OF THE COURT OF APPEALS

The Court of Appeals heard the appeal, and rendered its decision in June 1856. It was a highly technical ruling based solely on procedural issues. Unlike the decision of the Supreme Court, it did not reach the question of whether the three counts that were dismissed had been done so properly. The Court *implied* that the Oyer and Terminer judge had erred in not proceeding to trial on the first count of the indictment immediately after dismissing the other three counts. The Court of Appeals *held* that the Supreme Court had erred in permitting an appeal (on a writ of error) from Oyer and Terminer before any final judgment had been rendered there. Put simply, the Court of Appeals held that the Supreme Court should have refused to hear the appeal because no verdict had been rendered at the trial court level: "A writ of error can only be brought by a defendant to review a *final* judgment rendered upon an indictment."[39]

It may be looked at in this way: when defendants are brought to trial on a multicount indictment, there are not separate trials for each count. There is a single trial on all counts, and a jury, having heard the whole body of evidence, renders a verdict on each count. A judge at any stage may dismiss a count. What the Court of Appeals considered inappropriate was allowing the prosecution to appeal the dismissal of the three counts before trial had been held on the other count—and a judge going along with this by letting part of a case be appealed before the rest of the case was decided. The decision therefore reversed that of the Supreme Court and remanded the case back to Oyer and Terminer so that Merrill and Russell could be tried on the first count.[40]

In theory, moreover, this decision also vacated the Supreme Court's decision regarding the legality of the other counts and the constitutionality of the statutes, although it did not explicitly do this. Arguably, therefore, there was nothing in the Court of Appeals decision precluding the trial court from reinstating the three dismissed counts when the trial resumed—nor anything mandating their reconsideration.

THE CASE IS DROPPED

Despite the ruling of the Court of Appeals clearing the way for the trial's resumption, this never occurred. That fall a new District Attorney, John O. Mott, was elected, replacing Odell.[41] Mott was a Democrat; Odell, a Whig. In the politics of the period, Whigs were much more inclined to be favorable to African Americans. Though the kidnappers had been located and indicted "and the public, whose sympathies were all with the victim and his rescuers, looked eagerly for their trial and punishment. It seems . . . that a nolle prosequi has been entered upon the indictment."[42] The case was dropped in May 1857, nearly a year after the ruling by the Court of Appeals.[43]

Many factors may have gone into the decision to drop the case, and numerous theories were (or can be) advanced as to why: 1) Northup had been done in by the kidnappers; 2) Northup was away and not available as a witness; 3) the recently decided Dred Scott case had created a new legal climate; 4) the case was getting cold and the new District Attorney felt that on the merits he could not proceed, facing an unresolved statute of limitations issue and a case likely to be restricted to the one count of inveiglement; 5) the District Attorney came to believe that Northup was a party to the kidnapping; and 6) the political climate had shifted, public attitudes toward Northup had moved from sympathy to hostility, and the prosecutor was sympathetic to this shift or to the white kidnappers. It is likely that a combination of some of these factors was responsible.

First, suggestions were made nearly 20 years afterward that the trial did not continue because the kidnappers had killed Northup. Noting Northup's apparent disappearance, the *Bench and Bar of Saratoga*

County said, "What his fate was is unknown to the public, but the desperate kidnappers no doubt knew."[44] Even later, John Henry Northup, Henry Northup's nephew, in 1909 wrote about Northup: "The last I heard of him," he "was lecturing in Boston . . . All at once he disappeared. We believed that he was kidnapped and taken away, or killed or both."[45] But the evidence is very strong that Northup had *not* been the victim of Merrill and/or Russell a second time. In the summer of 1857, several months after the case was dropped, he was alive, since numerous newspapers reported events regarding a talk he was to make in Streetsville, Ontario.[46] The kidnappers would have had very little motive to kill Northup after the trial was dismissed. Free on bail since February 1855, had they wanted to kill him, surely they would have done so between then and May 1857. In any event, Northup was alive when the case was dropped.

Second, was the case dropped because Northup had lost interest in it, was away on speaking engagements, or was not cooperating with the new District Attorney—and was therefore not available or willing to participate in the trial? This seems highly unlikely. To be sure, Northup traveled a lot and gave many speeches (see Chapter 7) and the case had dragged on for several years, but it stretches credulity that he would have not been present (or a willing witness) at the trial for this reason. Having sought justice for a long time, he had an emotional stake in getting a verdict against the kidnappers, he had a financial stake in the companion civil suit, and the publicity attending a trial and guilty verdict would have helped promote his book and lectures. Northup may have found the many delays disillusioning, but when the state's highest court ruled, in effect, in his favor, it's difficult to believe he would not have moved decisively to assist the prosecution any way he could.

Third, could the Dred Scott case have influenced the D.A.'s action? Newspapers at the time implied that the case against the kidnappers was dropped as a result of the U.S. Supreme Court's infamous March 1857 decision, which affected the status of blacks in American courts.[47] The *Albany Evening Journal* observed, "In the case of the kidnappers of Solomon Northrup, we learn that a nol. pros. [will not prosecute] had been entered. Is this one of the effects of Judge TANEY's decision?"[48] The *Liberator* noted, "He [Northup] brought suit some time ago against his kidnappers . . . but since the Dred Scott decision, he has been obliged to abandon all hope of bringing them to justice, because he cannot sue in the United States courts."[49]

The impact of Dred Scott must be taken seriously. It did constrict and undermine the legal rights of African Americans to sue in Federal courts, and the precedent could have been used to argue against those rights in state courts. It should not, however, have affected the state's kidnapping case against Merrill and Russell. Northup was not a party to that case, only a complaining witness. Dred Scott would not have undermined New York law against the felony crime of kidnapping, even kidnapping blacks. However, even if the Dred Scott precedent did not apply to the Northup case directly, the direction in which the U.S. Supreme Court was moving could easily have impressed a prosecutor who, for political reasons, was apathetic about the case. It is reasonable to conclude that in one way or another, Dred Scott may have been part of the picture.

Fourth, might the District Attorney have reasonably decided to drop the case on the merits? He would have had several reasons for caution before proceeding. Although the Court of Appeals had arguably wiped the slate clean in terms of the three disputed indictments, going back to a trial judge and asking him to reinstate the indictments might not have seemed advisable in light of the Supreme Court's ruling on their merits. He could reasonably have decided that he had only one count on which to proceed. Secondly, the statute of limitations issue had not been definitively resolved and could have presented barriers. Third, the case had dragged out for some time, and public support for bringing the kidnappers to justice had waned. Nevertheless, although it could be argued that the case was "getting cold" (the kidnapping happened in 1841 and the arrests in 1854), the witnesses were still alive, and the evidence therefore intact. Moreover, the case was strong: the kidnappers had been identified by several witnesses; there was at least one witness besides Northup to the "inveiglement" in Saratoga; and the interrogatories, although sought by the defendants, provided evidence of Northup's sale to Birch. The evidence supporting the "inveiglement" charge therefore seems strong enough to take to a jury and it alone could have brought a serious sentence. Caution should be used in second guessing a prosecutor, but Odell certainly thought he had enough evidence to go to trial, and Mott had access to the same evidence.

Fifth, the case may have been dropped because the District Attorney and others came to believe that Northup was complicit in the kidnapping. Several newspapers suggested this. For example, "The Albany *Evening Journal* made some inquiries . . . which we will answer by saying that since the indictment was found, the District-Attorney was placed in possession of facts that, whilst proving their guilt in a measure, would prevent a conviction. To speak more plainly, it is more than suspected that Sol. Northup was an accomplice in the sale, calculating to slip away and share the spoils, but that the purchaser was too sharp for him, and instead of getting the cash, he got something else."[50]

This "conspiracy theory" had been advanced by Birch during his trial in Washington (and was mentioned in *Twelve Years*). Birch's self-serving story (with all the details about how willing the slave he bought from "Brown" was to be sold) attested to facts that, if true, would support this conspiracy contention. Birch's tale was on record. There was even one story circulated in 1902 after Merrill's death (a story that could have been around during the trial) that Merrill wrote Northup a letter from the Saratoga County jail, inviting him to come see him. "By a pre-arranged plan, two witnesses were secreted near the cell by Merrill's friends, who overheard Solomon admit that he had consented to be sold. When these facts became known, Merrill obtained his freedom without delay."[51] The latter point is not true: Merrill and Russell were released from jail about 15 months *before* the case was dismissed.

The conspiracy theory can be convincingly dismissed (as discussed in the concluding section of this chapter), but the question is not its validity, but its believability. Such stories may have made the District Attorney doubtful of Northup, or been used as an excuse for his action.

Finally, there seems to have been a shift in public opinion. Had the negative publicity associated with the second play reached Saratoga County, it could have hurt Northup's image. Moreover, the case had been politicized. Henry Northup had been very careful to make the rescue a bipartisan effort, but he could not control partisan sentiment once the kidnappers were discovered. Attacks on Northup and support for the kidnappers were voiced at the time of the 1855 trial: "Democratic newspapers opened their first racist attack on Northup calling for the acquittal of Merrill and Russell. Whig newspapers, in turn, came to Northup's defense."[52] This was a very polarized society soon to erupt in the Civil War, and polarization existed within New York. It was, in part, based on race, with Whigs, like Seward, championing the rights of African Americans, and Democrats appealing to the white vote, often on nativist and racial grounds. Needless to say, it was in the interest of the kidnappers, facing initial popular hostility, to encourage politicization and slander Northup, using race as an obvious vehicle. The more polarized the sentiment, the tougher it would be to get a unanimous jury verdict against them.

The exact reasons why District Attorney Mott abandoned the case are unknown, but there were several legal and trial-strategic reasons that could have cumulated to reinforce preconceived political perceptions. The unquestionable political reality was that backing Northup by prosecuting the kidnappers would be unpopular within Mott's own party and among his own partisan press.

CONCLUSION

The clear balance of evidence supports Northup's innocence on the conspiracy claim and supports Merrill's and Russell's guilt on the kidnapping charge.

The accusation that Northup conspired to sell himself and share the proceeds seems ridiculous on its face. The story, however, was widespread at the time and continued to have traction later (probably encouraged by supporters of the kidnappers themselves and aided by racial prejudice),[53] so it should be examined carefully. Such kidnapping stratagems seem to have been employed on a few occasions, but there are no apparent convictions along those lines. There are many reasons to disbelieve the allegation.

First, there is Northup's own definitive denial: "I do solemnly declare before men, and before God, that any charge or assertion, that I conspired directly or indirectly with any person or persons to sell myself . . . is utterly and absolutely false."[54] Its appearance in the text suggests Wilson was convinced of his innocence. The entire book has such a ring of authenticity that Northup should be credited in this, as in other regards.

Henry Northup, an experienced attorney, also obviously believed Northup, or he would not have been so willing immediately to proceed to trial when Birch, charging conspiracy, filed suit in Washington, D.C. Nor, having heard the claim in Washington, would he have proceeded so vigorously against the kidnappers in New York had he doubted Northup in this regard; he'd have realized they could argue conspiracy at their trial.

Moreover, Northup's own eager participation in the identification and arrest of Merrill and Russell shows no hesitancy in confronting them; he would not have done so if they'd had something on him. He could have failed to positively identify the two men, and the case—and risk of his exposure—would have dissipated.

Additionally, if Northup colluded, then he exercised much creative writing in his description of the trip to Washington. Why provide such accurate descriptions of Merrill and Russell, and of their antics in Albany? Why express so much uncertainty about whether Merrill and Russell had deliberately tricked him? The book would have sold just as well without such details. To be sure, Prindle testified at the hearing about Northup's lack of concern, when departing, about being kidnapped and enslaved (which might have been the case had he been in cahoots), but it may simply have been an expression of Northup's characteristic self-assurance.

Conspirators ordinarily avoid halls of justice, rather than seeking them out, since legal proceedings are likely to uncover their complicity. As Northup wrote in relation to the Washington, D.C. trial, "it is an outrage upon probability to suppose I would have run the hazard, not only of exposure, but of a criminal prosecution and conviction."[55] Surely, the same logic applied in 1854—stronger, even, because Northup's success as an author and speaker would have been threatened. Had he conspired, he likely would have avoided litigation.

Regarding the kidnapping itself, it's difficult to imagine an intelligent and in some ways worldly man trusting anyone enough to be sold into slavery for a sum of money, upon the promise that they would rescue him and share the profits. Such a scheme offered Northup little security, and high risk. To be viable, it would require a much greater level of trust than was possible between Northup and these strangers.

And then there are the logistics of the kidnapping. The strategic advantages of the design and location of Gadsby's hotel—one of Washington's most expensive—for the purpose of the kidnapping is described in Chapter 3. Had Northup been part of the plot, there would have been no need to stay there.

There is also the evidence and testimony of Birch himself. For Northup to participate, Merrill and Russell would have had to offer him a plausible "exit strategy." A key component would have been the free papers. Without them there was no proof of his free status. Obviously, Northup could not appear available for sale with these papers in his possession. He would have had to give them to Merrill and Russell and let them redeem him. But how would they accomplish this? They couldn't sell him, appearing the next day with free papers to redeem him. One of them would have had to sell him and the other redeem him with the free papers, accompanied by some plausible story. This, however, would rule out the two of them appearing together in front of Birch. But Birch's testimony is clear that he saw both men together (and even knew their aliases). Seeing the two of them with Birch, Northup would have known instantly that something was amiss—because that scenario would have precluded rescue. He would have bolted, or halted the transaction. This is one of the most important pieces of evidence against the conspiracy theory.

Finally, the only plausible alternative to a rescue using the free papers would have involved the physical abduction of Northup from slavery. That Northup would have placed his freedom at risk for such a dubious scenario seems highly implausible.

The case against the conspiracy theory is very strong, and so is the case that Merrill and Russell were indeed the kidnappers. To summarize the evidence, taken in sworn testimony and subject to cross-examination:

they were identified as the ones who accompanied Northup to Washington; they were seen with him there using assumed names; they were encountered on their return trip, without Northup and in affluent circumstances; and Merrill bragged about Northup's sale price, hinting at a figure similar to what Birch gave. Birch, in sworn testimony, gave one kidnapper's alias correctly, and listed the other's correctly on the *Orleans* manifest. Radburn testified that Northup was Birch's slave in Williams' Pen. The *Orleans* manifest listed Birch as Northup's shipper. Birch's books, however, contained no entry for a purchase of Northup, an omission fully consistent with a kidnap. A court of law will never pronounce on the matter, but it does seem beyond a reasonable doubt, before history, that Northup's story is true, with Merrill, Russell, and Birch complicit in his kidnapping.

Northup therefore was denied justice once again—denied the right to have his kidnappers brought to trial and dealt with according to law. It is truly ironic that the legal system of Louisiana, presented with evidence, found in his favor, but the legal systems of Washington, D.C. and New York State were unable to provide him with remedies, despite the efforts of excellent counsel.

9

Financial Problems, the Underground Railroad, and the Mystery of Northup's Fate

The failed trial of Merrill and Russell must have been a huge disappointment to Northup. The outcome of his civil suit against the kidnappers is unknown, but no documentation has been found showing it went to trial or that Northup received any compensation.

By 1857, his speaking engagements were dwindling, if not over, as were his theatrical ventures. He may still have been receiving book royalties, but after several years of publicizing his story, his earnings, after expenses, were probably small. The speaking engagements, partly aimed at promoting his book, were also aimed at supporting the abolitionist cause; some of the proceeds may have done that. The plays were far from financially successful and may even have left him in debt. By 1854, Northup was financially strained.

FINANCIAL PROBLEMS

Early in 1854, abolitionist Gerrit Smith, then a member of Congress, and Congressman Wade submitted citizens' petitions seeking "compensation to Solomon Northup for twelve years' captivity and suffering as a slave. . . ."[1]

The text of one such petition appeared in *Frederick Douglass' Paper:*

> To the Honorable Senators and House of Representatives in Congress assembled:

The undersigned, your petitioners, legal voters of the State of New York, respectfully represent to your Honorable body that Solomon Northrup, a citizen of this State, and at the time of his seizure a resident of the county of Saratoga, was, in the spring of 1841, kidnapped and carried into slavery, sold in the slave market of Washington, and was for twelve years detained in slavery in different parts of the State of Louisiana.

And we, respectfully request some suitable action of your Honorable body to indemnify him by some adequate compensation for the time thus, spent in the unrequited service of worse than Egyptian taskmasters.[2]

These petitions were rejected by the committees considering them.[3] Although the idea of petitioning Congress was not new—an article in 1853 noted Northup's plans to "bring his case before Congress, by petitioning for an allowance"[4] —his financial circumstances in 1854 may have given it added urgency.

In May 1854, a time when he was on a speaking tour and coordinating a theatrical production in Syracuse, he borrowed $450 (a personal loan, and two different mortgages on the property purchased in 1853). The first mortgage, on May 8, was for $200,[5] and the second, on May 24, for $150.[6] The second was to be repaid within three months. He was apparently unable to pay them, and the holder of the first foreclosed that fall.[7] On December 30, 1854, a foreclosure notice was delivered to his daughter at his home. An auction was held on January 30, 1855, at Wait Carpenter's Glens Falls Hotel and the property seems to have been purchased by Albert Cheney, a prominent local politician, for $24.

Northup obtained the personal loan from William Arlin on May 16, 1854. In court proceedings, which arose when Arlin sued for nonpayment, Northup said the loan was taken out to pay off someone named Fuller in Schenectady. Northup said he had not repaid Arlin because Arlin had not paid off Fuller, as they had agreed. The case was submitted to a referee, who found against Northup.[8] There were two other judgments against Northup that year, perhaps also arising from personal loans.[9] Taken together, it appears that in the spring and summer of 1854, Northup borrowed a substantial amount of money, and several months later, when the trial of his kidnappers was active in the local courts, judgments were entered against him for these debts. The timing of these debts suggests that they were needed to defray expenses incurred producing his play, which had opened in April 1854. The play was not a great success, and keeping it going and paying bills after it closed may have demanded cash. The prospect of further financial challenges may have been why the Glens Falls property purchased in 1855 was bought, not in Northup's name, but in that of his wife Anne.[10]

In addition, there is evidence that Northup was a generous person who tried to help others in need, especially fugitive slaves. A newspaper observed that "We hear he is generous and pitiful [pitying] to his fugitive brethren; that he gives of his substance to those who have fled from slavery, saying: 'I know what it is, I can feel for you.'"[11] This reinforces the conclusion that Northup's play and appearances were not undertaken strictly for personal gain and that money was not uppermost in his life.

The last reference to public activities by Solomon Northup is the traumatic 1857 speaking attempt in Canada, closely following the prosecutor's decision to drop the case against the kidnappers. After that, Northup seems to disappear from public view.

Northup's life from his rescue until 1857 consisted of intense activity: the early public appearances, the writing of the book, the lectures promoting both it and the abolitionist cause, the production of a play, the activities surrounding the arrest of the kidnappers (with the attendant hearings and appeals), more speeches, and the involvement with a second play. These activities, and perhaps others for which no records survive, also involved substantial travel, which required separation from his family.[12] He was leading the life of a very active, confident, energetic—even entrepreneurial—man, quite consistent with the Northup of *Twelve Years*. There were disappointments, such as the plays and the trial, but he continued fighting back; there is no sign of a slackening in his activities. Then he dropped from public notice in the fall of 1857. As John Henry Northup recalled: "All at once he disappeared."[13] This comment was made many years afterward, but the use of the phrase "all at once" is striking. John Henry also speculated that Northup had been abducted or murdered, though evidence against this, as noted, is very strong.

What might have happened? For celebrities, fame fades with time, and, in this case, so also does the historical record. Based on what evidence does exist, some conclusions can be drawn.

By the summer of 1857, Northup had reached a turning point in his life. The court case was finished, opportunities for speaking engagements had diminished, his plays had flopped, his book sales were trending down, and his finances were tenuous. In July he turned 50 years old, a milestone of sorts for any man. What had he to show for all the energy he had expended in so many activities during the previous four years? His life in freedom had been exciting and eventful, but it may have reached a point where a different direction was clearly indicated. He was no longer in a position to make a life solely out of the story of his enslavement and rescue, either financially or as a contribution to a cause. He had probably also become quite aware of the growing racial tensions and polarizations occurring in the region as the country headed toward civil war. In what direction should he go? Should he return to his preslavery existence, working as a farmer or artisan? Would it be possible and rewarding to resume his Saratoga life? His race prevented him from building a life in either capacity that would have equaled the status he had enjoyed as a national celebrity.

He could have accepted this reality and its consequences, but this was a man whose whole history revealed a high level of energy and sense of self-worth. His celebrity status, despite the setbacks, would have reinforced this. Still, there were grounds for disillusionment: he had been denied justice in the courts, perhaps for political and racial reasons; some of his white public had abandoned him; he'd been subjected to racially motivated attacks in the partisan press. On the national scene events seemed to be moving in the wrong direction, with the recent Dred Scott decision, "bleeding Kansas," and repeated examples of the enforcement of the fugitive slave law. There were certainly sufficient causes for disillusionment.

THE UNDERGROUND RAILROAD

Such prospects and perceptions might have overwhelmed any person, but it appears that they did not overwhelm Northup. Instead, there is evidence that he decided to devote his efforts to helping fugitives escape the type of enslavement he himself had experienced, by becoming an active participant in the underground railroad. This new undertaking would not earn him any money. It would separate him from his family and it would be largely anonymous, denying him the satisfaction of public recognition. It could be dangerous. But it also would give Northup something to do that was fully compatible with his love of adventure and accomplishment. He would be matching wits with slave-catchers. Day after day, he and a few others would see the results of his efforts. He would be striking a blow for freedom, and for his fellow African Americans. It would be a logical extension of the activities of a "generous" man who "gives of his substance to those who have fled from slavery." His personal contact with major players in the abolition movement—Frederick Douglass, Henry C. Wright, Gerrit Smith, and others—may have provided motivation and opportunity to become involved. But his activities would be shrouded in secrecy. To do this job effectively, he would indeed have to "disappear."

The evidence is not perfect, yet it's persuasive. Northup certainly had motivation to help fugitive slaves. His own experiences would have been sufficient for this, and they would have been reinforced by events described daily in the papers and discussed generally through-out the antislavery community. He may have been further motivated as a result of contact with one of his neighbors in the small and tight-knit African American community in Glens Falls.

This neighbor, John Van Pelt, was a black barber who owned property adjoining that of the Northup family.[14] It is almost certain that Northup would have known him. Van Pelt had a history of involvement in the antislavery movement. In the 1840s, while living in Saratoga Springs, he was a subscription agent for an antislavery newspaper, *The Northern Star and Freeman's Advocate*.[15] Van Pelt had worked in Saratoga (possibly Northup knew him there), but his barbershop was destroyed by fire in 1844,[16] and Van Pelt apparently moved to Glens Falls at some point after that.

Van Pelt had direct experience with the problems of fugitives because his wife was a fugitive slave. In an incident related by Samuel Boyd, she may have been the target of a stranger who was a suspected slave-catcher. The stranger asked some boys for directions to the Van Pelt home. Suspicious of the stranger, they gave him bad directions and one boy, Addison Stoddard, ran home to tell his father, who was active in the underground railroad. Soon the wife, along with her three children (who were also liable for capture) were spirited out of town and the Van Pelts moved to Canada for a while.[17]

This story is consistent with information for the Van Pelt family from the 1855 New York State Census. Van Pelt's birthplace is given as Albany County, but that of his wife is Virginia. Three of their children were born in New York State, but one, three-year-old Francis, was born in Canada, suggesting that the above incident happened in the early 1850s. A younger child was born in Warren County, New York, around 1854, indicating when the Van Pelts returned to Glens Falls.[18] Northup had just returned from slavery, and surely would have heard the story. Knowledge of the fear and disruption experienced by acquaintances of his may have brought home the suffering being endured by fugitive slaves. Van Pelt later recruited local African Americans for the famous 54th Massachusetts Regiment, the first military regiment that accepted black men in the Civil War.[19] One of the men he recruited, Charles Stanton, was the stepson of Northup's daughter Margaret. Northup must have been aware of his neighbor's antislavery activism, and of his wife's rescue by the underground railroad. Northup's own incentives to help fugitives could only have been strengthened by his association with Van Pelt.

Direct evidence of Northup's involvement with the underground railroad is provided by Wilbur Siebert, who researched the railroad extensively and wrote several books: *The Underground Railroad from Slavery to Freedom, The Underground Railroad in Massachusetts,* and *Vermont's Anti-Slavery and Underground Railroad Record.* In the last of these, Siebert writes that Northup, along with another black man, "Taylor Groce," worked with a white Methodist minister named John L. Smith to help fugitive slaves make their way through Vermont to Canada. The information came from a letter which the minister's son wrote to Siebert in the 1930s.[20] Siebert's book gives an incorrect name for the black man who worked with Northup: his name was actually "Tabbs Gross." John R. Smith, the minister's son, recalled "Tabbs Gross and Solomon Northrup except for my father were the only ones I ever saw that belonged to the [underground rail] road."[21] Rev. Smith served as one of three members of the (anti-slavery) Vermont Methodist Episcopal Church's Slavery Committee.[22]

Siebert received two letters written by John R. Smith, one of which stated "my father belonged to the under Ground Rail Road till the war ended it." He also wrote "It was a great thing to know that a slave was hid up in the house." The letters also indicate that his father had assistance. "Two of the greatest workers were Tabbs Gross and Solomon Northrup."[23]

Smith's letters also recount information about these men's histories. Northup "was kidnaped [sic] in Mass. when a boy and taken to South Carolina and sold into slavery. Was smart, ran away and got into Boston and put in his time helping other slaves get north." In another letter, he wrote (more accurately) "Northrup was born free north and kidnapt [sic] and sold off South. got away and put in his time helping others get north." Although the gist of Northup's story is correct, Smith obviously got a few details wrong. But clearly the person he wrote of was kidnapped *and* escaped slavery. Although kidnappings were not infrequent, escape was rare. This strongly suggests that he knew *the* Solomon Northup. Despite the mangled information about Northup's background (Smith admits that he had "forgotten so much about it"), everything else about this story checks out.

Northup's story was well-publicized, and Smith could have read or heard about his book. Since his letters were written after many years had passed, he might have intermingled what he knew about Northup with his memories of his father's activities. But it is not likely that this would be the case with Gross, whose life history was less accessible to Smith, living in rural Vermont. Smith wrote of Tabbs Gross that he "had quite a family and had them all in Canada. He bought two or three of them but kept on helping others get away. He was a man of some education. He spoke in my fathers desk [pulpit] once at least. . . ."[24] Gross is also referred to (though not by name) in notes from an interview with John R. Smith. In them, mention is made of a black man who worked with Rev. Smith: "The man who first made this underground railroad was a negro who got himself, his wife and children clear thru to Canada and then got people from the south thru the N.E. [New England] States to Canada."[25] Except for items in newspapers (mostly away from Vermont), little contemporaneous information about Gross was available to the general public. It is difficult to imagine how Smith could have remembered so accurately this man's background, other than by knowing him personally.

The story of Gross is perhaps as interesting as that of Northup, and a brief summary confirms Smith's recollections of him. "Theodore (Tabb) Gross . . . was born a slave on a Maryland plantation." His last master was "a minister from Germantown, Kentucky, who struggled with the idea of slavery; he urged Gross to preach and to obtain an education. In 1850 Gross convinced his master to sell him his freedom. Gross was allowed to travel north, where he raised the $1,000 necessary for his purchase by appealing to congregations in Ohio, Indiana, Pennsylvania, and New York." In 1852, he relocated to California, and raised the money needed to purchase his wife and four children. In 1860, Gross undertook a speaking tour in England to raise money to purchase the freedom of Lewis Smith, whom he had met as a slave.[26]

Rev. Smith's parsonage in Hartland, Vermont, on the Connecticut River, was apparently an important station on the underground railroad. John R. Smith recalled that "I never knew when a slave came to the house or when he left. Some times my father carried him, and sometimes someone came or he left on foot, always towards Canada. I never saw but one or two, but knew when one was hid up in the house."[27] This suggests fugitives were accommodated with some level of frequency.

There are other credible stories of residents in the Hartland area providing aid to fugitives. One of the letters collected by Siebert, written by Hartland Postmaster Walter F. Hatch, includes some notes about underground railroad activity. Most of the information is somewhat vague, but one story, about a man named Edmond Barrell, presented some specific information. Barrell had, according to the recollection of his son, assisted at least one fugitive—a 25-year-old man who said he was the offspring of a slave woman and her white master. Mary Hatch (Hatch's mother) recalled another incident in the late 1850s when her grandparents left food for a black man they had found asleep in their barn near Windsor, Vermont.[28]

The details of Northup's association with Rev. Smith are unknown. His son recalled in a letter to Hatch, that the first year of the war was the most active year. He also mentioned that his father had lived in Hartland the first two years of the Civil War. He further stated that "My father only stayed two years in a place so his activity on the road [underground railroad] changed very often from place to place."[29] Biographical information on Rev. Smith shows that he was indeed at Hartland in 1861 and 1862.[30] This evidence points to Northup working out of (or through) Hartland during those years. The biographical information also says that Smith was in the "traveling ministry," mentioning a series of appointments, lasting from one to three years each. Northup and Gross may have worked with him in other Vermont towns. For example, Smith's son wrote that Northup "came to see my father once after the emancipation." If Northup visited him after the Emancipation Proclamation in 1863, then it would have been in Lunenburg, Vermont, also on the Connecticut River, where Smith served after leaving Hartland.

Northup may have become involved with Smith through Tabbs Gross, since Gross was the man "who first made this underground railroad." Northup could have met Gross (a recognized figure in the antislavery movement) through several different channels. In 1855, Gross made several speaking appearances in upstate New York, including one at Rochester's Corinthian Hall, on April 16.[31] In June, he was at Canandaigua where he either lost or was robbed of $700, which he had raised to buy the freedom of a slave.[32] Also in June, he spoke in Elmira at the First Methodist Episcopal Church and at the Independent Congregational Church.[33] In July, he was listed as a subscriber to *Frederick Douglass' Paper.*[34] Gross visited St. Johnsbury, Vermont, in June 1856, successfully raising funds for the purchase of his daughter.[35] Also, in 1858, he was in Utica raising funds to purchase the freedom of the children of ex-slave Lewis Smith, and reportedly planned to go to Albany.[36]

Northup's experience with slavery had taught him to be aware of relevant networks. He certainly would have had familiarity with the antislavery network in the New York and New England African American community as a result of traveling throughout the region. The above newspaper listings make it likely Frederick Douglass would have known Gross and could have introduced them or credentialed them to each other.

Given Northup's personal experiences as a slave, the experiences of fugitives and their families known to him, his willingness to take risks, his apparent and unexplained disappearance from public life, and the recollections of a relative of an agent on the underground railroad, it seems reasonable to conclude that Northup was indeed actively involved in aiding fugitive slaves to attain freedom in Canada.

What work might Northup have done on the underground railroad? Although the evidence we have connects him with the Hartland, Vermont, station, he may have been active in other locales as well. Rev. Smith served a number of different parishes in Vermont. Northup, perhaps in association with him, may have conducted fugitives up and down the whole Connecticut Valley. He may have worked the line moving fugitives from station to station, or he may have organized the route in a supervisory capacity. His life experiences had prepared him for reading people and situations, maintaining confidences, planning and making things work.

The underground railroad ceased operation during the Civil War. If Northup began his participation around 1858, he may have been at it for several years. His life would have been intrinsically rewarding, but lacking in financial wealth. By 1865, when he was 58 years old, his fame—already fading in 1857—would have been lessened even more by the Civil War, reducing his ability to earn money by telling his story. By that time it is unlikely that he was earning any money from his book. Having worked on the underground railroad, possibly for years, he may have had no savings, and by this time, there was no property held in his name. His music had always been a supplement to other income and never his principal source. At his age, it would not have been easy to again take up farming or any of the trades for which he was skilled. The condition of his health is unknown. To be sure, his children were now all grown and on their own, and Anne still had employment, but it is likely that Northup faced serious economic circumstances in a world with few social safety nets. His years on the railroad meant he had sacrificed much for the sake of others.

THE MYSTERY OF NORTHUP'S FATE

After the mid-1860s, there is no known evidence as to Northup's fate. How long he lived, where he died, or where he is buried are all unknown. More is known about Anne during this period (see

Appendix B). In an 1871 deposition, Anne stated that Northup *was* her husband (and not that he *had been* her husband). The 1875 New York State Census, and notices of her death in 1876 refer to her as a "widow." This evidence suggests that he died sometime between 1871 and 1875, but it is not conclusive. Anne may have referred to Northup as her husband, even were he deceased, and the writers of her death notices may have used the word "widow" simply because Northup may not have been in the area for some time and it was taken for granted that he was dead. It is possible that he and Anne did not live together on a sustained basis. With all of his speaking engagements and then the time he spent on the underground railroad, they would have been separated for long periods of time.

Some have speculated as to the date of his death and as to his fate. Some suggestions can be dismissed with a reasonable degree of certainty. Sue Eakin and Joseph Logsdon conclude he had died by 1863 because his wife had sold property that year (actually in 1864).[37] But the property sold was in Anne's name alone, so she could sell it independently. The Smith letters indicate he was still alive at that time. The story that he was murdered by the kidnappers is not credible (see Chapter 8).

One unpleasant possibility is that Northup may have been kidnapped a second time and again became a slave. Some newspaper articles in 1858 mention that this may have happened: Northup "has been again decoyed south, and is again a slave."[38] But this is unlikely. It is rather doubtful that he would have allowed himself to be "decoyed" south again. Although the supposition cannot be dismissed completely, it seems reasonably certain that he was in Vermont in the 1860s, and, therefore, was never again in slavery.

An entry in Field Horne's index to Saratoga newspapers mentions the possibility in 1854 of Northup going to England.[39] There are no indications that he actually went at that time, and he likely did not, considering his reported presence in Syracuse. Perhaps he went later on. Henry Northup visited England with some frequency; Solomon might have accompanied him on a voyage. But he would not have gone after the Civil War, when the interest in antislavery speakers would have been low.

Finally, it may be that he died destitute, far from family and friends, perhaps under tragic circumstances. Some notices of Anne's death, reprinted in several newspapers, contained disparaging comments about Northup's lecturing, implying that he'd become a nuisance.[40] Given the financial challenges he probably faced, Northup may well have died in difficult financial conditions, but were he still together with his wife, it is highly unlikely that he was destitute, since Anne continued working. Even if she were unable or (less likely) unwilling to support him, he would almost certainly have had the option of living with one of his children. If he spent his final years apart from his family, it would have been by choice, not from necessity.

It is, of course, possible that escalating challenges and continuing disappointments may finally have combined to break this remarkable man. He could have given up, resorted to drink, and sunk below the surface. But his whole life's history of dealing pragmatically with adversity while surmounting serious odds argues against it. The fact that he is unaccounted for in the public record of his region after the mid-1860s may only mean that he sought adventure far from home.

The mystery of his fate remains unsolved.

Appendix A

Notices of Appearances by Solomon Northup

Key:

FDP=Frederick Douglass' Paper

Where only a month is listed, the article did not provide a specific appearance date.

Cities are in New York State, unless otherwise specified.

Articles containing more than a brief announcement of Northup's appearance are marked (D) for "Description."

*Relates to a play about Northup's life.

**Date is not specified on the poster, but the authors believe that this play, at which Northup was present, was held about the same time as a performance held at Worcester, which featured almost the identical cast.

2/1/1853: Troy

FDP, 2/11/1853 (D)

2/4/1853: Albany

FDP, 2/18/1853 (D)

10/1/1853: Syracuse

Syracuse Evening Chronicle, 10/1/1853; *The Wesleyan,* 10/6/1853 (D); *Liberator,* 10/14/1853

1/1854: Lockport

Syracuse Daily Journal, 1/7/1854

1/1854: Buffalo
Syracuse Daily Journal, 1/12/1854

1/12/1854: Buffalo
FDP, 1/27/1854 (D)

1/13/1854: Rochester
Rochester Daily Union, 1/13/1854

2/2/1854: Syracuse
Syracuse Daily Journal, 1/28/1854; *Syracuse Evening Chronicle,* 1/30/1854; *Syracuse Daily Journal,* 1/31/1854; *Syracuse Evening Chronicle,* 2/2/1854 (D)

2/25/1854: St. Albans, VT
FDP, 3/3/1854 (D)

3/24/1854: Utica
Albany Evening Journal, 3/25/1854

4/1854: Moore's Forks
FDP, 5/5/1854 (D)

4/1854*: Syracuse
Syracuse Evening Chronicle, 4/21/1854

4/1854*: Syracuse
Syracuse Evening Chronicle, 4/28/1854 (D)

4/1854*: Syracuse
Syracuse Daily Standard, 7/19/1856 (D)

4/10/1854: Oswego
Oswego Times and Journal, 4/10/1854

4/26/1854*: Syracuse
Syracuse Daily Standard, 4/24/1854 (D); *Syracuse Daily Standard,* 4/25/1854

4/29/1854*: Syracuse
Syracuse Evening Chronicle, 4/29/1854

4/30/1854*: Syracuse
Syracuse Daily Standard, 5/1/1854

5/1854*: Syracuse
Syracuse Daily Standard, 5/2/1854

5/1854*: Syracuse
Syracuse Evening Chronicle, 5/5/1854 (D)

5/1854*: Syracuse
FDP, 5/26/1854 (D)

7/7/1854: Gloversville
Northern Christian Advocate, July 26, 1854

9/15/1854: Hamilton
Utica Morning Herald, 9/18/1854; *Oneida Weekly Herald*, 9/19/1854; *Syracuse Evening Chronicle*, 9/19/1854

1/1855: Montpelier, VT
Green Mountain Freeman, 1/23/1855

3/1855: Concord, NH
Syracuse Daily Standard, 3/31/1855

3/10/1855: Boston, MA
Boston Daily Atlas, 3/12/1855; *FDP*, 3/16/1855 (D)

3/15/1855: Boston, MA
Liberator, 3/23/1855 (D)

3/19/1855: Boston, MA
Liberator, 3/23/1855

3/24–25/1855: Worcester, MA
Liberator, 3/23/1855

3/31/1855: Worcester, MA
National Aegis, 4/4/1855

4/5/1855: Leominster, MA

Liberator, 3/30/1855

10/1855**: Fitchburg, MA

Poster, American Antiquarian Society

2/23/1856: Montpelier, VT

Vermont Watchman and State Journal, 2/22/1856

12/1856: St. Albans, VT

St. Albans Messenger, 12/11/1856 (D)

8/1857: Streetsville, Canada

Detroit Daily Free Press, 8/26/1857 (D)

8/1857: Streetsville, Canada

Charleston Mercury, 8/29/1857 (D), *Albany Evening Journal*, 9/5/1857 (D), *Pittsfield Sun*, 9/10/1857 (D), *New Hampshire Patriot*, 9/16/1857 (D)

Appendix B

Solomon Northup's Family

In the course of researching Solomon Northup, some information about his family members was discovered, which will no doubt be of interest to readers of this book.

Anne (Hampton) Northup

In *Twelve Years a Slave*, Northup mentions that his wife had resided in Sandy Hill, which is now called Hudson Falls, and also that she had lived in Salem, with the family of Rev. Alexander Proudfit. Indeed, the 1825 New York State Census shows, in the Proudfit household, one person of color, undoubtedly Anne.[1]

In the affidavits included at the back of Northup's book, Orville Clark identifies Anne as the daughter of William Hampton, a neighbor of his in Sandy Hill. There is a William Hampton, Jr.—probably a brother to Anne—buried in the same cemetery as Northup's father, Mintus.[2] Clark says the fathers of Solomon and of Anne were "reputed and esteemed in this community as respectable men."[3]

Northup makes some mention of what his family (wife Anne, and children Margaret, Elizabeth, and Alonzo) did during his absence, but it is minimal, and can be filled out a little more. It turns out that Northup's family had not been in the Saratoga/Glens Falls area the entire time he was away. Something very interesting happened. Information about Anne's life (and the lives of her children) during Solomon's absence is provided in the testimony given by her and her two daughters in the court proceedings involving the estate of Madame Eliza Jumel.[4] Madame Jumel was a wealthy and eccentric woman who lived in a mansion in New York City. She also owned a house in Saratoga (where she was a neighbor of Rev. Alexander Proudfit, whose family Anne had lived with in Salem, New York).

In 1841, Anne and her family lived at the Pavilion Hotel in Saratoga, and Anne was likely employed there as a cook. Madame Jumel, while staying at the hotel that summer, met them, and made arrangements that fall to have the older daughter, Elizabeth, go to her mansion in New York City and work as her servant. Not long afterward, Elizabeth was joined there by her mother and siblings, who stayed a year or less. Elizabeth remained with Madame Jumel until the fall of 1843. The contrast between Solomon's and his family's living arrangements at this time could not be greater: Solomon living in a primitive slave cabin, and his family living in a luxurious riverside mansion.

Each family member was employed in some way by Jumel: Anne as a cook, Elizabeth as a servant, Alonzo as a footman and errand boy, and Margaret served as a playmate for young Eliza Chase, a relative of Jumel residing in Hoboken, New Jersey. Although the children had duties, their presence may also have fulfilled a desire by Jumel to have young children in her household.[5]

Northup mentions that Clemens Ray, whom he met in the slave pen in Washington, D.C., made contact with his family while making his way to Canada. Specifically, he says that Ray stayed overnight with Northup's brother-in-law. This probably was Harry Hampton, who later on is listed in the same household as Anne.[6] In 1850, Hampton resided in the town of Moreau in Saratoga County.[7] Perhaps that was where Ray visited him, while the Northups were at Jumel's, since Northup makes no mention of Ray seeing other members of his family.

Probably in the fall of 1842, Anne returned to Saratoga with two of her children, Alonzo and Margaret. Margaret had ceased to be the playmate of Jumel's relative, and lodged briefly with a black family in Harlem until Anne retrieved her and took her home. Eventually, Elizabeth also returned to Saratoga.

Margaret got married to a widowed man named Philip Stanton, and in the late 1840s the extended family moved to Glens Falls. Northup explains that, during his absence, his family had relocated to Glens Falls, New York, where his wife worked as a cook at Wait Carpenter's Hotel. Indeed, census records reflect this with an entry for "Anne Northrop" at the hotel/household headed by Wait Carpenter.[8]

Anne is also listed in Saratoga in 1850, living, along with daughter Elizabeth, in the household of Rosanne Swift, a black woman.[9] (Citizens are not *supposed* to be enumerated in two different places, but it does happen.) This could be an indication that Anne was spending time in both places, or that she was in a state of transition on the date of the census (September 6). In 1850, Philip Stanton, a 29-year-old "mulatto," heads the household that follows that of Swift. With him are Margaret Stanton (Anne's other daughter) and children Charles and Solomon. Northup writes in *Twelve Years a Slave* that Margaret had married and had a son, whose name he gives as Solomon Northup "Staunton."[10]

Stanton, Margaret's husband, purchased property in Glens Falls (in the town of Queensbury) on May 7, 1851.[11] The deed identifies him as a resident of Queensbury, suggesting that he had already been living there, perhaps as a tenant. There is also a mortgage (discharged in 1864) between the married couple and Anne Northup, dated July 16, 1852.[12] The home purchased was on School Street, not far from Carpenter's hotel. So by the early 1850s, Anne was living and working in Glens Falls.

After Northup's rescue and return, he lived in Glens Falls with his family, when he wasn't traveling to give lectures. Property in Glens Falls, which he purchased about the time his book was being published, was unfortunately sold at a foreclosure sale early in 1855 when Solomon did not keep up with the mortgage payments.[13]

In May 1855, however, property adjoining Stanton's lot was purchased in the name of "Anne Northup" for $400.[14] Since Solomon's name doesn't appear on the deed, this suggests that either he wanted to protect the property from creditors (and there had been several judgments against him), or that he expected to be away from the area and wanted to insure that his family had a home to live in.

The 1855 New York State Census for Queensbury (which included Glens Falls), taken on June 9, 1855, lists Solomon (age 49), Anne (age 48), and Alonzo (age 21) as a separate family living in the same house as Stanton's family.[15] Northup's occupation is given as "carpenter," and none is given for either Anne or Alonzo.

On September 25, 1857, Anne was advanced $49.75 by the Glens Falls Bank, which she promised to repay with interest. She had not done so by March 20, 1859, and a few days later Benjamin P. Burhans, the bank president, obtained a judgment against her which, with interest and court costs, amounted to $61.22. The records give no indication of why she borrowed the money. On this document, as well as on the affidavit with her testimony for the Jumel trial, Anne's signature appears as an 'X', indicating that she had never learned to write. This may be why none of the letters Northup sent from Louisiana had been addressed directly to her.[16]

In the 1860 Federal Census for Queensbury, Anne is listed as head of household, with Stanton's family listed as the next household. Solomon is not listed, but a 50-year-old Harry Hampton (whose race is given as "mulatto," as is Anne's) is part of the household. Hampton is likely Anne's brother (and thus, Solomon's brother-in-law). Anne's occupation is "cook," and Harry's is "farmer."[17] She likely was still employed at Wait Carpenter's hotel, which was very near to the Northup and Stanton properties on School Street.

Anne probably had a summertime job as well, since she is probably the person listed in 1860 as "Anna Northrop" in the household of H.S. Wilson, a "hotel keeper," in the town of Bolton on Lake George. Her occupation is "cook."[18] Living and working in Bolton during the summers would be consistent with her testimony in the Jumel trial in the 1870s, when she said "my residence, for the summer, is at Bolton, in the county of Warren."[19]

Presumably, in 1860 Anne was primarily living in the home that was purchased in her name in May 1855, which, at the time of the 1855 census, she may not yet have occupied.

In 1864, Anne sold her property in Glens Falls. On March 31, it was sold to Maria Baker for a consideration of $600.[20] The following day, Philip and Margaret Stanton sold their adjoining property to Julia Schermerhorn.[21] Anne moved with the Stantons to property they'd purchased in Moreau, just across the Hudson River.[22]

The 1865 New York State Census shows Anne living with the Stantons in Moreau. Her relationship to the head of household, Philip Stanton, is "mother-in-law." No occupation is listed for her, but— significantly—she is listed as having been married once, and the column labeled "Now Married" is checked.[23]

Interestingly enough, Northup's relatives left Glens Falls just before a terrible fire destroyed much of the village. The blaze on May 31, 1864 reportedly started in the kitchen of the Glens Falls Hotel. Anne perhaps had still been working there prior to, perhaps even after, the move to Moreau.[24]

In 1871, Anne was called on to give evidence (as a deposition) in the lawsuit involving the Jumel Estate case. A Saratoga newspaper reported that "the wife and daughter of the once notorious Sol. Northrup" gave evidence relating to offspring of Madame Jumel.[25] It has also been stated that Anne provided evidence bearing on Jumel's sanity, which was an issue in the case.[26]

The year 1875 finds Anne (listed as "Anna") living with the Stantons in Kingsbury (which includes the village of Sandy Hill). A notation indicates that she was "widowed" at this time. Her husband apparently died sometime before 1875.[27]

Anne seems to have maintained a presence in the Glens Falls/ Moreau area. The following notice of her death appeared in a local newspaper:

"Mrs. Northup (colored) of Reynolds Corners died very suddenly August 8, at the house of Wm. Hamilton. Having washed the day before, she was preparing the clothes for ironing, standing by a table. About 11 o'clock she spoke of its being near dinner time, and partly settling back into a chair she expired immediately. She was the widow of the famous Sol. Northup."[28] (Reynolds Corners is the neighborhood in Moreau where Stanton's property was located.) On a map of the area, a William Hampton's property is located very near to that owned by Stanton.[29] There were several men named William Hamilton in Moreau, but the death notice likely refers to the one at this location. Anne possibly was a domestic servant in Hamilton's household, since she died at his home. But she may also have gone to people's houses to do their laundry.

Evidence relating to her year of birth is inconsistent,[30] but at the time of her death she was probably close to 75 years old.

Elizabeth Northup

Very little is known about Elizabeth, Northup's oldest child. In 1860, she was 30 years old and living with her mother and 50-year-old Harry Hampton (probably her uncle, but possibly her husband, since ditto marks—possibly erroneously—indicate her name is "Elizabeth Hampton") in Glens Falls.[31] In 1865, she is not among those listed in the Stanton household in Moreau, although her mother is.[32]

At some point, Elizabeth married a man named Price, and resided at 54 Thompson Street, New York City in the early 1870s.[33] She *may* have married again later, since a death notice for a Lizzie Thomas was printed in a Rochester paper in 1901. It says Thomas died at the age of 50 (whereas Elizabeth would have been around 70 by then). However, the item does say that besides her husband George S. Thomas and her two children, she was survived by "her brother, Alonzo Northrup, of Weedsport."[34] (Alonzo had relocated to Weedsport in the mid-1870s, and resided there until his death.) Though there was another Alonzo, a son of Alonzo, and hence, a grandson of Solomon, *that* Alonzo did not have a sister named Lizzie or anything that would result in a Lizzie nickname.

Margaret (Northup) Stanton

Margaret, Northup's second child, married Philip Stanton, sometime after the death of his first wife, Betsey Oakley (who died on February 24, either in 1847 or 1848).[35] The 1850 Census for Saratoga Springs shows Philip, aged 29, and Margaret, aged 19, listed just below the household of Rosanne Swift, whose household included Anne and Elizabeth Northup. Also, in the Stanton household are 9-year-old Charles (Philip's son from his first marriage), Solomon, aged 1, and Jane and Adaline Niles.[36]

Stanton purchased property in Glens Falls in 1851.[37] The 1855 New York State Census shows his family (joined by Solomon, Anne, and Alonzo Northup) living in Glens Falls. In addition to Charles and Solomon, the Stantons had a four-month-old son Pilay, according to census records. They are recorded as having lived in Glens Falls for eight years (which conflicts with information in the 1850 Federal Census, when they were shown to be living in Saratoga).[38]

The Stantons were still living in Glens Falls in 1860 (Anne, Harry Hampton, and Elizabeth are listed just above them in the Federal Census). Son Pilay is not listed, but there is a daughter, aged 2, named Florence. Philip's occupation is given as "teamster."[39]

The Stantons sold their property in Glens Falls on April 1, 1864.[40] Anne had sold hers the day before.[41] On April 1, Philip also *bought* property in nearby Moreau. This property was purchased from Maria Baker and Julia Schermerhorn, Jonathan Austin's widow and daughter, respectively.[42] (These were the same parties that had bought the Northup and Stanton properties in Glens Falls.) Later that month Stanton took over a lease of land that had belonged to Jonathan Austin.[43]

They all moved to Moreau, to the area known as Reynolds Corners. The 1865 New York State Census shows a household consisting of Philip, Margaret, Thomas (about the same age as Solomon Stanton would be, so he may also have been known by that name), Florence, and Anne Northup. Philip's occupation is "farmer."[44]

On an 1866 map of Moreau, the property of "P. Stanton" is labeled near the northeast corner of the intersection that forms Reynolds Corners.[45] Stanton's name appears in a Saratoga County Directory as a farmer, with 33 acres of land.[46]

The Stantons (Philip, Margaret, Solomon, and Florence) were living in Moreau in 1870, though Anne is not listed with them.[47] Court testimony indicates that Margaret was ill for a time in the early 1870s, and a man had to come to her home at Reynolds Corners to record her statement for the Jumel trial.[48]

Several real estate transactions were undertaken by the Stantons in the Glens Falls area: the discharge, in 1871, of a lease Philip had taken on in April 1864;[49] the recording, on September 5, 1873, of a substitute deed for a plot in the Glens Falls Cemetery that had been purchased in 1867;[50] and the sale of the Moreau property on June 7, 1874.[51] The property was sold to Thomas Brice for $1,650.

Not long afterward, property was conveyed from Thomas and Emily Brice of Sandy Hill to Margaret A. Stanton of Moreau (with no mention of Philip). A deed, dated June 17, 1874, indicates that Mrs. Stanton paid $1,500 for the Sandy Hill property.[52] Philip later described these two transactions as an exchange.[53]

A mortgage document shows that in 1877, the Sandy Hill property was used to leverage a deal for the Stantons to take over property on South Broadway in Saratoga Springs.[54] A move to Saratoga Springs at this time is consistent with a list of residences Stanton provided as part of his application for a "dependent father's" pension, based on the Civil War service of his son Charles.[55] Papers in the pension file also reveal that the Stantons relocated to Washington, D.C. in the late 1870s. Philip worked as a nurse at Freedmans Hospital.

Margaret died on March 14, 1879. She was interred (possibly some years after her death) at Norfolk, Virginia's West Point Cemetery, and death and burial records show her as a resident of the District of Columbia when she died. Her occupation is given as "hair weaver."[56]

Stanton later resided with his daughter Florence (often referred to as Flora) and her husband, Dr. Philip L. Barber at their home in Norfolk, Virginia.[57] He died on February 11, 1893, and was interred at West Point Cemetery.[58]

Another child of Philip and Margaret Stanton, Solomon Northup Stanton,[59] lived in Fort Edward, New York in 1875. He and his wife Mary are a household in a house owned by Owen Tinney.[60] Mary may have died, because on August 25, 1893, a Solomon Northup Stanton married Elizabeth Adams in Council Bluff, Iowa. His birthplace was New York State, he was born in 1848, and his parents were Philip Stanton and Margaret "Northrup."[61] This man, Northup's grandson, is very probably the Solomon N. Stanton who died in Omaha, Nebraska (not far from Council Bluff) in September 1893.[62]

Alonzo Northup

Northup's son Alonzo is listed with his parents on the 1855 New York State Census for Glens Falls.[63] The same year, Alonzo is referred to in a letter from "S.B.R." dated May 30, sent from Stockton, California addressed to the "East Genesee [sic] Conference" of the Methodist Episcopal Church in central New York. "We received eleven young men, of great promise, on probation, at this [California] Conference. One of who is a son of Mr. Northup, the author of the life of Solomon

Northup, of late notoriety. I doubt not this young man will honor the name of his illustrious and honorable father."[64]

Alonzo does not appear with his mother on the 1860 Census.[65] He may have left the family, as there are affidavits in his military pension file from several residents of central New York who said they knew him prior to his enlistment in the army. A Wayne County man named A. Forman Hoyt said that before the Civil War, Alonzo had worked with him and his father on a canal boat.[66]

He seems to have had a presence in the Glens Falls area in the early 1860s, however, because on February 15, 1864, he enlisted in the Army at Queensbury. Enlistment documents list two occupations for him: "laborer" and "boatman."[67] In his pension application, Alonzo stated he had lived in Glens Falls and Fort Edward prior to enlisting, and that after his discharge, he resided at Reynolds Corners (Moreau), Fort Edward, then Reynolds Corners again, and moved to Weedsport in 1871.[68]

Military records show that Alonzo served in the 26th Regiment of United States Colored Troops, employed as a teamster. He saw action in the Battle of Bloody Bridge at Johns Island, South Carolina in July 1864. At the end of August 1865, he was mustered out. Shortly after leaving the army, Alonzo married Caroline Victoria Robison at Jersey City, New Jersey.[69]

He returned home, and apparently lived in Glens Falls for a time, since tax records include an entry for him in 1865.[70] In 1870, Alonzo and wife Victoria were residing in Fort Edward, with a six-month-old child, Anna.[71]

By 1875, the family had relocated to Weedsport in Cayuga County. They may still have spent some time in the Glens Falls/Saratoga area until about 1874, though, since the youngest child was born sometime that year in Saratoga County.[72] Alonzo's occupation at this time was "mason tender."

Alonzo and Victoria raised quite a large family in Weedsport. Alonzo eventually received an invalid pension for his military service. After his death, his wife received a widow's pension.[73] Alonzo died on October 17, 1909, and his interesting heritage was referred to in a brief obituary: "Alonzo Northrup, an aged colored man, died this morning at his home in Mechanic street from a complication of diseases. His father, Solomon Northrup, was stolen and held as a slave for twelve years. Alonzo's age is not known, although he is thought to have been about 80 years old. His son Harry is well known in Central New York as a baseball player. Besides his wife he is survived by three sons and one daughter."[74] His wife died on April 2, 1932.[75] Husband and wife are buried in Weedsport Rural Cemetery.

Appendix C

Publishing History of
Twelve Years a Slave

While not meant to be a definitive history of the publication of *Twelve Years a Slave*, these notes relating to 19th-century editions of the book may prove interesting. Information on the evolution and demise of the Derby and Miller firm is from Karl Kabelec, "Book Publishing History Interesting," *Auburn Citizen* (July 4, 1976): 22.

1853

Publisher: Auburn: Derby and Miller; Buffalo: Derby, Orton & Mulligan; Cincinnati: Henry W. Derby; London: Sampson Low, Son & Company.

Derby and Miller was operated by James C. Derby and Norman C. Miller in Auburn. Derby, Orton & Mulligan was an affiliated company in Buffalo, operated by George Hunter Derby, William Orton, and Eugene Mulligan.

The 1853 edition was dedicated to Harriet Beecher Stowe, and referenced her book, *A Key to Uncle Tom's Cabin*, which was published about the same time.

1854

Publisher: Auburn and Buffalo: Miller, Orton & Mulligan; London: Sampson Low, Son & Company.

Late in 1853, Derby left the publishing company; hence the name change.

The 1854 edition contained a direct quote mentioning Northup taken from *A Key to Uncle Tom's Cabin* on the dedication page.

1859

Publisher: New York: C. M. Saxton.

After the dissolution of Miller, Orton & Mulligan in the late 1850s, C. M. Saxton gained some of its titles, including *Twelve Years a Slave*.

1879

Henry Bleby, *Scenes from Transatlantic Life* (London: Wesleyan Mission House, 1879).

This book consists of two stories. The first is a fairly short tale of the experiences of the author while a Christian missionary in the Bahamas.

The major part of the book consists of a paraphrased version of *Twelve Years a Slave* titled "Vicissitudes of a Lowly Life," with the text adjusted to the third person. The author states in the introduction: "The incidents contained in the other and larger story were brought to his notice by an eminent Minister of one of the New England Congregational Churches, who was well acquainted with several of the parties mentioned therein." Sadly, Bleby does not provide the name of the minister he refers to, who seems to have known Northup personally.

Bleby learned about Northup during an 1858 visit to the United States, at a time when "this case of kidnapping was exciting considerable public interest."

1881

Publisher: Philadelphia: John E. Potter & Company.

On the title page, the author's name is given as "S. Northup." No year of publication appears, but the book was announced in 1881, in *The Literary World* (September 10, 1881): 314; and *Publishers Weekly* (September 17, 1881): 368.

Though the table of contents lists the illustrations, as in the earlier editions, no illustrations appear in the body of the book. Also, the song "Roaring River" is not included. The book appears to have been printed from the original plates, or reproductions of them.

A publisher's preface is included, but makes no reference to Northup specifically. "Slavery is now one of the institutions of the past," it notes. The reason given for issuing a new edition is that "at this time . . . the exciting questions of color, race, and of social standing are forever settled on American soil by . . . the Constitution."

It is possible that this edition was published to take advantage of the book's lapse of copyright. The length of an original copyright at the time was 28 years, as given in "30. Duration of Copyright," *Copyright Law Revision, Studies Prepared for the Subcommittee on Patents, Trademarks and Copyrights of the Committee on the Judiciary, United States Senate, Eighty-sixth Congress, Second Session Pursuant to S. Res. 240.* (Washington: United States Government Printing Office, 1961), 58. The copyright probably wasn't renewed when the original term expired in 1881. The book had originally been copyrighted by Derby and Miller, and that company was no longer in business.

1890

An edition appears to have been published by Talty & Wiley in 1890. The publisher appears to have been located in Dallas, Texas.

1900

An edition was published by New York publisher International Book Company in 1900. Reproductions of the cover which the authors have seen look very similar to the John E. Potter edition from 1881.

Notes

Chapter 1

1. The narrative in this chapter is faithfully based on Northup's own account in *Twelve Years a Slave*, Sue Eakin and Joe Logsdon, eds. (Baton Rouge: Louisiana State University Press, 1968). Cited hereafter as *TYS*.

2. James H. Birch was born on October 8, 1803, and died on December 20, 1870. He is buried in the Congressional Cemetery in Washington, D.C.

3. For an account of possible spellings of Radburn, see Chapter 3.

4. *TYS*, xxxvii.

5. Northup's wife, Anne, had received no formal schooling and could not read.

6. Northup refers to Tibaut as "Tibeats." This is one of several misspellings in the book. See *TYS*, 73.

7. This extended description quotes and paraphrases Northup's from *TYS*, 74.

8. Anderson Leonard Chafin, see *TYS*, 77n.

9. *TYS*, 83–85.

Chapter 2

1. Edith Hay Wyckoff, *The Autobiography of an American Family* (Fort Edward, New York: Washington County Historical Society, 2000), 1. Henry B. Northup's line of descent from Stephen is: Henry (1663–1740), who married Mary Kingsley; Immanuel (1699–1790), who married, as his third wife, Anna Carr Holmes (d. 1780); Carr (1747–1774), who married Sarah Clark (1747–1826); John Holmes (1774–1834), who married Anna Wells and was the father of Henry B. Northup. Immanuel, his third wife Anna, and son Carr are buried in North Kingston, RI; Captain Henry was the son of Immanuel and his second wife, Sarah Gould. He married Mary Gard(i)ner. They are buried

in Hoosick Falls, NY. Clarke and his wife Mary are buried on their farm in Slyborough, NY. John Holmes and his wife Anna were buried on their farm in Hebron, and then moved to the Union Cemetery in Fort Edward; also buried there: Henry B. Northup, his brother Nicholas Carr Northup (an affidavit signer), and their spouses.

2. Rhode Island during the American Revolution passed a law that emancipated any slave volunteering to serve in the armed forces for the duration. At least two African American North(r)ups served in the Revolution from Rhode Island. See the Records of the Rhode Island Historical Society: Jeremiah Olney Papers, manuscript 690, 1794; list of non-white veterans of the American Revolution, 50.

3. See Wyckoff, *passim.* John Holmes Northup, father of Henry B., and his brother Clarke Northup, employer of Mintus, moved to Washington County. Captain Henry moved to Hoosick Falls in Rensselaer County.

4. Charles B. Moore, comp., *Cemetery Records of the Township of Kingsbury, Washington County, New York* (Queensbury, New York: Historical Data Services, 1996), 4. However, Mintus completed an affidavit in 1821, which said he was 45 years old, Robert O. Bascom, *The Fort Edward Book* (Fort Edward, NY: J. D. Keating, 1903), 162. This would make his year of birth to be 1776.

5. There seems to be little doubt that Mintus was born into slavery. Solomon says so: *TYS,* 5. Copies of the will that freed him are extant. Census records for 1790 do not show a Mintus Northup living in North Kingston, Rhode Island. In a presentation made before the Fort Edward Town Board on April 25, 1821, Mintus stated, however, that he had always understood that he had been born a free man in North Kingston, and that since his arrival at the age of 20 years "he had acted and continued to act as a free man." It is easy to understand why he wanted to clarify his status as a free man in Fort Edward on this occasion. His affidavit is similar to paperwork completed by other black citizens the same day, see L. Lloyd Stewart, *A Far Cry from Freedom: Gradual Abolition, (1790–1827), New York State's Crime Against Humanity* (Bloomington, Indiana: Authorhouse, 2006), 171–178. That these were all completed the day after Election Day (held in April 1821) suggests some blacks had been challenged at their polling places, and immediately afterward set about getting the proper documentation of their free status—less than a year before New York suffrage property requirements for blacks were raised. Timothy Eddy, a prominent citizen of Fort Edward, swore that he had known Mintus for at least 20 years and that he had always been considered to be free during that time. Eddy was correct: Mintus in 1821 had been free for 23 years. Mintus was also correct when he stated that he had acted as a free man from the age of 20. Judge John Baker declared that, in light of these affidavits, Mintus was indeed free under the laws of New York, Robert O. Bascom, *The Fort Edward Book* (Fort Edward: J.D. Keating, 1903), 162. These documents are extant at the Fort Edward, New York, Town Clerk's office.

6. The 1790 Census shows Captain Henry Northup living in North Kingston, Rhode Island, and owning five slaves, Department of Commerce and Labor, Bureau of the Census, *Heads of Families at the First Census of the United*

States Taken in the Year 1790: Rhode Island (Washington: Government Printing Office, 1908), 44–46.

7. See the last will and testament of Henry Northup, March 3, 1797, Rensselaer County Historical Society.

8. "And to my servant man by the name of Mintus I will and bequeath his freedom from servitude from and after the first day of September one thousand seven hundred and ninety eight." From the county records of Rensselaer County, copy in possession of authors; also reproduced in Wyckoff, 121. In this same will, he manumitted a servant girl by the name of Binar, effective upon the death of his wife, Mary. In doing this, Captain Henry followed the precedent of his father, Immanuel Northup, who manumitted two servants in his will (copy in possession of authors).

9. Clarke Northup was the son of Carr Northup, Captain Henry's half-brother.

10. A Quaker meeting was established in Granville in 1800, and a house for worship was built in 1806. See Crisfield Johnson, *History of Washington County, New York* (Philadelphia: Everts & Ensign, 1878), 211. About 11 families were Friends during Northup's time in Granville. Johnson states that "every meeting supports its poor," a local example of the Quaker tradition of sharing.

11. Mintus probably accompanied a group of settlers from Granville to Essex County around 1804. If so, it's likely he was in Granville some time before that date—at least long enough for him to become well acquainted with the Adirondack colonizers.

12. The Federal Census for 1840, lists, in Argyle, NY, a "Susanna Northrop," over 50 years of age, head of household, living with a younger man between the ages of 24 and 36. They are persons of color. We believe that Susanna is the widow of Mintus and the younger man, their son Joseph, Solomon's brother. Solomon's mother and brother later lived in Oswego County, where she died before Solomon's return from Louisiana, *TYS*, 257. Mintus and his family lived on the Argyle road on the east side of Fort Edward.

13. The 1852 Affidavits of Anne Northup, Henry B. Northup, Nicholas Carr Northup, and Orville Clark all attest to her free status. Anne states that she never was a slave, *TYS*, 257, 260–261.

14. Northup refers to his birthplace as "Minerva" though the area was called "Schroon" at the time of his birth. Minerva was not incorporated and named until 1817. Had Solomon been asked after 1817 where he had been born, he might well have said, "in what is now Minerva."

15. Mabel Jones, "A Brief History of Minerva," in Mable Jones, *Minerva, Essex County, N.Y.* (Minerva: np, 1957), 5, available on HeritageQuest. The 1804 date is also given by H. Perry Smith (ed.), *Essex County: History of Essex County With Illustrations and Biographical Sketches of Some of Its Prominent Men and Pioneers* (Syracuse: D. Mason & Co., 1885), 633.

16. Winslow C. Watson, *Military and Civil History of the County of Essex, New York* (Albany: J. Munsell, 1869), 212–213.

17. Smith, 634.

18. Watson, 212.

19. Jones, 4–6.

20. Smith, 634.

21. Since Northup was born there, the family was still in Schroon in 1807. They probably moved before he reached the age of two, so 1808 is a good estimate for their departure. The Federal Census lists them in Granville in 1810.

22. The home of Clarke Northup still stands on the north side of County Route 23 in the Slyborough section of Granville. The home of Mintus Northup was located on the south side of Aldous Road, a short distance away. It was near a small pond, but no longer stands. See Map 1.

23. Wyckoff, xxv.

24. Ulysses P. Hedrick, *A History of Agriculture in the State of New York*, Printed for the New York State Agriculture Society, 1933 (New York: Hill and Wang, 1966), 283.

25. Warren Cardwell, long-time owner of John Holmes Northup's home, told the authors that there was a room in his house where, by tradition, black families had stayed.

26. *TYS*, 259–260.

27. Henry B. attended Granville Academy, a private school, before matriculating at Middlebury College.

28. Henry Northup moved to Sandy Hill in 1831 at about the time that Solomon and Anne moved to nearby Moss Street, a village located a mile or so north of Sandy Hill. Anne also was in charge of the kitchen at Sherrill's coffee house, located just down the street from Henry's law office. Attorneys pleading before the court frequented it, as did politicians, including: Orville Clark, General Hughes, and Henry B. Northup, "In a Reminiscent Mood," *[Glens Falls] Morning Star* (January 8, 1894). Henry would have known Anne for an extended period in this capacity. See also Wyckoff, 121–122.

29. See the essay by Warren Cardwell on the rescue of Solomon Northup in the files of the Washington County Historical Society.

30. The affidavit of Sandy Hill's Josiah Hand, written in connection with the rescue effort in 1852, gives "previous to the year 1816" as the date when he first knew Mintus and Solomon, and says Mintus ran farms in Kingsbury and Fort Edward dating from that time. This locates him in Kingsbury in about 1816. The affidavit of Benjamin Ferris (who lived in the north part of Sandy Hill) gives 1816 as the date when he first knew Mintus. Orville Clark says he knew Mintus in 1810 and 1811, and knew him well after 1818. The latter could be when Mintus moved to Fort Edward. The best evidence suggests that 1816 was the date Mintus brought his family to Kingsbury.

31. Kingsbury is north and east of Hudson Falls, known as "Sandy Hill" in Northup's time. Moss Street was a village located to the west of today's Route 4, just over a mile northeast of the triangular green in Hudson Falls. The Alden family owned property in section 34 of the original survey of Kingsbury, and we believe the Alden farm Northup mentions was on what is now County Route 35 roughly a mile north of its intersection with NYS Route 32, and a bit more than a half mile south of its intersection with Wait Road. This would place the farm at about two miles from the Sandy Hill green—an easy walk from the village.

32. William L. Stone, *Washington County, New York, Its History to the Close of the Nineteenth Century* (np: New York History Co., 1904), 325.

33. Stone, 326.

34. *TYS,* 5.

35. *TYS,* 5.

36. *TYS,* 262.

37. He was the son of Nicholas C. Northup, Henry Northup's older brother. Born in 1822, he was about seven when Mintus died. His recollections are in a letter he wrote in 1909. See, Wyckoff, 121.

38. Wyckoff, 121.

39. *TYS,* 5.

40. Nathaniel H. Carter, William L. Stone, and Marcus T.C. Gould, *Reports of the Proceedings and Debates of the Convention of 1821, Assembled for the Purpose of Amending the Constitution of the State of New York* (Albany: E. & E. Hosford, 1821), 189–191.

41. Washington Hunt, Annual Message, January 7, 1851, in Charles Zebina Lincoln, *Messages from the Governors: Comprising Executive Communications . . . ,* Vol. 4 (Albany: J. B. Lyon, 1909), 620.

42. Northup states, *TYS,* 4, that he was born in July 1808, and that he was married on December 25, 1829, at the age of 21. However, in sworn depositions (reprinted in his book), the date of his marriage is given as December 25, 1828, by his wife Anne, Josiah Hand, and Timothy Eddy (who performed the marriage). Care would have been taken in preparing legal depositions. Eddy, a longtime town official, would have had access to the records. We conclude the marriage actually took place in 1828, and that Northup (or David Wilson) was somehow mistaken when the manuscript was written. Moreover, in sworn testimony during a hearing held in Ballston Spa, New York, on July 11, 1854, Northup said he had reached the age of 47 on "the 10th of this month," from "The Northup Kidnapping Case," *New York Herald Tribune* (July 14, 1854), attributed to the *Saratoga Whig.* That would mean he was born on July 10, 1807. This being the case, he would indeed have been 21 years old at the time of his marriage—in 1828, not 1829. Further, in a letter from John Thompson, an acquaintance of Henry B. Northup, Solomon's age in August 1853 is given as "about 46," in agreement with the 1807 birth year, *Keesville Republican* (August 13, 1853). Northup, *TYS,* 7, mentions that, with a wife to support, he was "deprived of the advice and assistance of my father." Mintus died on November 22, 1829, Charles B. Moore, comp., *Cemetery records of the Township of Kingsbury, Washington County, New York* (Queensbury, New York: Historical Data Services, 1996), 4. See also the depositions of Anne Northup and Nicholas C. Northup, *TYS,* 257, 261, which give this date (the deposition of Timothy Eddy also gives the year as 1829). This death date for Mintus would mean that if the Northups were married in December of 1828, Mintus would have been alive for about 11 months following their marriage. However, he may have been in a condition of decline during his last months, and it is not surprising that Northup more than a quarter of a century later associated the time of his marriage with that of the loss of his father.

43. *TYS*, 6.

44. *TYS*, 6.

45. *TYS*, 46–48, 174–178.

46. Wyckoff, 121.

47. *TYS*, 6.

48. Johnson, 208.

49. See Samuel S. Randall, *The Common School System of the State of New York* (Troy: Johnson and Davis, 1851), 12–13, 17.

50. Leo H. Hirsch, Jr., "The Free Negro in New York," *Journal of Negro History*, Vol. 16, No. 4 (Oct. 1931), 415–453.

51. See Ansel Judd Northrup, "Slavery in New York: A Historical Sketch," *State Library Bulletin*, History No. 4, May, 1906. Although this law would not have affected free people, it was consistent with there being growing sentiment in favor of black education in New York.

52. Hirsch, Jr., 426ff.

53. By 1820, when Northup turned 13 years old, there were 6332 School districts in New York; 5489 of them filed reports that year. In the districts that filed reports, 304,559 students were enrolled, out of a relevant population of 317,633, namely children 5 through 15 years old. Thus, by this time, the system was fully functioning. See Randall, 91.

54. Johnson, 208.

55. Johnson, 326.

56. Hedrick, 198.

57. Johnson, 326.

58. Hedrick, 198.

59. *TYS*, 6.

60. See affidavit of Orville Clark, *TYS*, 262.

61. The 1800 Census shows a household of four free non-whites. By 1810, there were six, and by 1820, a total of eight, probably Anne, her parents, and five brothers. One brother was probably Harry, who in 1860 is enumerated in Anne's household. Another was probably William, Jr., who died in 1824 and is buried in the same cemetery as Mintus Northup (Moore, p. 2).

62. His elegant house where Anne lived still stands in Salem, New York, east of the center of the village, on the north side of the road to West Rupert, Vermont (County Route 153).

63. *TYS*, 6.

64. Proudfit (late in life) and his son lived in Saratoga next door to Madame Jumel, for whom Anne worked as early as 1841. Anne may have been introduced to Jumel by one of the Proudfits.

65. The Old Fort house was built in 1772–1773 by Patt Smyth. It is named for Abraham and Abby Fort, who bought it in 1839. It was a noted edifice where Washington County courts anciently met and where everyone of importance, it seems, stayed during the period of the American Revolution, including Franklin, Washington, Arnold, Schuyler, and even Burgoyne. It is unknown how much of the house was rented by the Northups.

66. The vocational relationship between seasonal farming and seasonal artisanship is well discussed in Martin Bruegel, *Farm, Ship, Landing* (Durham & London: Duke University Press, 2002), 43–49.

67. *TYS*, 10.

68. *TYS*, 7–8. He worked on the section superintended by William Van Nort-wick. David McEachron was in charge of the detachment in which Northup worked. Van Nortwick, one of the numerous "Superintendents of Repairs" for the Erie and Champlain Canals, contracted in 1825 to construct Section 16 of the Champlain Canal, which went south from Fort Edward to Fort Miller. See *Legislative Documents of the Senate and Assembly of the State of New York,* Fifty Third Session, 1830, Vol. 1 (Albany: E. Croswell, 1830), Report #40; and Edwin Williams, *New-York Annual Register for the Year of Our Lord 1833, Containing an Almanac, Civil and Judicial List* (New York: Peter Hill, 1833), 276.

69. *TYS*, 8.

70. Evelyn Dinsdale, "Spacial Patterns of Technological Change: The Lumber Industry of Northern New York," *Economic Geography,* Vol. 41. No. 3 (July 1965): 252–274, at pp. 256–263.

71. Dinsdale, 262.

72. Dinsdale, 258.

73. For details on raft construction, see William Fox, *A History of the Lumber Industry in the State of New York,* published by the U.S. Department of Agriculture, Bureau of Forestry as Bulletin 34 (Washington: Government Printing Office, 1902), 19–20.

74. *TYS*, 8.

75. *TYS*, 70–71.

76. *TYS*, 8.

77. *TYS*, 8.

78. *TYS*, 209.

79. *TYS*, 8.

80. *TYS*, 8.

81. Northup states that this was in the winter of 1831–1832, which would not have been the winter following his first year of rafting, as the text implies. His first year of rafting was 1829, assuming he was married in December 1828. If he actually did this in the winter of 1831–1832, then this woodcutting enterprise would have been during one of the winters after they moved to Kingsbury—which is possible, but at variance with the text. The best evidence is that it was during the winter of 1829–1830.

82. The following descriptions are based on Fox, 16–17 and 33–38.

83. Fox, 38.

84. Fox, 16. For some of the dangers of lumbering, see also, Michael Beaudry, *The Axe Handler's Handbook* (Springville, UT: Horizon Publishers, 2005), 32, 37–38.

85. *TYS* gives the date for the move as the spring following the winter of 1831–1832. Anne's Memorial, however, gives 1830 as the date (*TYS*, 256). If their marriage date was December 1828, the work experience following marriage was: Champlain Canal repairs that same winter; rafting the following summer, woodcutting the following winter, with move to Kingsbury the following spring—that would bring him to Kingsbury in the spring of 1830. Decisively, the 1830 Federal Census has him there at this time.

86. 1830–1834.

87. *TYS*, 9.

88. Single-bottom plows with wrought iron moldboards were common in New York by the 1820s, Hedrick, 288–293; Bruegel, 105–109. See Wyckoff, p. 21.

89. Bruegel, 109.

90. Made from 5 × 5 beams and large iron spikes, made by a local blacksmith. The spikes broke up the soil and then smoothed it. See Hedrick, 293–294, and picture facing 292.

91. Dry corn stalks would yield two to three tons of fodder per acre, far more than Northup would have needed for his livestock. Ebenezer Emmons, *Natural History of New York,* Vol. 2, (New York: D. Appleton & Co. and Wiley and Putnam, 1848), 159.

92. Bruegel, 47.

93. One person with a scythe and cradle could cut about two acres per day. See David S. Cohen, *The Dutch-American Farm* (New York and London: New York University Press, 1992), 128.

94. Emmons, II, 115.

95. Bruegel, 105.

96. *TYS,* 9.

97. Elizabeth would have been nine years old ("in her tenth year") in the spring of 1841 (*TYS,* 11); Margaret, seven years old (*TYS,* 11, 251); and Alonzo, five years old (*TYS,* 11). This would mean that Elizabeth would have been in her "first year" in the spring of 1832, so she would have been born in 1831 or 1832. Margaret would have been born in 1833 or 1834. Alonzo, just five years old in March 1841, would presumably have been born in 1835 or 1836.

98. It is likely that Anne did most of these—including helping in the fields. For a description of farm wives' chores in early 19th century New York, see Bruegel, 52–54, especially, 114–125.

99. *TYS,* 9.

100. After his rescue, when his story became publicized and then politicized, regional strands of racism surfaced and were aired in the newspapers.

101. *TYS,* 7.

102. *TYS,* 5.

103. Bruegel, 49.

104. Quoted by Bruegel, 48–49.

105. Bruegel, 49.

106. Bruegel, 75ff.

107. Bruegel, 95.

108. He uses it in a passage where he wishes to compare the life at Kingsbury with that to come in Saratoga, and he may be exaggerating the former to emphasize the difference from the latter. "Solomon Northup, of Kingsbury" is listed under the heading "TO EXONERATE FROM IMPRISONMENT [for debt]," legal notice in the *Albany Argus* (November 4, 1831).

109. Anne's Memorial says they moved to Kingsbury in 1830 and remained there "about" three years before moving to Saratoga. The specificity of the March 1834 date in the book, and more general reference in the Memorial leads us to credit the 1834 date.

110. *TYS*, 10. Census records show them living there as a family of five in 1840 (1840 Federal Census, New York State, Saratoga County, Village of Saratoga Springs, 262).

111. See Appendix B.

112. Jon Sterngass, *First Resorts* (Baltimore: Johns Hopkins University Press, 2001), 8.

113. This account of early Saratoga is based on Sterngass, 7–12, and Theodore Corbett, *The Making of American Resorts* (New Brunswick, New Jersey: Rutgers University Press, 2001), 83ff.

114. Corbett, 62–67.

115. Lafayette visited there in 1825; Joseph Bonaparte spent five seasons there during this period. See Sterngass, 20, and William L. Stone, *Reminiscences of Saratoga and Ballston* (New York: Worthington and Company, 1890), 176, 227ff.

116. F. Daniel Larkin, *Pioneer American Railroads: The Mohawk and Hudson and the Saratoga and Schenectady* (Fleischmanns, New York: Purple Mountain Press, 1995), 52, gives July 12, 1832 as the date the Schenectady to Saratoga Railroad opened for business. This would have been between Schenectady and Ballston Spa. Stone, 178–179, including notes, gives July 7, 1832 as the Ballston date. He says that the first steam engine arrived in Saratoga on July 4, 1833. The line was probably finished to Saratoga by the spring of 1833, with horses used until the arrival of steam (see Stone, 182–183).

117. Its first trip carrying members of the public was on August 9, 1831. See Larkin, 39.

118. The trip from Albany to Saratoga was about three-and-a-half hours, including a horse-drawn crossing of the Mohawk in Schenectady, car by car. Larkin, 52.

119. Sterngass, 18.

120. Sterngass, 18–19.

121. Sterngass, 21.

122. Sterngass, 19.

123. Corbett, 91.

124. Sterngass, 21.

125. Corbett, 132.

126. Corbett, 91.

127. Corbett, 144. There were 48 free blacks in the Saratoga area in 1790, constituting 28 percent of the free blacks in the entire Albany area, while the Saratoga portion of the slave population in the Albany area was only 8 percent (Corbett, 146–147). This means that Saratoga's blacks were disproportionately free at the end of the 18th century.

128. Corbett, 148.

129. Corbett, 148.

130. Corbett, 149, concludes that 4/5 of Saratoga's blacks came from New York, with most of the rest from the free states of Massachusetts, New Jersey, and Pennsylvania. Hardly any were from the south.

131. Corbett, 144.

132. Corbett, 144.

133. *TYS,* 9.

134. *TYS,* 9. Corbett, 145, says "Even in the eighteenth century the kitchen was the domain of female slaves; there black women developed their skills as cooks, seamstresses, and laundresses—skills that eventually would be in high demand at resorts." Anne's skills in the kitchen may have been grounded in a long regional family and cultural tradition; this tradition may also have made it easier for her to find acceptance and employment opportunities in a supervisory capacity as a cook.

135. *TYS,* 12. Sandy Hill was the county seat; the county court met there periodically.

136. The "Tourist or Pocket Manual for Travelers," published in 1831, described Washington Hall as follows: "In a more retired position is Washington Hall of which I. Taylor is proprietor; pleasantly situated at the north part of the village where the invalid and those who do not mingle with the gay throng, who pursue pleasure instead of health may be accommodated in the best style" (quoted in Durkee, Cornelius E., compiler, *Reminiscences of Saratoga,* Reprinted from *The Saratogian,* 1927–1928, 69). According to the Durkee compilation, Taylor sold it in 1836 to Joel Root.

137. *TYS,* 9.

138. Corbett, 90–91.

139. In the mid-1830s, there were strong barriers to entrance to the buildings trades (Corbett, 130ff.), which may have started to ease by the 1840s. Given Northup's carpentry work later in the South, he may have had some carpentry experience in Saratoga, which could have afforded some opportunities even for African American carpenters.

140. Sterngass, 14. Johnson in 1831 wrote the music for "the abolitionist standard 'the Grave of the Slave,' whose lyrics condemned the cruel demands of masters and preached, 'death to the captive is freedom and rest.'" Sterngass, 29.

141. Corbett says, 150–151: "The 1850 census describes black men's occupations in detail. Black males were attracted to Saratoga Springs because they had the skills required for resort work. All had manual occupations, which we can categorize as 23 percent skilled, 70 percent semiskilled, and 7 percent unskilled. The skilled included barbers, stonecutters, a tailor, a butcher, a blacksmith, and a farmer. The semiskilled workers were waiters, musicians, teamsters, a cook, and a soda maker. The unskilled were porters and laborers. Given the limitation of the census, we can see that black men usually had a skill, particularly in resort services, and they rarely competed for unskilled jobs."

142. Corbett, 150.

143. *TYS,* 9.

144. *TYS,* 9. It was completed in 1835. This line ran north from Waterford along the Hudson (and east of the old Champlain Canal) to Mechanicsville, where it curved west, probably along the right of way of the modern Boston and Main Railroad, just below Anthony's Kill. It then traveled about a half-mile south of Round Lake and thence, northwest across part of Malta until it joined the Saratoga and Schenectady Railroad just south of Ballston Spa. See

Nathaniel Bartlett Sylvester, *History of Saratoga County* (Philadelphia: Everts and Ensign, 1878), 8. Today, a section of its rail bed is known as the Zim Smith Trail, and is used for recreational purposes.

145. *Solomon Northup v. Washington Allen*, Box A33, Saratoga County Clerk's Office.

146. *TYS*, 8.

147. At Whitehall, Allen hired David Morehouse to replace Northup, and Morehouse had hired extra help, using only one man whom Northup had engaged. Because he had incurred expenses as a result of discharging Northup, Allen refused to pay the full amount ($50) due under the contract. Northup filed a writ of attachment to collect what he had been owed.

148. Court documents say: "The parties prosecuted and defended in their individual characters." *Solomon Northup v. Washington Allen*, Box A33, Saratoga County Clerk's Office.

149. Fox, 20–21.

150. Index to Convictions, Vol. 1, 1809–1902, Saratoga County Clerk's Office.

151. *TYS*, 10.

152. *TYS*, 10–11.

153. *TYS*, 9.

154. Approximately half of the African American population of Saratoga lived in their own household at mid-century. Corbett, 149.

155. "Evidently whites with similar occupations saw no difficulty in living with blacks, who might even be their landlord." Corbett, 150.

156. Corbett, 148.

157. *TYS*, 10.

158. *TYS*, 10–11.

159. *TYS*, 11.

Chapter 3

1. *TYS*, 12.

2. Northup's testimony after the arrest of Merrill and Russell in 1854 was that he met them *at* Moons' Tavern. It is entirely possible, and consistent with both accounts that they approached him near the tavern and that the trio went inside to talk. See accounts of the examination, attributed to the *Saratoga Whig*, printed in *The Albany Evening Journal* (July 13, 1854) and the *New York Daily Tribune* (July 14, 1854).

3. *TYS*, 13–14.

4. *TYS*, 12.

5. *New York Daily Tribune* (July 14, 1854): 7.

6. *TYS*, 12.

7. *TYS*, 12.

8. *TYS*, 209.

9. *TYS*, 8, 209.

10. *TYS*, 13.

11. *TYS*, 14.

12. *TYS*, 13.

13. *TYS*, 14, which does not mention the name of the hotel, only that it was "southward of the Museum." Later on, however, Northup identified it as the Eagle, stating that he *thought* this was where they stayed in Albany, see *New York Daily Tribune* (July 14, 1854). The Eagle hotel or tavern was, in fact, south of the Museum.

14. See Ulysses P. Hedrick, *A History of Agriculture in the State of New York*, printed for the New York State Agriculture Society, 1933 (New York: Hill and Wang, 1966), 172-173. According to Hedrick, passengers from Albany crossed the Hudson, left the ferry landing on the east bank at 5:00 A.M., breakfasted at Kinderhook, lunched at Rhinebeck, and ate supper when they stopped for the night at Fishkill.

15. See *TYS*, 16.

16. *TYS*, 14.

17. The custom house in the spring of 1841 was in temporary quarters on Pine Street, one street north of Wall Street and running parallel to it. It was directly across the street from today's Federal Hall.

18. The "free papers" were issued by the Customs Office because black sailors going ashore in southern ports needed them to avoid being seized as fugitive slaves. Records of free papers exist in the National Archives for that era, but not for New York for April, 1841.

19. Northup says that the free papers episode *did* contribute to raising his confidence in the kidnappers, *TYS*, 16.

20. See Constance McLaughlin Green, *The Secret City* (Princeton: Princeton University Press, 1967), 25, 32.

21. Frederick Douglass, *Life and Times of Frederick Douglass, Written by Himself* (Hartford: Park Publishing, 1881), 199–200.

22. See Robert Reed, *Old Washington, D.C. in Early Photographs 1846–1932* (New York: Dover Publications, 1980) 72.

23. There was a curfew on African Americans in Washington that forbade their presence on the streets late at night. See Green, 18, 32. See also, Letitia Woods Brown, *Free Negroes in the District of Columbia* (New York: Oxford University Press, 1972), 140; see "By the Mayor of the City of Washington, A Proclamation," August 20, 1827, in which the terms of the curfew and the need for free papers is set forth (in the possession of the Historical Society of Washington, D.C.). In addition, Merrill and Russell may have wanted to insure that Northup didn't spend the money they gave him before they could reclaim it.

24. *TYS*, 16–17.

25. He'd been president for only 32 days.

26. *TYS*, 17.

27. *Washington Daily National Intelligencer* (April 9, 1841).

28. Ibid.

29. John Quincy Adams, *Memoirs of John Quincy Adams, comprising portions of his diary from 1795 to 1848*, Charles Francis Adams, ed., Vol. 10 (Philadelphia: J. B. Lippincott & Co., 1876), 459.

30. "By five o'clock, nothing remained but empty streets and the emblems of mourning upon the houses. . . . ," from *National Daily Intelligencer* (April 9, 1841).

31. Charles Dickens, "American Notes," in *American Notes and Pictures from Italy* (London: Oxford University Press, 1957), 116.

32. Such as the Patent Office and Treasury colonnade.

33. Dickens, 116.

34. *TYS*, 17.

35. The funeral procession took place on Wednesday, April 7, 1841, according to both the *National Daily Intelligencer* (April 9, 1841) and the diary of John Quincy Adams, *op. cit.*

36. Anthony Reintzel, *The Washington Directory and Government Register for 1843* (Washington, J.T. Towers, 1843), 32. The entry reads, "Gadsby's Hotel, n side Penn av. btw 4 1/2 and 6 w. cor 6."

37. The City Directory for 1834 lists no fewer than seven Congressmen resident at Gadsby's: see E.A. Cohen & Co., *A Full Directory For Washington City, Georgetown, and Alexandria* (Washington City: Wm Greer, 1834).

38. Amy LaFollette Jensen, *The White House and Its Thirty-Five Families* (New York: McGraw-Hill, 1970), 60, and *Niles' National Register* (February 13, 1841): 372.

39. The hotel was demolished in 1942. See James M. Goode, *Capital Losses: A Cultural History of Washington's Destroyed Buildings* (Washington: Smithsonian Institution Press, 1979), 168–70, for details about the old Gadsby Hotel, the National Hotel, and the new Gadsby's. A photograph of the hotel in 1940 appears in Charles Suddarth Kelly, *Washington, D.C., Then and Now* (New York: Dover Publications, 1984), 20. Kelly mentions the Dickens visit.

40. See Goode, 168–69; Dickens, 115–116. Errors in the Goode work include the hotel's location and the year Dickens stayed there. The material about Goode, Dickens, and the hotel, although appearing in footnote 25 at p. 411 of Sue Eakin's *Solomon Northup's Twelve Years a Slave and Plantation Life in the Antebellum South* (Lafayette, LA: University of Louisiana at Lafayette, 2007) comes from a manuscript by Cliff Brown, shared with her in 2005.

41. Gadsby was indisputably a slave-owner; whether he was a slave dealer is a matter of dispute. See Goode, but also documents by T. Michael Miller and by Carla Jones in the possession of Office of Historic Alexandria. Gadsby's former place of business, the City Hotel (Gadsby's Tavern) in Alexandria, Virginia, is now a museum, in which hangs his portrait.

42. Samuel Nelson, the Supreme Court Justice who helped Henry Northup with the rescue, lived or had his office in the second Gadsby's Hotel in 1853 at the time of the rescue.

43. For the locations of these hotels, see Map 3.1, which, together with Map 3.2, is based, in part, on "Map of the City of Washington of the District of Columbia Established as the Seat of the Government of the United States of America, 1839"; "Map of the City of Washington Established as the Permanent Seat of the Government of the United States of America, 1846, Engraved and Published by D. McClelland, Washington"; and "Map of the

City of Washington, D.C. by James Keily, Surveyor, Lloyd Van Derveer Publisher, Camden, New Jersey, 1850"; all on microfilm at the Martin Luther King Library, Washington, D.C.

44. Gaither & Addison, *The Washington Directory and National Register for 1846* (Washington, John T. Towers, 1846), 25. The entry reads, "Birch, James H. United States Hotel, n side Penn av, btw 3 and 4 1/2."

45. The Historical Society of Washington, D.C. has a woodcut advertisement of the United States Hotel believed to be from 1849 (Machen Collection. Acc. 81.01.271). It says "Tyler & Birch, Proprietors" below the depiction of the hotel. He is the only Birch in the 1846 City Directory who gives the hotel as his address (Gaither & Addison). The woodcut shows the hotel on the corner, as portrayed in Map 3.1.

46. The Baltimore and Ohio station was located on Pennsylvania Avenue from 1835 until 1852 (see Map 3.1), when a new station was constructed at the corner of New Jersey Avenue and C Street. See Robert Reed, *Old Washington, D.C. in Early Photographs 1846–1932* (New York: Dover Publications, 1980), 72.

47. Goode, 164–166.

48. Including those operated by Robey, Shekell, and Lloyd, as noted elsewhere. Also, see in this regard, W. B. Bryan, "A Fire in an Old time F Street Tavern and What It Revealed" (*Records of the Columbia Historical Society*, Vol. 9, 1906): 198–215, especially 200ff. With respect to other parts of the District of Columbia, T. Michael Miller, "Slave Traders Operating in Alexandria, D.C.—Virginia & Washington, D.C."(in possession of the Office of Historic Alexandria) lists Eli Legg Tavern and Hodgkins Tavern (later Indian Queen Tavern) in Alexandria; and McCandless Tavern in Georgetown. The last was used by Birch: see *National Daily Intelligencer* (July 1, 1834): 4.

49. See *National Daily Intelligencer* (July 9, 1833): 3, (July 1, 1834): 4; (December 7, 1835): 4.

50. Advertisements for "Birch & Shekell" offering "Cash for Negroes," *National Daily Intelligencer* (May 1, 1838) and (May 17, 1838).

51. *TYS*, 245. Shekell, responding to interrogatories, referred to his establishment as the "7 Street Steam Boat Hotel," Records of *People v. Alexander Merrill and Joseph Russell*, Court of Oyer and Terminer, Saratoga County, New York, on file at Saratoga County Clerk's Office (Box A83).

52. Four buildings in Washington were, variously, called "Steamboat Hotel." Two were near the river (see Map 3.2 and Chapter 4, note 6). The others were on the east side of Seventh Street between Pennsylvania Avenue and North B Street (now Constitution). One was Shekell's Tavern, previously owned by Isaac Beers, also called Mechanics Hall. The other was owned by Thomas Lloyd and probably subsequently by John West. See advertisements, *National Daily Intelligencer* (December 7, 1835): 4; (December 16, 1836): 1; (July 9, 1833): 3; and City Directories for Washington in 1843, 1846, and 1850. Birch gives each location, at different times, as his place of business. Since Shekell's Tavern was apparently not called the "Steamboat Hotel" in 1841, it is understandable that Northup could truthfully protest, *TYS*, 249, that he was never in the Steamboat Hotel. Shekell appears in the Federal Censuses of 1840 and 1850; the latter gives his age as 45.

53. Various locations for Thorne, from City Directories, appear on Map 3.1.

54. *TYS*, 245–247.

55. *TYS*, 16–17.

56. Birch was an experienced dealer at this time. His advertisements in the *National Daily Intelligencer* begin as early as July 9, 1833.

57. The Auxiliary Guard was created by Congress in August 1842, more than a year after the kidnapping, to fulfill this need. James H. Birch served as its head for two years after 1854. The city police patrolled by day and the Auxiliary Guard by night until 1861 when they were consolidated. See Wilhelmus Bogart Bryan, *A History of the National Capital*, Vol. 2 (New York: Macmillan Company, 1916), 274–275, 402–403, 403n.

58. W. C. Clephane, in "Local Aspect of Slavery," in *Records of the Columbia Historical Society*, Vol. 3, (1900): 241, states " . . . it was a common thing for free negroes to be seized in the District of Columbia and transported from here to other places in these slave vessels." Kidnapping free blacks and selling them into slavery had been punishable according to an act of Congress since 1831. Also see Bryan, 207.

59. *National Daily Intelligencer* (November 21, 1839). Another ad noted Williams also conducted business from "A. Lee's lottery office, five doors east of Gadsby's' hotel," *The [Washington, D.C.] Globe* (August 24, 1836).

60. See Clephane, 239–240. Clephane says the house had three stories, while Northup said it had two.

61. *National Daily Intelligencer* (November 21, 1839). Center Market (or the market house) was located across the Mall from Williams' Slave Pen between Seventh and Ninth Streets on North B Street (now Constitution Avenue), where the National Archives now stands. The Washington end of the Long Bridge was where Maryland intersected Fourteenth Street.

62. *The [Washington, D.C.] Globe* (August 24, 1836).

63. *TYS*, 23.

64. Paul Finkelman and Donald R. Kennon, *In the Shadow of Freedom: The Politics of Slavery in the National Capital* (Athens, Ohio, Published for the United States Capitol Historical Society by Ohio University Press, 2011), 211.

65. Clephane says that the pen was said to be located on the southeast corner of Eighth and B Streets, 239–240. This would be the outbuilding. A William H. Williams appears in the tax records of the District of Columbia for 1839, 1840, and 1841 (National Archives) as an owner of property in this block, thus supporting the location and giving us a full name for the owner. The Federal Censuses for the District of Columbia for both 1840 and 1850 list a William H. Williams. The 1850 Census (Ward 7, Dwelling 382) gives his occupation as "slave trader" and his age as 50.

66. *Albany Patriot* article, quoted in Mary Kay Ricks, *Escape on the Pearl: The Heroic Bid for Freedom on the Underground Railroad* (New York: William Morrow, 2007), 88.

67. *TYS*, 22. We are assuming this went along side of the house out to Seventh Street because Northup was led through it and taken from it into the house the night he left.

68. Clephane, 238–239. The City Directory for 1834, at p. 47, locates a tavern operated by Washington Robey on this spot. The entry reads, "Robey

Washington, Tavern, e side 7 w, btw B and C s." Note that Goode, 166, re-
verses the addresses of the Williams and Robey slave pens given by Clephane,
on whom Goode chiefly relies; Goode also erroneously renders Clephane's
"Southeast" as "Southwest" in the same description. Maps 3.1 and 3.2 portray
Robey's slave pen and tavern as two separate buildings, although they might
have been parts of a single complex.

69. Although Robey is listed in the tax records for 1839, the records for 1840
and 1841 have a penciled notation "dead" next to his name. See *Corporation of
Washington, Assessment of Real and Personal Property for the Year 1839, Residents
(M–Z)*; also, 1840 and 1841.

70. See 1836 engraving, Historical Society of Washington, D.C., Photo
Collection #3242, entitled "Slave House of J.W. Neal & Co.," giving location,
"Sixth and B St. SW 200 block 7th and Maryland bounded by Maryland Ave."

71. See T. Michael Miller, "Slave Traders Operating in Alexandria, D.C.—
Virginia & Washington, D.C.," *passim.*

72. Green, 29, confirms the locations: "The principal slave pens lay . . .
across the road from the place where the Smithsonian Institution would rise
in the 1840's."

73. See Birch's responses to interrogatories, Records of *People v. Alexander
Merrill and Joseph Russell*, Court of Oyer and Terminer, Saratoga County, New
York, on file at Saratoga County Clerk's Office (Box A83). The firm of Price
and Birch was located at 283 Duke Street, Alexandria (1860s numbering); extant, it is now 1315 Duke Street. See Janice G. Artemel, Elizabeth A. Crowell,
and Jeff Parker, *The Alexandria Slave Pen; The Archaeology of Urban Captivity*
(Washington, D.C.: Engineering Science, Inc., 1987), 30–41, for the sequence of
interconnected slave dealerships there from Franklin & Armfield in the 1830s
through Price and Birch in the 1850s.

74. There were also slave pens *north* of the central axis of the city. Note
Thorn's entry in the 1850 City Directory: "Thorn, B.A., trader, e side 8w, btw
In and NY av," which places him north of the central business district. Slave
pens located north of the city would have been strategically placed for business with Maryland; those south, for business with Virginia and south.

75. Washington City Directory, 1843; 1846 (as "Burch"), and 1841 tax rolls
for this same block, 435, ("Birch"). Spelling of the name is not always con-
sistent, but Birch's signature on court documents related to the 1854 trial in
Saratoga County shows the surname as "Birch," Records of *People v. Alexander
Merrill and Joseph Russell*, Court of Oyer and Terminer, Saratoga County, New
York, on file at Saratoga County Clerk's Office (Box A83) and Saratoga County
Historian's Office. The spelling on his tombstone is also "Birch."

76. Eliza is a major figure in *TYS*. According to her account, given by Northup, she had been the slave and mistress of a wealthy individual, Elisha
Berry, living in comfortable circumstances, "in the neighborhood of Washington." He lived separately from his wife and daughter, both of whom were
deeply resentful of Eliza. Emily was his child. Berry fell on hard times and
Eliza, in a division of property, had become the slave of his daughter's husband, Jacob Brooks. The daughter, who hated her half-sister Emily, prevailed
upon Brooks to sell Eliza and her children to Birch, which he did (conveying

her to Washington on the cruel pretext that he was about to manumit her). For evidence as to who Berry and Brooks might have been, see Eakin, notes 37, 38, 40, and 41, which give information about men bearing these names.

Chapter 4

1. Or possibly on one of the subsequent three nights. The slave manifest of the brig *Orleans* for the voyage bearing Northup to New Orleans is dated April 27, 1841. By Northup's account, it took a day to reach Richmond from Washington, leaving in the middle of the night; they sailed the next day. This would mean he departed from Washington the night of April 25 to 26. Another manifest, prepared at Norfolk, where more slaves were boarded, bears the date May 1, although Northup recalled only a single day of sail between the two ports. These two documents would place Northup's departure from Washington no earlier than April 26 and no later than April 29.

2. *TYS*, 33.

3. Ebenezer "Radburn" is identified as "Rodbury" in the *New York Daily Times* (January 20, 1853): 1, and the *National Era* (February 3, 1853). We adapt the *Times* spelling, although we find neither name in the city directories of 1834, 1843, 1846, 1853, or 1858, nor in the Federal Censuses of 1840 and 1850. An "Ebenezer Rodbirde" appears in D.C. tax records, but his property is on the opposite side of the city from Williams' Slave Pen.

4. *TYS*, 34.

5. 1846 City Directory (Gaither & Addison), 77.

6. According to Gail Redmann, at the Washington Historical Society, this bridge was built in 1835, replacing one built in 1809. The 1834 City Directory confirms that the Long Bridge was built before the kidnapping. In it there appears the following entry: "Fielder Birch, tavern, n side Md av, near Long Bridge." Near the wharf were two different Steamboat Hotels. According to the City Directory of 1846, one was located at "cor Gs and 11w" and operated by Peter Jones; the 1850 City Directory locates the other at "Cor Fs and 12w," and it was operated by Joe Corson (Map 3.2). The 1858 listing gives the first location. Birch, who moved around a lot, gives the hotel as his residence in the 1858 Directory. By then, the slave trade was outlawed in the District of Columbia, and Birch, while still a D.C. resident, operated a slave business in partnership with Charles M. Price in Alexandria. This Steamboat Hotel location would have given him easy access to his business across the river.

7. *TYS*, 34.

8. This almost certainly would have been a steamboat owned and operated by the Washington and Fredericksburg Steamboat Company, which provided the principal service between the capital and Aquia Creek. After 1845, it was renamed as the Potomac Steamboat Company and was controlled by the Richmond Fredericksburg & Potomac Railroad.

9. Charles Dickens, "American Notes," in *American Notes and Pictures from Italy* (London: Oxford University Press, 1957), 128.

10. Dickens, 128.

11. *TYS,* 35. According to Dickens, 131, these stages carried nine passengers, eight inside and one outside. Birch, together with his slaves would have been only six, including two children, so the carriage would not have been crowded.

12. Dickens, 130.

13. *TYS,* 35–36.

14. This would have been on the Richmond, Fredericksburg, and Potomac Railroad, chartered in 1834, with service between Richmond and Fredericksburg starting on January 23, 1837. The railroad was finished as far as the Potomac (at Aquia Creek) on September 10, 1842, six months after Dickens' trip and a year and a half after Northup's. The coaches taken by Dickens and Northup were probably owned by the railroad. This famous railroad continued to exist into modern times (now part of the CSX System).

15. Dickens, 62, states that his train from Boston, MA, to Lowell, MA, was also segregated.

16. Dickens, 134.

17. Dickens, 133.

18. *TYS,* 36. In all probability, this was William Harris Goodwin, a Richmond slave trader. Northup describes him as "about fifty years of age." Goodwin in 1841 would have been 45 years old. See "A Guide to the Templeman and Goodwin Slave Dealers Account Book, 1849–1851," Accession Number 11036, A Collection in Special Collections, The University of Virginia Library. The source of Goodwin's middle name comes from a note 7 on p. 92 of a dissertation about the Amistad, in our possession, but for which we do not have a citation. The spelling "Goodin" is not necessarily an error. Theophilus Freeman at one time operated under the name "Goodin & Co." There may have been two different slave dealers with approximate names, or Goodwin and Goodin might have been the same person, using two different spellings for some purpose of legal deception.

19. *Richmond Whig* (August 26, 1834). A Civil War-era map of Richmond shows the location of Seabrooks warehouse. A slightly different location for the pen, the corner of Broad and Union Streets, is given in: Maurie D. McInnis, *Slaves Waiting for Sale* (Chicago and London: The University of Chicago Press, 2011), 55 and 99.

20. Templeman and Goodwin boasted that "the buildings are strong and airy, and consist of several apartments . . . together with a comfortable Hospital," *Richmond Whig* (August 26, 1834).

21. Scott Nesbitt, Robert Nelson, and Maurie McInnis, "Visualizing the Richmond Slave Trade," American Studies Association, San Antonio, November 2010: http://dsl.richmond.edu/civilwar/slavemarket_essay.html.

22. See McInnis, 55 and especially 72.

23. "An Advertisement for the Sale of Eleven Slaves, February 17, 1812," web page, Virginiamemory, Library of Virginia, http://www.virginiamemory.com/online_classroom/shaping_the_constitution/doc/slavead.

24. Trammell, John, *The Richmond Slave Trade: The Economic Backbone of the Old Dominion* (Charleston: History Press, 2012), 52.

25. *TYS*, 39–40.

26. See *Ship Registers and Enrollments of New Orleans, Louisiana,* Vol. 4, 1841–1850, prepared by the Survey of Federal Archives in Louisiana, Service Division, Works Progress Administration, Number 1098. We are sure this is the correct *Orleans:* 1) The registered weight in this description is the same as that on the slave manifest for the journey that carried Northup south; 2) Luther Libby, given as an owner in 1846 in this description, was mate on the Northup voyage (no doubt the "Biddy" referred to by Northup), and signed the "Manifest of slaves intended to be transported on the Brig Orleans . . . ," dated April 27, 1841, National Archives and Records Administration, Washington, D.C., Slave Manifests of Coastwise Vessels Filed at New Orleans, Louisiana, 1807–1860, Microfilm Serial: M1895, Microfilm Roll: 8.

27. According to the slave manifest at the time of Northup's journey.

28. See George Hendrick, and Willene Hendrick, *The Creole Mutiny* (Chicago: Ivan Dee, 2003), 77. The *Creole* was a brig slightly smaller than the *Orleans* and, like the *Orleans,* was used frequently in the intercostal transportation of slaves between Richmond and New Orleans.

29. *TYS*, 43.

30. Both documents were printed in *The Liberator* (December 2, 1842).

31. The Richmond manifest is dated April 27, 1841, the Norfolk, May 1, 1841—four days apart, as noted. Northup says that it was a one-day journey between Richmond and Norfolk. We cannot account for this discrepancy. Possibly such manifests at times were prepared a few days in advance.

32. The manifest executed on April 27 at Richmond states there were 41 slaves on board. The number "39" was scratched out and two added to the total, presumably accounting for two children added at the end of the list.

33. We assume the list of Barnes' slaves ends at number 28 and Birch's begins with number 29. Entry number 20 is for three persons, including in all probability the children listed as 40 and 41. There were actually 43 slaves leaving Richmond, and the correction was made on the Norfolk manifest. Since the brig had not left American waters, this would not have been a problem, considering the purpose of the manifest. According to an 1830s letter published in the *Liberator* (December 2, 1842), G.W. Barnes is mentioned in connection with Goodwin.

34. On the Norfolk manifest, the last two entries are Lucinda and Robert Jones. The latter is certainly the Robert mentioned by Northup who died on the voyage, as reported by Wickham on arrival in New Orleans. A careful examination of both manifests shows that these two entries were added after the previous five in the handwriting of the person who wrote the entries on the Richmond manifest. It seems that somehow they were left off the list and that, after realizing the mistake, Wickham added them after the voyage was underway (to the Norfolk manifest, since the Richmond one was already too crowded with names). Although "dittoed" to G.W. Apperson, Robert is definitely in Birch's consignment and presumably Lucinda is also.

35. He is listed as number 33.

36. She appears as number 38.

37. She appears as number 39.

38. There is a "Rudal Ames," appearing as number 35, who might be Eliza's son Randall, but he is listed as being 15 years old. Elick Pinney, age 11, is the more likely candidate.

39. Henry Williams (number 29), Lethe Shelton (number 30), Mehala Irvin (number 31), and Caroline Parnell (number 32); Caroline was probably Caroline and Mehala was Mary. Lethe might have been Lethe, but Northup describes her as a woman, while the manifest dittoes Lethe as a male (which could have been a mistake). That would leave Henry Williams to be David.

40. Including Elick Pinney, 11 years old (number 36), possibly Randall.

41. The only one of the four mentioned by Northup as having come aboard at Norfolk that we can clearly match with the Norfolk manifest is Maria, who was listed as Mary McCoy, the only female among the five. There is another slave with the first initial "A," who might be Arthur, but given the extensive renaming that would be quite conjectural. The shipper of the five Norfolk slaves was listed as G. W. Apperson, the owner as S. Johnson.

42. *TYS*, 42.

43. The Richmond manifest lists a "Jim White" (number 28), a "Cuff Singleton" (number 1), and a "Jane" (number 23), who might have been these three, but, again, there is no guarantee here, given the frequent reassignment of names.

44. Jesse Torrey, *American Slave Trade* (London: J. M. Cobbett, 1822), 66ff.

45. Harriet Beecher Stowe, *A Key to Uncle Tom's Cabin* (London: Samson Low, 1853), 420.

46. Carol Wilson, *Freedom at Risk: The Kidnapping of Free Blacks in America, 1780–1865* (Lexington: The University Press of Kentucky, 1994).

47. *TYS*, 44.

48. See Howard Jones, *Mutiny on the Amistad* (New York: Oxford University Press, 1987), Chapter 10.

49. Justice Story did indeed endorse "the ultimate right of all human beings in extreme cases to resist oppression, and to apply force against ruinous injustice." He even conceded that men might commit "dreadful acts" to win freedom (Jones, 190). But whether or not such reasoning would have been applied in this case is questionable.

50. Governor Seward in the *Creole* affair sympathized with the slaves who seized the ship and publicly condemned Webster for issuing the protest, Glyndon G. Van Deusen, *William Henry Seward* (New York: Oxford University Press, 1967), 66.

51. The *Creole* was registered at 157 and 25/95 tons; the *Orleans* was registered at 195 and 79/95 tons, as noted.

52. Some of the slaves on the *Creole* were owned by George Apperson, who also had slaves on the *Orleans* with Northup.

53. Hendrick and Hendrick, 120.

54. Hendrick and Hendrick, 7, list a captain, first and second mate, and crew of six. Northup says the *Orleans* had a crew of six and does not mention a second mate.

55. Robert Jones' death is noted on the Norfolk manifest.

56. According to the *Daily Picayune* (May 25, 1841) and the Inspector's signatures on the Richmond and Norfolk manifests.

57. *TYS*, 49.

58. "Dictionary F," *Dictionary of Louisiana Biography*, Louisiana Historical Association web site, http://www.lahistory.org/site23.php. Retrieved October 10, 2012.

59. *TYS*, 50. John Brown, an escaped slave, gives a much more detailed description of what is believed to be Freeman's slave pen. See *TYS*, 52n, and Sue Eakin, *Solomon Northup's Twelve Years a Slave and Plantation Life in the Antebellum South* (Lafayette, Louisiana: Center for Louisiana Studies, University of Louisiana at Lafayette, 2007), 415–16, note 30. However, Brown's description and Northup's description do not tally very well, giving rise to the possibility that these were two different slave pens. Freeman's slave pen in the Brown description was formed by a block of houses, the center of which was filled in to the level of an elevated first floor of the surrounding buildings. Northup describes Freeman's slave pen, however, as being very similar to Goodwin's, with a fence and two small buildings in its yard. These discrepancies suggest that either Freeman changed slave pens between the time Northup was there and the time Brown was, or the slave pen was seriously altered.

60. Hendrick and Hendrick, 50–51.

61. In 1842, his finances started to unravel with a series of lawsuits against him by his creditors. Courts began ruling against him, beginning in January 1843, and on January 18, 1844, he was declared insolvent, with assets of $137,991.73 and debts of $186,698.72—notable sums indicative of the scale on which he operated. He apparently tried to protect some of his assets by transferring a portion of them to his manumitted former slave, turned concubine, turned wife, but the creditors attacked this scheme and tried (unsuccessfully, as it turned out) to have her freedom revoked. There was a legal feeding frenzy over his assets, with recurrent lawsuits throughout the 1840s and early 1850s. These suits included charges of malfeasance, including "simulated sales and donations," see Judith Kelleher Schafer, *Slavery, the Civil War, and the Supreme Court of Louisiana* (Baton Rouge: Louisiana State University Press, 1994), as cited in Eakin, 413–414, note 28. At times he was sent to jail by his creditors to prevent a possible flight. In fact litigation continued until 1861 when the Civil War interrupted it and Freeman did, in fact, flee New Orleans (*Dictionary of Louisiana Biography* web site, cited above). Northup himself recounts that on his return journey, in early 1853, he and Henry Northup visited Freeman's slave pen and actually saw Freeman on the street. He says that "from respectable citizens we ascertained he had become a low miserable rowdy—a broken down disreputable man" (*TYS*, 243). This description is certainly consistent with his legal circumstances at the time.

62. Hendrick and Hendrick, 51.

63. The Northup and Eliza sales could be used as evidence in support of this observation.

64. *Dictionary of Louisiana Biography* web site, cited above. These observations, of course, may emanate, in part from Northup's account.

65. Johnson, 63.

66. Hendrick and Hendrick, 51–54, building on Brown's account.

67. For Northup's description of his stay in New Orleans, see *TYS*, 51–60.

68. For an excellent discussion and description of slave auctions, see McInnis. This impressive book focuses on abolitionist art (both engravings and paintings) portraying slave auctions.

69. For a detailed description of New Orleans slave market practices and especially the examination of slaves by prospective purchasers, see Walter Johnson, *Soul by Soul: Life inside the Antebellum Slave Market* (Cambridge: Harvard University Press, 1999), Chapter Five, "Reading Bodies and Marking Race." Johnson, who cites Northup, among many others, explores a full range of motivations and practices by prospective slave buyers.

70. For an extensive description of slave auctions, illustrated with engravings and paintings from the era, see McInnis, 55 and 72.

71. Practices in such private quarters could go beyond the bounds of Victorian era description. See McInnis, 128; and especially, Johnson, Chapter Five, passim.

72. Revealing that he could play the fiddle may have been a deliberate ploy by Northup, who might have figured that this would maximize his chances of being bought by someone from New Orleans, as opposed to someone in the back country, so he might have a greater chance of stowing away on northbound boats.

73. *TYS*, 55, and footnote 2. See also Eakin, 423, note 60.

74. The disease is recorded as *variola* on the hospital records, a synonym for smallpox.

75. *TYS*, 55–56.

76. *TYS*, 58. Northup's quoting Freeman's use of the phrase "fancy piece" in this context is an important reference. "Fancy girls," was the trade name for slaves, often mulattos, who were sold to be concubines or for sexual exploitation. The word "fancy" did not refer to style of dress, but to those who are "fancied." See McInnis, 138–139, and citation of Johnson. The threat that Emily was to be held for eventual sale for this purpose would be doubly cruel to her mother.

77. Edward Bennett, Notary, *Notorial Acts of New Orleans* (June 23, 1841), XVII, 670. The bill of sale is reproduced in *TYS*, 253.

Chapter 5

1. *TYS*, 183.

2. *TYS*, 101.

3. See *TYS*, 85, 104, 106, 118, and 183. When Northup fled from Tibaut through the swamp, he confronted the reality that he had no pass—without one, he could not seek help at a white person's dwelling for fear of being turned in (*TYS*, 104). When he encountered a young white man upon emerging from the swamp, he had to bluff his way past him (*TYS*, 106). Wiley, another

slave of Epps's, tried to escape and was caught when he could not produce a pass upon demand (*TYS*, 183). On one occasion Northup started defiantly to leave Tibaut without a pass, but Tibaut, probably fearing the expense needed to redeem Northup from custody, wrote one out for him just as he was leaving (*TYS*, 118).

4. *TYS*, 181.

5. *TYS*, 180–181, n. 1.

6. *TYS*, 101–102, 110–112, 170, 181–184, 186–187.

7. *TYS*, 101–103.

8. Other slaves took similar precautions with their plantation dogs. Celeste, a runaway who appeared at Northup's cabin, also had apparently reached an accommodation with the dogs from her plantation, *TYS*, 187.

9. *TYS*, 65.

10. *TYS*, 101.

11. See Peter Kolchin, *American Slavery 1619–1877* (New York: Hill and Wang, 2003), 158.

12. *TYS*, 184–185, 187–188.

13. *TYS*, 186.

14. *TYS*, 188–189.

15. *TYS*, 181–183, 185–186.

16. *TYS*, 190.

17. *TYS*, 25–27.

18. *TYS*, 37–38.

19. Epps was not fined for owning Northup.

20. *TYS*, 63.

21. *TYS*, 239. This would have been easier said than done with Henry Northup on the scene, but with no one on the spot to champion his cause, Northup could easily be disposed of.

22. He could not have walked to freedom, given the pass system and no real underground railway operation in Louisiana. He could not have taken a train: the local line to Alexandria was not then connected to the larger rail network that could have taken him north. Successfully stowing away in a series of freight trains and making the journey between their terminals would not have been an attractive option.

23. *TYS*, 149–150.

24. *TYS*, 63.

25. *TYS*, 175.

26. *TYS*, 175–179.

27. *TYS*, 204ff.

28. *TYS*, 211.

29. *TYS*, 111.

30. *TYS*, 69.

31. Northup mentions working for or with the following people: a Mr. Avery, Samuel Bass, Anderson Chafin, Randal Eldret, Edwin Epps, Mary Epps, William P. Ford, Martha Ford, a Mr. Hawkins, Francis Myers, Peter Tanner, Adam Taydem, John Tibaut, and William Turner. Obviously, there may have been others. In some cases, he describes the relationship in some detail; at times, it is not described at all.

32. *TYS*, 79.
33. *TYS*, 70.
34. *TYS*, 108-109.
35. *TYS*, 74.
36. *TYS*, 74, 121, 150.

37. Such behavior was not uncommon in the slave culture. Frederick Douglass and Henry "Box" Brown describe encounters with lower class whites. Confrontations, such as those between Northup and Tibaut, "were usually opportunistic encounters involving . . . impulsive response to intolerable provocation. Confrontations were often followed by flight as resisters, pondering the likely consequences of their actions, opted to give their enraged targets a chance to cool off. . . . these two forms of resistance [confrontation and flight] occurred so often, and with such consistency, that they may be regarded as pervasive features of antebellum slavery. . . . " Kolchin, 160. Nor were Northup's actions irrational. Indeed, "Slaves who gained a reputation for standing up to authority often gained a measure of respect and tolerance from white authorities and secured for themselves greater freedom of action." Kolchin, 164. Under Ford, Northup established a pattern of commendable, indeed remarkable, behavior. Hence, it was easier for Ford to blame Tibaut for the confrontation, and for Peter Tanner to make light of it.

38. *TYS*, 138.
39. *TYS*, 206.
40. *TYS*, 136–137.

41. See also, *TYS*, 138 where Northup states that Epps *did* perceive his slaves as animals.

42. At times he seemed intellectually insecure with respect to Northup himself, as evidenced by his sarcasms, *TYS*, 177.

43. Northup's descriptions of frequent whippings by Epps are plausible. See Kolchin, 120–121.

44. *TYS*, 135.
45. *TYS*, 181–183.
46. *TYS*, 196–199.
47. Kolchin, 103.
48. See *TYS*, 170, 172–173.
49. *TYS*, 172.
50. See *TYS*, 192, 222.
51. *TYS*, 129.

52. Ira Berlin, "Introduction, Solomon Northup: A Life and a Message," in Solomon Northup, *Twelve Years a Slave* (New York: Penguin Books, 2012), xxvii.

53. *TYS*, 116.
54. *TYS*, 169.
55. *TYS*, 200.
56. *TYS*, xvi.

57. Northup's first-hand descriptions of Ford (*TYS*, 56, 58, 62, 64, 68–70); Tibaut (*TYS*, 74); Epps (*TYS*, 122–123, 138–139, 151, 173–174, 178); and Peter Tanner (*TYS*, 93–94) ring true and appear to be the product of a careful

observer with a stake in the accuracy of his observations. His character descriptions of his slave companions are also insightful (see, for example, *TYS*, 29–32, 139–144, 188). He read Bass carefully and accurately (*TYS*, 204–209).

58. *TYS*, 176–177.

59. Walter Johnson, *Soul by Soul: Life Inside the Antebellum Slave Market* (Cambridge, MA: Harvard University Press, 1999), 66–68, 72–75.

60. These skills, and the regional intellectual and cultural attitudes that underlay them are humorously, but in many ways sympathetically, described in Twain's *A Connecticut Yankee in King Arthur's Court*.

61. *TYS*, 69.

62. *TYS*, 70–71.

63. *TYS*, 73.

64. *TYS*, 97.

65. *TYS*, 73.

66. *TYS*, 78–79.

67. *TYS*, 203ff.

68. *TYS*, 121, 133, 219, 240.

69. *TYS*, 114, 147; 203ff.

70. *TYS*, 161–162.

71. *TYS*, 123–124.

72. *TYS*, 159–161.

73. *TYS*, 148, 159.

74. *TYS*, 125, 135.

75. *TYS*, 153.

76. *TYS*, 1967, 154–155.

77. *TYS*, 149, 165, 222.

78. His reputation lasted beyond his stay in Louisiana. See, *TYS*, 190n.

79. *TYS*, 87–88.

80. *TYS*, 89.

81. *TYS*, 112.

82. *TYS*, 173. This particular conversation was to protect Patsy, not Northup, but is an example of slave conversation in the field aimed at mutual protection.

83. For an excellent brief description of the importance of knowledge to survival, see Berlin, xxvii–xxix.

84. See *TYS*, 190, where he says, "More than once I have joined in serious consultation, when the subject [insurrection] has been discussed, and there were times when a word from me would have placed hundreds of my fellow-bondsmen in an attitude of defiance." This assertion, no doubt, contains hyperbole, but it is probably true that he did consult on this subject with trusted acquaintances—suggesting that he was well-connected with what was going on in the region, and kept well-informed.

85. He was designated "Platt Hamilton" on the *Orleans* manifest—but presumably only knew of himself as "Platt" in New Orleans. He then would have become Platt Ford, then Platt Tibaut, then Platt Epps. See, for example, *TYS*, 165.

86. See, for example, *TYS*, 67, 92.

87. *TYS*, 60.

88. *TYS,* 77.
89. *TYS,* 119–120.
90. *TYS,* 140–142.
91. *TYS,* 142–143.
92. The whipping of Patsey is not easily tied chronologically to other events, but it comes toward the end of the narrative and seems to have taken place near the end of Northup's stay. He refers to the episode as "not long ago." *TYS,* 195.
93. *TYS,* 195–199.
94. See, for example, *TYS,* 20, 50, 100, 110. He recognizes the genuine and beneficial features of Ford's religious convictions (as well as the extensive hypocrisy of other professed Christians), and notes that Epps's brutal whipping of Patsey took place on the Sabbath, (*TYS,* 198).
95. *TYS,* 116.
96. *TYS,* 117.
97. Berlin makes this important point about pride, xxix.
98. The incident that led to Tibaut's murderous attack on Northup (*TYS,* 98–99) was when Northup was planing sweeps and Tibaut told him he had not planed them down enough. Northup insisted that they were planed to the line (which, it proved, they were). Tibaut swore at Northup, so Northup said "mildly" that he would plane it down some more if Tibaut wanted him to—and planed off one more shaving. Now the sweep was too narrow and spoiled. It is hard to give credence to Northup's assertions here of total innocence. It is much more likely that Northup did this to teach Tibaut a lesson—that the latter didn't know what he was doing and he had better leave Northup alone. This message, of course, produced the explosion.
99. Berlin, xxx.
100. Berlin, xxxi.
101. Johnson, 66.
102. A more accomplished literary work that integrates the description of technique with the narrative line is *Moby Dick.*
103. *TYS,* 140–141.
104. *TYS,* 237.
105. *TYS,* 243.
106. *TYS,* 186–88.
107. *TYS,* 186.
108. *TYS,* 6.
109. *TYS,* 165–166.
110. *TYS,* 6.   ʔ
111. *TYS,* 149.
112. *TYS,* 166.
113. *TYS,* 165.
114. *TYS,* 166. Some of these words may be Wilson's, but the sentiment they convey is unmistakably Northup's. His descriptions of the music and dances at Christmas celebrations make valuable contributions to our understanding of this important aspect of slave culture, as Alan Singer pointed out to the authors.

Chapter 6

1. *TYS*, 47–48.
2. *TYS*, 40, 252.
3. *TYS*, 48.
4. See John Taylor, *William Henry Seward, Lincoln's Right Hand* (Washington and London, Brassey's, 1991), 65–69; and Glyndon Van Deusen, *William Henry Seward* (New York: Oxford University Press, 1967), 93–97.
5. Chapter 375 of the Laws of 1840, signed into law by Seward in May, 1840.
6. Crisfield Johnson, *History of Washington Co., New York* (Philadelphia: Everts & Ensign, 1878), 424.
7. Edith Hay Wyckoff, *The Autobiography of an American Family* (Fort Edward, New York: Washington County Historical Society, 2000), 57.
8. Wyckoff, 57.
9. Taylor, 47–48; Van Deusen, 65–67.
10. Taylor, 52–53.
11. New York Whigs were generally more sympathetic to African American rights than New York Democrats.
12. *TYS*, 210; see also 225.
13. Nathaniel Bartlett Sylvester, *History of Saratoga County* (Philadelphia: Evarts and Ensign, 1878), 192.
14. According to Minnie Bolster, a descendent of Cephas Parker, Parker and Perry's store was in the Pitney House hotel (later, a boarding house) on West Congress Street (now called Grand Street) near the neighborhood where Northup and Anne resided (conversation with David Fiske, November 13, 2012). Parker married a Pitney, and his father-in-law ran the boarding house. The Pitneys had owned this property since the 1820s. See Theodore Corbett, *The Making of American Resorts* (New Brunswick, NJ: Rutgers University Press, 2001), 91–93. See also, 66. The Saratoga Springs City Directory of 1868–69 lists Parker as living on Walnut Street near Washington, with Perry at that time running a meat market with partner David Rouse.
15. *TYS*, 225.
16. Wyckoff, 46–50.
17. Laws of the State of New York Passed at the Seventy-Sixth Session of the Legislature (Albany: Weed, Parsons and Company, Printers, 1853), 1155–1156, side heading: "Henry B. Northup." Northup was also reimbursed $392.37 for expenses.
18. Henry, son of the first Stephen, is recorded as having given six shillings in 1700 toward the expense of a Quaker meetinghouse (Taunton Historical Society Records, cited in Northup family records).
19. *TYS*, 256–263.
20. Northup was the first elected District Attorney of Washington County, the position previously having been appointive (Johnson, 113). He served from 1847 until 1850. Also, see Wyckoff, 57.
21. *Sandy Hill Herald* (October 5, 1852), (July 31, 1860), (June 4, 1888); Johnson, 109, 430–431.

22. *Sandy Hill Herald* (June 14, 1888); Johnson, 213.

23. Papers in possession of the Washington County Historical Society.

24. J.R. Cronkhite, "The Clark Families of Sandy Hill," paper in possession of Fort Edward Historical Society; also "Notes on Springside & the Clark Family," paper in possession of the Fort Edward Historical Society; *History and Biography of Washington County and Queensbury, New York* (Gresham Publishing Co., New York, 1894); Johnson, 114, 430, 431; *Sandy Hill Herald* (October 13, 1835), (January 25, 1859), (July 31, 1860).

25. Johnson, 113, 436, 444–445.

26. Johnson, 323. The Hoag family appears to have been Quaker, Johnson, 463–464, which may account for part of his willingness to sign the petition to the governor.

27. See his obituary, in possession of Fort Edward Historical Society in writing of James Cronkhite, Genealogy file; *Sandy Hill Herald* (January 19, 1841), (February 20, 1844), issues of November 1852, *passim;* Johnson, 424.

28. Johnson, 502; The State of New York, *The State Government from 1879: Memorial Volume of the New Capitol,* 55–56; *Sandy Hill Herald* (February 20, 1844), (March 19, 1844), (April 2, 1844), (October 26, 1852); Gresham, 1894, 195; Wyckoff, 118.

29. Daniel Sweet had an assessed property valuation of $4,500 in 1863, 10 years after the Northup rescue. This assessment made him the 13th largest taxpayer out of 262 on the town rolls (including commercial properties)— which would put him in the top 5 percent of taxpayers in the town.

30. See Allen Corey's *Gazetteer of the County of Washington,* 1849 and 1850; Johnson, 112, 424.

31. Wyckoff, 116; *Sandy Hill Herald,* January 19, 1841.

32. Johnson, 115, 120, 317; *Sandy Hill Herald* (October 29, 1829).

33. For example, Anne at different times was in charge of the kitchen at Sherrill's Coffee House and at the Eagle Hotel; on the same block as the Coffee House and almost across the street from the Hotel was the meat market of Peter Holbrook—who probably supplied both establishments. Holbrook's is the first signature on the petition.

34. Clark, as a pillar of the Presbyterian Church, could have spoken to Baker, Ferris, and Holbrook, all active in that church; he, Almon Clark, and Hughes were also Masons. Having Clark approach Baker, his fellow-Democrat, would have been diplomatic, given that Baker's paper had been sarcastically critical of Henry Northup during the recent congressional campaign.

35. The home where Justice Samuel Nelson grew up was in Hebron, New York, on what is currently called Middle Road, which travels roughly north-south about half way between Routes 22 and 31. It is no longer standing, but its cellar hole is (in 2005) on the west side of Middle Road opposite NYT Telephone Pole 31 between First Light Road (or Smith Hill Road) to the north and Lazzari Way to the south. It is approximately .8 miles south of Benn Road and 1.6 miles north of Chamberlain Mills Road. The Nelson homestead was about a mile by a road (now partly abandoned) across the hill from the farmhouse where Henry B. Northup grew up. This information was provided by Harold Craig through Warren Cardwell.

36. Allen Johnson and Dumas Malone, *Dictionary of American Biography* Vol. 13, (New York: Charles Scribner's Sons, 1930), 422–423; *National Cyclopedia of American Biography* Vol. 2 (New York: James T. White & Co., 1892), 470–471.

37. *TYS*, 227.

38. The account in *Twelve Years a Slave,* referring to Waddill, states, "After reading the letters and documents presented him . . . . " Since the Memorial, the Petition, the Affidavits, and the Commission might properly be called "documents," this sentence tends to support the conclusion that there were "letters" of introduction to him from people in Washington.

39. Johnson and Malone, Vol. 17, 405–407.

40. *TYS*, 227.

41. Johnson and Malone, Vol. 4, 354.

42. The following account of Solomon Northup's rescue is based largely on *TYS*, 225–242.

43. Cochrane acted as an agent of the State of New York in 1856 to retrieve Charles Granby, an African American thought to have been kidnapped from Rochester. Cochrane is credited with examining 200 of the slaves present at a particular plantation in Louisiana. See, "Abduction and Enslavement of Two Citizens of New York," *Albany Evening Journal* (January 31, 1857): 3. Granby had not been kidnapped at all, but was living in Illinois.

44. *TYS*, 231. Waddill may have made successful inquiries of the Marksville postmaster regarding who mailed the letter, and this story provided cover for him. The postmaster might also have confirmed Bass's identity after Waddill deduced it.

45. *TYS*, 237–238.

46. "The Case of Mr. Northrup," *The New York Daily Times* (January 21, 1853) and the *National Era* (January 27, 1853), both citing the "*Wilmington, N.C., Commercial* of January 18," states, "Mr. H. B. Northup, of Washington County, New York, arrived at the Carolina Hotel, in this town, on Saturday morning, en route from Red River, via New Orleans, Mobile, and Charleston, for New York."

47. "Arrivals at the Hotels," *Washington Daily Evening Star* (January 20, 1853): 2, lists under the entry for the National Hotel, "H B Northup NY."

48. In 1855, Senator Henry Wilson said flowers were for sale at the location, "Senator Wilson's Anti-Slavery Lecture," *Wisconsin Free Democrat* (May 23, 1855).

49. Northup's admittance as an attorney in Washington was noted in "Supreme Court of the United States," *New York Daily Times* (January 20, 1853).

50. Benjamin K. Morsell (not "Mansel" as given in *TYS*, 244), had an office on Louisiana Avenue in the same neighborhood as Shekell's tavern and Shekell's home at the time of the trial. See Alfred Hunter, *The Washington and Georgetown Directory, Strangers Guide-Book for Washington, and Congressional and Clerk's Register* (Washington, Printed by Kirkwood and McGill, 1853), 72. B.K. Morsell also resided in the neighborhood before the period of the trial (see Map 3.1); see Anthony Reintzel, *The Washington Directory and Government Register for 1843* (Washington, J.T. Towers, 1843), 43; Gaither & Addison, *The Washington Directory and National Register for 1846* (Washington, John T. Towers, 1846), 63.

51. Joseph H. Bradley, born in Washington, D.C., in 1803 was the son of Abraham Bradley, the United States First Assistant Postmaster General. According to the *New York Herald* (April 4, 1887, 10), Bradley was connected by blood and by marriage to many prominent Washington families. He was, however, not averse to representing notorious clients. In the 1860s, he defended John M. Barrett, accused of being one of the Lincoln assassination conspirators. At the conclusion of the trial, Bradley was disbarred by the judge for being "disloyal to the government," whereupon he challenged the judge to a duel (which did not take place). It was several years before he could resume practice in D.C. He died in 1887.

52. "From Washington," *New York Daily Times,* January 19, 1853, 8.

53. When Birch appeared before Goddard and Morsell, he, like them, was a sitting Justice of the Peace; he was appointed in 1851 and reappointed in 1854. See Charles Bundy, "History of the Office of Justice of the Peace," *Records of the Columbia Historical Society,* Vol. 5, (1902): 273.

54. The charge, that Northup conspired with Hamilton and Brown to defraud Birch, was reported extensively. In addition to the account in the *New York Daily Times,* it was reported in the *Washington Republic,* reprinted in "Kidnapped," *Alexandria [Virginia] Gazette* (January 21, 1853): 2, and the *Boston Herald* (January 24, 1853): 1.

55. A story with a January 18, 1853 dateline says Henry and Solomon planned to leave D.C. the next day, "From Washington," *New York Daily Times* (January 19, 1853), 8. He would have passed through Albany on the 20th, reaching Sandy Hill that night, *Albany Evening Journal* (January 21, 1853). The January 20 date Northup gives for his departure from Washington appears to be in error, *TYS,* 251.

56. It being January (1853), it is unlikely that there would have been boat travel on the Hudson. Henry's arrival at Albany was noted: "accompanied by Solomon, the poor fellow who has been twelve years in bondage." Solomon was described somewhat patronizingly as, "of medium stature, with a well-formed head and intelligent countenance." *Albany Evening Journal* (January 21, 1853).

57. *Albany Evening Journal* (January 21, 1853).

Chapter 7

1. *Albany Evening Journal* (January 21, 1853).

2. *Frederick Douglass' Paper* [cited hereafter as *FDP*] (February 18, 1853).

3. *FDP* (February 18, 1853).

4. *Sandy Hill Herald* (March 8, 1853).

5. *Albany Evening Journal* (June 10, 1870); *New York Times* (June 18, 1870).

6. *[Auburn, New York] Daily American* (September 16, 1855), attributed to the *Albany Argus.*

7. *New York Times* (January 27, 1858).

8. Letter from John Thompson, *Essex County Republican* (August 13, 1853).

9. *Albany Evening Journal* (June 10, 1870).

10. *New York Daily Times* (April 22, 1853).

11. *Syracuse Evening Journal* (January 30, 1854).

12. Letter from John Henry Northup to Edith Carman Hay, quoted in Wyckoff, 136.

13. *New York Daily Times* (April 15, 1853).

14. *FDP* (April 29, 1853).

15. *FDP* (September 9, 1853).

16. *FDP* (July 29, 1853).

17. *Liberator* (September 9, 1853).

18. *Rome [New York] Citizen* (July 20, 1853).

19. *[Montpelier, Vermont] Watchman & State Journal* (January 26, 1855).

20. *Salem Press* (July 26, 1853), attributed to *Albany Evening Journal*.

21. Letter from John Thompson, *Essex County Republican* (August 13, 1853).

22. *Northern Christian Advocate* (July 13, 1853).

23. *Buffalo Daily Courier* (August 3, 1853).

24. *Syracuse Evening Chronicle* (July 18, 1853).

25. James C. Derby, *Fifty Years Among Authors, Books, and Publishers* (London: G. W. Carleton, 1884), 63.

26. *Syracuse Evening Journal* (August 12, 1853).

27. *National Era* (August 25, 1853); *FDP* (August 26, 1853).

28. *[Elyria, Ohio] Independent Democrat* (December 7, 1853).

29. *[Elyria, Ohio] Independent Democrat* (December 7, 1853).

30. *Wesleyan* (November 17, 1853).

31. *Syracuse Daily Standard* (January 12, 1855).

32. *Syracuse Standard* (April 4, 1853).

33. *Wesleyan* (July 20, 1854).

34. Letter from John Thompson, in *Essex County Republican* (August 13, 1853).

35. Warren County, New York, Deeds, Book U, p. 297.

36. *War Talks in Kansas* (Kansas City, Missouri: Franklin Hudson, 1906), 162.

37. Elias Porter Pellet, *History of the 114th Regiment, New York State Volunteers* (Norwich, New York: Telegraph & Chronicle Power Press, 1866), 77.

38. Joseph Logsdon, "Diary of a Slave: Recollection and Prophecy," in *Seven on Black: Reflections on the Negro Experience in America,* by William G. Shad and Roy C. Herrenkohl, eds. (Philadelphia: Lippeincott, 1969), 43.

39. *FDP* (July 29, 1853).

40. Photocopy of inscription provided to author (Fiske) by Connecticut bookseller John D. Townsend.

41. *Auburn Weekly Journal* (October 5, 1853).

42. *Liberator* (October 14, 1853); *Wesleyan* (October 6, 1853); *Syracuse Evening Chronicle* (October 1, 1853).

43. *Wesleyan* (October 6, 1853).

44. *Syracuse Evening Chronicle* (January 30, 1854).

45. *Syracuse Daily Journal* (January 31, 1854).

46. *Syracuse Evening Chronicle* (February 2, 1854).

47. *FDP* (January 27, 1854).

48. *FDP* (March 3, 1854), attributed to the *Vermont Tribune.*

49. Field Horne, *Index to News of Saratoga Springs, New York 1819–1900.* (Privately printed, 1998).

50. *Green Mountain Freeman* (January 23, 1855).

51. *Syracuse Daily Standard* (March 31, 1855).

52. *FDP* (March 16, 1855); *Liberator* (March 23, 1855); *Liberator* (March 30, 1855).

53. *Boston Daily Atlas* (March 12, 1855); *FDP* (March 16, 1855).

54. *Liberator* (March 23, 1855).

55. *Lewis County [New York] Republican* (April 29, 1854).

56. *[Rome, New York] Sentinel* (May 1, 1854). Other papers also said Northup portrayed himself in the play: *Syracuse Daily Standard* (April 24, 1854); *Syracuse Daily Standard* (April 25, 1854); *FDP* (May 26, 1854).

57. *Syracuse Evening Chronicle* (April 21, 1854); *Syracuse Daily Standard* (July 19, 1856).

58. *Syracuse Daily Standard* (May 1, 1854).

59. *Syracuse Daily Standard* (May 2, 1854).

60. *Syracuse Daily Standard* (May 3, 1854).

61. *Syracuse Daily Standard* (May 3, 1854).

62. *Syracuse Daily Standard* (May 4, 1854).

63. *Syracuse Evening Chronicle* (April 28, 1854).

64. *Syracuse Daily Standard* (July 19, 1856).

65. Item 9169 from *American Broadsides* database, American Antiquarian Society collection.

66. For example: the hero Bass appeared early, in Saratoga, when in reality he appeared only toward the end of Northup's years in Louisiana; Tibaut ("Tibbeats") murders Freeman in his slave pen; and Eliza dies on the Epps plantation.

67. Item 23755 from *American Broadsides* database, American Antiquarian Society collections.

68. *Barre [Massachusetts] Patriot* (November 17, 1855).

69. *Springfield [Massachusetts] Republican* (November 10, 1855).

70. *St. Albans Messenger* (December 11, 1856).

71. *Albany Evening Journal* (September 5, 1857).

72. Attributed to the *Streetsville Review,* via the *Louisville Journal,* in the *Detroit Daily Free Press* (August 26, 1857); and the *New Hampshire Patriot* (September 16, 1857).

73. *Charleston Mercury* (August 29, 1857); *Pittsfield Sun* (September 10, 1857).

74. *[Holmes County, Ohio] Republican* (August 27, 1857).

Chapter 8

1. St. John was originally from Fish House, a village on the border between Broadalbin and Northampton, Fulton County, New York. His father, Alexander St. John, had been the surveyor who laid out the town of St. Johnsville, New York, and it was named for him. See *History of Montgomery and*

Fulton Counties, N.Y., (Heart of the Lakes Publishing, Interlaken, NY, 1981), 172. The family house, which still exists, is in Northampton, where St. John testified that he had been brought up.

2. "Trial of the Suspected Kidnappers of Solomon Northup," *Albany Evening Journal* (July 12, 1854).

3. Testimony of Northup and St. John, reported in the *New York Daily Tribune* (July 14, 1854): 7.

4. See also the introduction of Sue Eakin and Joe Logsdon, *TYS*, xvii–xviii.

5. Attributed to *Zion's Herald,* printed in *North Christian Advocate* (July 26, 1854): 19. In a very few places, throughout our presentation of Parks's account, we have provided alternative punctuation and capitalization. The account itself is dated July 10, 1854.

6. Washington Frothingham, *History of Fulton County* (Syracuse: D. Mason, 1892), 391.

7. Attributed to *Zion's Herald,* printed in *North Christian Advocate* (July 26, 1854): 19.

8. The site of the village, located in the town of Mayfield near the border of Broadalbin, Fulton County, New York, is now under the waters of the Great Sacandaga Lake. Thaddeus St. John in court testimony said Merrill had grown up in Northampton, New York, *New York Daily Tribune* (July 14, 1854).

9. *New York Daily Tribune* (July 11, 1854). The fact that Saratoga County officials were involved in helping to locate Merrill is an indication of the extent to which the investigation had been conducted after St. John came forward with his evidence. For another account of Merrill's arrest, see *Albany Evening Journal* (July 9, 1854).

10. Attributed to the *Albany Evening Journal,* in *Utica Morning Herald* (July 12, 1854). Russell in the account mentions the inauguration; this would have taken place before the funeral of William Henry Harrison. Russell (or the reporter) had conflated the two events: he witnessed the public funeral ceremonies.

11. Thaddeus St. John testified that he had known Russell from childhood, and that Russell had been brought up in the town of Edinburgh in Saratoga County, which borders Northampton in Fulton County. The village of Edinburgh is about 10 miles north of Fish House where St. John grew up. See, *New York Daily Tribune* (July 14, 1854): 7.

12. Merrill was represented by William Wait, Russell by John Brotherson. The *Saratoga Whig's* account of the trial was carried in numerous papers, and one of the most complete versions (the one on which we rely) appeared in *New York Daily Tribune* (July 14, 1854): 7.

13. *New York Daily Tribune* (July 14, 1854): 7. On the basis of this last testimony, the prosecution attempted to introduce into evidence the bowie knife and loaded revolver found when Merrill was arrested, Henry Northup stating that they would be evidence proving that Merrill had long engaged in kidnapping and other crimes and that he was therefore always armed for offense and defense. The account does not state if his motion was successful.

14. *New York Daily Tribune* (July 14, 1854): 7.

15. *New York Daily Tribune* (July 14, 1854): 7.

16. *New York Daily Tribune* (July 14, 1854): 7.

17. *The Wesleyan* (July 20, 1854).

18. *Frederick Douglass' Paper* (August 4, 1854).

19. Records of People *v.* Alexander Merrill and Joseph Russell, Court of Oyer and Terminer, Saratoga County, New York, on file at Saratoga County Clerk's Office (Box A83) and Saratoga County Historian's Office. A copy initiating the lawsuit is one of the few extant documents bearing Northup's signature.

20. Hon. John A. Corey, County Judge of the County of Saratoga, David Maxwell and Abram Sickler, Esquires, Justices of the Peace for Sessions in and for said county. James W. Horton served as clerk.

21. We find no newspaper accounts of the substance of the grand jury hearing. We find no court record of the substance of the testimony taken.

22. *New York Daily Tribune,* September 2, 1854, 4.

23. Decision of the New York State Court of Appeals in the case of People *against* Merrill and another, decided June, 1856 (14 NY 74, 75). See also, *TYS,* xxi.

24. Decision of the New York State Court of Appeals in the case of People *against* Merrill and another, decided June, 1856 (14 NY 74, 75).

25. *TYS,* xix.

26. Statements of Merrill and Russell, in Records of People *v.* Alexander Merrill and Joseph Russell, Court of Oyer and Terminer, Saratoga County, New York, on file at Saratoga County Clerk's Office (Box A83).

27. *Buffalo Dailey Courier* (October 5, 1854).

28. His testimony in January 1853, had been tentative and inconclusive. He probably testified then only to help Birch, and perhaps did not wish to be involved in further proceedings.

29. The following account of the responses to the interrogatories are taken from documents in the Records of People *v.* Alexander Merrill and Joseph Russell, Court of Oyer and Terminer, Saratoga County, New York, on file at Saratoga County Clerk's Office (Box A83).

30. *TYS,* 12–13.

31. It makes little sense that a slave under these circumstances in the middle of a business transaction would have played a fiddle for an entire hour simply to determine if he could actually play it.

32. We do not know why Birch gave the Alexandria address as the point of reception for Northup—Radburn in 1853 had confirmed Northup's story that he had been sent to Williams' Slave Pen.

33. Birch was still involved in the slave trade into the late 1850s, having moved his business to Alexandria, Virginia (as a partner in Price, Birch and Company) after a provision of the Fugitive Slave Law of 1850 banned the slave trade in Washington.

34. Eakin and Logsdon state that "the presiding judge ruled against the contested parts of the indictment in order to have the point of law clarified before the state supreme court," *TYS,* xxi.

35. *Temperance Helper* (February 22, 1855).

36. *New York Daily Express* (February 15, 1855); *New York Times* (February 15, 1855); *Temperance Helper* (February 15, 1855).

37. It was unlikely that D.C. officials would demand the surrender of Merrill and Russell, even had New York officials turned over to them the evidence in their possession. Birch, after all, had already been cleared of the charge of kidnapping. Northup's testimony would have been central to the case, and Northup, being black, could not testify against his kidnappers in the District courts.

38. Amasa J. Parker, *Reports of Decisions in Criminal Cases Made at Term, at Chambers and in the Courts of Oyer and Terminer of the State of New York,* Vol. 2 (Gould, Banks & Co., Albany, 1856), 590–605.

39. Decision of the New York State Court of Appeals in the case of People *against* Merrill and another, decided in June 1856 (14 NY 74, 76).

40. People *against* Merrill and another, June 1856 (14 NY 74, 78). See also, *Syracuse Daily Standard* (July 19, 1856).

41. Nathaniel Bartlett Sylvester, *History of Saratoga County* (Everts & Ensign, Philadelphia, 1878), 87.

42. *Syracuse Daily Courier* (July 3, 1857).

43. *Ballston Journal* (May 26, 1857).

44. E. R. Mann, *The Bench and Bar of Saratoga County; or Remembrances of the Judiciary, and Scenes in the Courtroom,* (Waterbury and Inman, Ballston, New York, 1876), 153.

45. Letter from John Henry Northup to Edith Carmen Hay, quoted in Edith Hay Wyckoff, *The Autobiography of an American Family* (Fort Edward, New York: Washington County Historical Society, 2000), 136.

46. Attributed to the *Streetsville Review,* via the *Louisville Journal,* in *Detroit Daily Free Press* (August 26, 1857); *Holmes County [Ohio] Republican* (August 27, 1857); *Charleston Mercury* (August 29, 1857); *Albany Evening Journal* (September 5, 1857); *Pittsfield Sun* (September 10, 1857); *New Hampshire Patriot* (September 16, 1857).

47. "Can't Sue," *The National Era* (July 9, 1857).

48. *Albany Evening Journal* (June 6, 1857).

49. "The Taney Hunt against Colored Americans," *The Liberator* (August 28, 1857). The *[Janesville, Wisconsin] Daily Morning Gazette* (June 19, 1857), asked "With Judge Taney's 'decision' staring him in the face, what else could he [the District Attorney] do?"

50. Attributed to the *Saratogian,* in *Syracuse Daily Courier* (July 3, 1857); repeated with slight variation in the *Lowell Daily Citizen and News* (June 17, 1857).

51. "Slavery Days Recalled," *Amsterdam Evening Recorder* (December 24, 1902).

52. *TYS,* xxi–xxii, and note 26, citing *Saratoga Whig,* February 16, 1855, reprinting an editorial from the *Ballston Democrat* "criticizing the position taken by the *Saratoga Republican* in regard to the trial."

53. There was a more colorful version of this story (and one probably not meant to be taken seriously, since it was told at a meeting of a group called

"The Tramps" who gathered in Tribes Hill, New York). In this tale, the plan was hatched when Northup was gambling with Merrill and Russell in Albany. As part of the scheme, Merrill worked with Northup so that he could convincingly act the part of a slave, in order to fool potential buyers. The article, containing numerous factual errors concerning Northup's story, appeared in "Reminiscences of a Lawyer," *Amsterdam Evening Recorder* (October 30, 1907).

54. *TYS*, 249.

55. *TYS*, 249.

Chapter 9

1. *Journal of the House of Representatives for 1854*, pp. 401, 404, and 537. Smith's petitions were filed on February 20 and 21; Wade's, on March 21.

2. *Frederick Douglass' Paper* (April 28, 1854).

3. *Journal of the House of Representatives for 1854*, p. 970; *Congressional Globe* (June 10, 1854); *National Daily Intelligencer* (June 12, 1854).

4. *Springfield [Massachusetts] Republican* (February 4, 1853).

5. Warren County, New York, Mortgages, Book N, p. 156.

6. Warren County, New York, Mortgages, Book N, p. 149.

7. Warren County, New York, Mortgages, Book N, p. 346; *Glens Falls Free Press* (November 4, 1854).

8. The referee, Edgar Cronkhite, investigated, and on October 23, 1854, reported that Northup had to repay the $100, plus interest amounting to $2.20. By January 8, 1855, Arlin still had not received what was due him, and Northup was ordered to pay the sum of $150.64, which included various court and document costs. Documents on file at Warren County, New York, Records Center.

9. On June 10, 1854, John T. B. Traphagan and Charles R. Bennett obtained a judgment for $44.87 (which included court costs of $1.03), and on October 9, Benjamin Carll, Jr., from Wayne County, New York, was awarded $156.75 (which included $53.80 in costs) by a court there. Records relating to these judgments are on file at the Warren County, New York, Records Center. Wayne County officials had notified Warren County of the judgment, since Northup owned property there. There are no surviving records in Wayne County relating to the judgment.

10. Warren County, New York, Deeds, Book X, p. 78.

11. *Syracuse Evening Chronicle* (April 28, 1854).

12. Interestingly, we see little evidence of his publicly performing on the violin, although he may have done so in conjunction with his speaking engagements and performances of his plays.

13. Edith Hay Wyckoff, *The Autobiography of an American Family* (Fort Edward, New York: Washington County Historical Society, 2000), 136.

14. Warren County, New York, Deeds, Book S, p. 379; Book N, p. 156.

15. *The Northern Star and Freeman's Advocate* (March 10, 1842); *The Northern Star and Freeman's Advocate* (December 8, 1842).

16. *[Newark, NJ] Sentinel of Freedom* (November 26, 1844); *[New York, NY] Spectator* (November 27, 1844).

17. Samuel G. Boyd, *In the Days of Old Glens Falls, as I Remember It* (Glens Falls, New York: Zonta Club of Glens Falls, 1927), 8. The incident was also described in a contemporary newspaper account, see Patrick Dowd (ed.), *Warren County (New York): Its People and their History Over Time* (Virginia Beach, VA: Donning Company Publishers, 2009), 163.

18. 1855 New York State Census, Warren County, Town of Queensbury, Household #111.

19. Dowd (ed.), 190.

20. Wilbur Henry Siebert, *Vermont's Anti-slavery and Underground Railroad Record* (Columbus Ohio: The Spahr and Glenn Company, 1937), 98–100.

21. John R. Smith, letter [to Wilbur H. Siebert], April 25, 1935, in the collection of Siebert's papers at the Houghton Library, Harvard University, Call Number MS Am 2420, Vol. 41 "The Underground Railroad in Vermont."

22. "Memorial Papers," *Minutes of the Vermont Annual Conference of the Methodist Episcopal Church* (Montpelier, VT: Walton 1858), 13.

23. John R. Smith, letter [to unknown recipient], April 25, 1935, in the collection of Siebert's papers at the Houghton Library, Harvard University, Call Number MS Am 2420, Vol. 41 "The Underground Railroad in Vermont." Harvard's Siebert collection contains two letters from John R. Smith. One is addressed to Walter F. Hatch, who was the postmaster in Hartland, Vermont (Siebert's research methodology often involved contacting local postmasters seeking information on underground railroad activity in their areas). The recipient of the other letter is not given, but it most likely was sent to Siebert. Notes from Hatch indicate that he was forwarding information, including Smith's letter, to Siebert.

24. John R. Smith, letter [to unknown recipient], April 25, 1935, cited in note 23.

25. Dora Webster, *Underground Railroad in Hartland,* undated manuscript in the collections of the Vermont Historical Society, Montpelier, Vermont.

26. "Speech by Theodore Gross," in *The Black Abolitionist Papers, Vol. 1: British Isles, 1830–1865,* C. Peter Ripley, editor (Chapel Hill: University of North Carolina Press, 1985), 485n.

27. John R. Smith, letter [to unknown recipient], April 25, 1935, cited in note 23.

28. Walter F. Hatch, letter [to Wilbur H. Siebert], [nd], in the collection of Siebert's papers at the Houghton Library, Harvard University, Call Number MS Am 2420, Vol. 41 "The Underground Railroad in Vermont."

29. John R. Smith, letter [to unknown recipient], April 25, 1935, cited in note 23.

30. "Memorial Papers," *Minutes of the Vermont Annual Conference of the Methodist Episcopal Church* (Montpelier, VT: Walton 1887), 52–53.

31. *Frederick Douglass' Paper* (April 13, 1855).

32. *Frederick Douglass' Paper* (June 19, 1855).

33. Quoted in Michael Horigan, "Antebellum Elmira, Part Two," *Chemung Historical Journal,* 48:2 (December 2002), 5288.

34. *Frederick Douglass' Paper* (July 27, 1855).

35. *[St. Johnsbury, Vermont] Caledonian* (August 9, 1856).

36. *Utica Daily Observer* (June 25, 1858).

37. *TYS*, xxiii; Warren County, New York, Deeds, Book 9, p. 528.

38. *Syracuse Daily Journal* (October 13, 1858); and a similar item in *Wyoming County [New York] Mirror* (November 17, 1858).

39. Field Horne, *Index to News of Saratoga Springs, New York 1819–1900* (privately printed, 1998). We were unable to locate this article.

40. Reports said: "The venerable wife of Sol. Northup, the slave who was taken from bondage several years ago, and after exhibiting himself through the country became a worthless vagabond, died last week at Reynolds Corners, at the age of 78 years." *New York Evening Telegram* (August 21, 1876); *Utica Morning Herald* (August 19, 1876); *Waterville Times* (September 14, 1876).

Appendix B

1. 1825 New York State Census, Washington County, Town of Salem.

2. Charles B. Moore, comp., *Cemetery Records of the Township of Kingsbury, Washington County, New York* (Queensbury, New York:, Historical Data Services, 1996), 2.

3. *TYS*, 262.

4. U.S. Supreme Court, *U.S. Supreme Court Transcript of Record Bowen v. Chase [98 U.S. 254]* (np: Gale MOML Print Editions, 2011), 242–250.

5. Jane Lancaster, Personal Correspondence with David Fiske, November 28, 2011, based on her research on the litigation over Madame Jumel's estate, and for a book on Madame Jumel's life; Jane Lancaster, "Madame Jumel: A 19th [Century] Woman Who Defied Convention," *Social Science Docket*, Vol. 11, No. 1, online at http://people.hofstra.edu/alan_j_singer/docket/docket/11.1.21_Madame_Jumel_A_19th_Woman.pdf; reference is also made of Anne and Alonzo being in the employ of Madame Jumel in William Henry Shelton, *The Jumel Mansion* Boston: Houghton Mifflin, 1916), 176–177; U.S. Supreme Court, *U.S. Supreme Court Transcript of Record Bowen v. Chase [98 U.S. 254]* (np: Gale MOML Print Editions, 2011), 242–250.

6. 1860 Federal Census, New York State, Warren County, Town of Queensbury, 9.

7. 1850 Federal Census, New York State, Saratoga County, Town of Moreau, 140.

8. 1850 Federal Census, Warren County, Town of Queensbury, 31.

9. 1850 Federal Census, New York State, Saratoga County, Village of Saratoga Springs, 211.

10. *TYS*, 251.

11. Warren County, New York, Deeds, Book S, p. 379.

12. Warren County, New York, Mortgages, Book M, p. 24.

13. Warren County, New York Mortgages, Book N, p. 346; *Glens Falls Free Press* (November 4, 1854).

14. Warren County, New York Deeds, Book X, p. 78.

15. 1855 New York State Census, Warren County, Town of Queensbury, Second Election District, Dwelling # 110.

16. Supreme Court, Warren County, *Benjamin P. Burhans, President of the Glens Falls Bank against Anne Northup,* March 25, 1859, Warren County, New York, Records Center.

17. 1860 Federal Census, New York State, Warren County, Town of Queensbury, 9.

18. 1860 Federal Census, Warren County, Town of Bolton, 299–300.

19. U.S. Supreme Court, *U.S. Supreme Court Transcript of Record Bowen v. Chase [98 U.S. 254]* (np: Gale MOML Print Editions, 2011), 244.

20. Warren County, New York, Deeds, Book 9, p. 528.

21. Warren County, New York, Deeds, Book 9, p. 527.

22. Saratoga County, New York, Deeds, Book 98, p. 154.

23. 1865 New York State Census, Saratoga County, Town of Moreau, Dwelling # 299.

24. For an account of the fire and aftermath, see H. P. Smith, *History of Warren County* (Syracuse: Mason & Co., 1885), 284ff.

25. *Saratogian* (September 28, 1871).

26. Shelton, 176–177.

27. New York State Census, 1875, Washington County, Town of Kingsbury, E.D. 3. Household # 199.

28. *Saratoga Sentinel* (August 17, 1876).

29. "Moreau," *Beers Atlas of Saratoga County, New York* (Philadelphia: Stone & Stewart, 1866), 49.

30. In her 1871 deposition for the Jumel Estate trial, Anne said she was 73, but in her memorial, she indicates she was born March 14, 1808, *TYS*, 256.

31. 1860 Federal Census, New York State, Warren County, Town of Queensbury, 9.

32. 1865 New York State Census, Saratoga County, Town of Moreau, Household # 266.

33. U.S. Supreme Court, *U.S. Supreme Court Transcript of Record Bowen v. Chase [98 U.S. 254]* (np: Gale MOML Print Editions, 2011), 242–243.

34. *Rochester Democrat and Chronicle* (July 6, 1901).

35. Pension File for Charles Stanton, Certificate #298,723, National Archives.

36. 1850 Federal Census, New York State, Saratoga Springs, 211.

37. Warren County, New York, Deeds, Book S, p. 379.

38. 1855 New York State Census, Warren County, Town of Queensbury, Second Election District, Dwelling # 110.

39. 1860 Federal Census, New York State, Warren County, Town of Queensbury, 9.

40. Warren County, New York, Deeds, Book 9, p. 528.

41. Warren County, New York, Deeds, Book 9, p. 527.

42. Saratoga County, New York, Deeds, Book 98, p. 154.

43. Saratoga County, New York, Deeds, Book 98, p. 156.

44. 1865 New York State Census, Saratoga County, Town of Moreau, Dwelling # 299.

45. "Moreau, " *Beers Atlas of Saratoga County, New York* (Philadelphia: Stone & Stewart 1866), 49.

46. Hamilton Child. *Gazetteer and Business Directory of Saratoga County, N.Y. and Queensbury, Warren County for 1871* (Syracuse: Journal Office, 1871), 214.

47. 1870 Federal Census, New York State, Saratoga County, Town of Moreau, 337.

48. U.S. Supreme Court, *U.S. Supreme Court Transcript of Record Bowen v. Chase [98 U.S. 254]* (np: Gale MOML Print Editions, 2011), 243.

49. Saratoga County, New York, Deeds, Book 176, p. 61.

50. Warren County, New York, Deeds, Book 27, p. 282.

51. Saratoga County, New York, Deeds, Book 138, p. 150.

52. Washington County, New York, Deeds, Book 76, p. 258.

53. Pension File for Charles Stanton, Certificate #298,723, National Archives.

54. Washington County, New York, Mortgages, Book 49, p. 292.

55. Pension File for Charles Stanton, Certificate #298,723, National Archives. Charles was the son of Philip and his previous wife, Betsey Oakley. Charles, served in the 54th Massachusetts, and was wounded at Fort Wagner. He died while a prisoner of war, and because Charles was unmarried and had no children, his father was entitled to a military pension, as well as his back pay.

56. Interment card for "M.A. Stanton," obtained from West Point Cemetery, Norfolk, Virginia; USGENWEB Archives Norfolk, Virginia, West Point Cemetery database (http://www.usgwarchives.net/va/norfolkcity/cemeteries/westpoint/wpcem-s.html: accessed 11 Dec 2012); "Search the Westpoint Cemetery Database," (http://www2.vcdh.virginia.edu/afam/Norfolk/search_cemetery.html: accessed 11 Dec 2012); "District of Columbia Deaths and Burials, 1840–1964," index, FamilySearch (https://familysearch.org/pal:/MM9.1.1/F7BW-FM3: accessed 11 Dec 2012), Margaret A. Stanton, 14 Mar 1879. Regrettably according to Bobette Nelson with the Norfolk, Virginia Bureau of Cemeteries an inventory of grave markers at West Point Cemetery revealed no extant markers for Margaret or Philip Stanton, though both are buried there.

57. "District of Columbia Marriages, 1811–1950," index and images, FamilySearch (https://familysearch.org/pal:/MM9.1.1/XLQQ-FZP: accessed 11 Dec 2012), Philip L. Barber and Florence A. Stanton, [August 3] 1886; "Norfolk News," *New York Freeman* (August 21, 1886): 4.

58. Pension File for Charles Stanton, Certificate #298,723, National Archives; "District of Columbia Deaths and Burials, 1840–1964," Margaret A. Stanton, 1879; Interment card for "Philip Stanton," obtained from West Point Cemetery, Norfolk, Virginia; USGENWEB Archives Norfolk, Virginia, West Point Cemetery database (http://www.usgwarchives.net/va/norfolkcity/cemeteries/westpoint/wpcem-s.html: accessed 11 Dec 2012); "Search the Westpoint Cemetery Database," (http://www2.vcdh.virginia.edu/afam/

Norfolk/search_cemetery.html: accessed 11 Dec 2012); *Indianapolis [Indiana] Freeman* (March 4, 1893): 8 [his name is incorrectly given as "Phillip B. Stratton"].

59. *TYS*, 251, which incorrectly gives the surname as Staunton.

60. 1875 New York State Census, Washington County, Town of Fort Edward, Dwelling # 381.

61. Iowa Marriages, 1809–1992, retrieved from familysearch.org, December 3, 2011.

62. *Omaha World Herald* (October 1, 1893).

63. 1855 New York State Census, Warren County, Town of Queensbury, Second Election District, Dwelling # 110.

64. *Northern Christian Advocate* [Auburn, NY] (July 18, 1855): 114.

65. 1860 Federal Census, New York, Warren County, Town of Queensbury, 9.

66. Pension File for Alonzo Northrup, Certificate # 1,041,353, National Archives.

67. Compiled Military Service Records of Volunteer Union Soldiers Who Served with the United States Colored Troops: Infantry Organizations, 26th Regiment. National Archives Collection.

68. Pension File for Alonzo Northrup, Certificate # 1,041,353, National Archives.

69. Compiled Military Service Records of Volunteer Union Soldiers Who Served with the United States Colored Troops: Infantry Organizations, 26th Regiment. National Archives Collection; Pension File for Alonzo Northrup, Certificate # 1,041,353, National Archives.

70. Tax Records, Glens Falls, Warren County, New York, Records Center.

71. 1870 Federal Census, New York State, Washington County, Town of Fort Edward, 206.

72. 1875 New York State Census, Cayuga County, Town of Weedsport, 1st Election District, Dwelling # 25.

73. Pension File for Alonzo Northrup, Certificate # 1,041,353, National Archives.

74. *Syracuse Post-Standard* (October 18, 1909).

75. "Mrs. C. Victoria Northrup," *Cayuga Chief* (April 8, 1932).

Bibliographical Note

What follows is a list of the most important references cited in this volume as well as a general outline of the resource base employed—especially the very diverse resource base that is directly relevant to the Solomon Northup story. For excellent examples of formal bibliographies on the institution of slavery more generally, and on kidnapping of free blacks into slavery, see the 2003 edition of Peter Kolchin's *American Slavery 1619–1877*, and Carol Wilson's *Freedom at Risk: The Kidnapping of Free Blacks in America, 1780–1865.*

Needless to say, a principal source for this volume is Northup's own account, which appears in several modern editions. The 1968 Eakin and Logsdon edition is, for several reasons, the unquestionable starting point for any contemporary attempt at biography. In addition to its important interpretive content, the introduction and notes verify and contextualize the factual basis of the story in *Twelve Years a Slave* and present an account of Northup's life after slavery. Eakin's 2007 sequel presents further valuable substantive and bibliographical information, although in many cases calls into question, in unconvincing ways, the factual basis of Northup's story and the motivations of David Wilson. Ira Berlin's introduction to the Penguin edition provides important contextualization to the story, especially with respect to the culture of slavery. We also note that Northup's account is frequently, perhaps increasingly, cited in the literature on slavery, as for example in Maurie D. McInnis, *Slaves Waiting for Sale,* and Walter Johnson, *Soul by Soul.*

A

Although this book, in focusing on Northup himself, relies heavily on original sources, there are works that have been especially useful in giving general background information about the social and economic environment in which Northup grew up and lived as a free man, the culture of slavery itself, and the context of his life after rescue. Journal references are listed throughout the notes; the following are the books most frequently cited for those purposes.

Adams, John Quincy. *Memoirs of John Quincy Adams: Comprising Portions of His Diary from 1795 to 1848*, edited by Charles Francis Adams. Vol. 10. Philadelphia: J. B. Lippincott & Co., 1876.

Artemel, Janice G., Elizabeth A. Crowell, and Jeff Parker. *The Alexandria Slave Pen: The Archaeology of Urban Captivity*. Washington, DC: Engineering Science, Inc., 1987.

Beaudry, Michael. *The Axe Handler's Handbook*. Springville, UT: Horizon Publishers, 2005.

Berlin, Ira. "Introduction, Solomon Northup: A Life and a Message," in Solomon Northup, *Twelve Years a Slave*. New York: Penguin Books, 2012.

Boyd, Samuel G. *In the Days of Old Glens Falls, as I Remember It*. Glens Falls, New York: Zonta Club of Glens Falls, 1927.

Brown, Letitia Woods. *Free Negroes in the District of Columbia*. New York: Oxford University Press, 1972.

Brugel, Martin. *Farm, Ship, Landing*. Durham & London: Duke University Press, 2002.

Bryan, Wilhelmus Bogart. *A History of the National Capital*. Vol. 2. New York: Macmillan Company, 1916.

Carter, Nathaniel H., William L. Stone, and Marcus T. C. Gould. *Reports of the Proceedings and Debates of the Convention of 1821 Assembled for the Purpose of Amending the Constitution of the State of New York*. Albany: E. & E. Rosford, 1821.

Cohen, David S. *The Dutch-American Farm*. New York and London: New York University Press, 1992.

Corbett, Theodore. *The Making of American Resorts*. New Brunswick, New Jersey: Rutgers University Press, 2001.

Derby, James C. *Fifty Years Among Authors, Books, and Publishers*. London: G. W. Carleton, 1884.

Dickens, Charles. "American Notes" in *American Notes and Pictures from Italy*. London: Oxford University Press, 1957.

Douglass, Frederick. *Life and Times of Frederick Douglass, Written by Himself*. Hartford: Park Publishing, 1881.

Eakin, Sue. *Solomon Northup's Twelve Years a Slave and Plantation Life in the Antebellum South*. Lafayette, LA: University of Louisiana at Lafayette, 2007.

Eakin, Sue and Joe Logsdon (eds.). *Solomon Northup, Twelve Years a Slave*. Baton Rouge: Louisiana State University Press, 1968.

Emmons, Ebenezer. *Natural History of New York.* Vol. 2. New York: D. Appleton & Co. and Wiley and Putnam, 1848.

Finkelman, Paul, and Donald R. Kennon. *In the Shadow of Freedom: The Politics of Slavery in the National Capital.* Published for the United States Capitol Historical Society. Athens: Ohio University Press, 2011.

Fox, William. *A History of the Lumber Industry in the State of New York.* Published by the U.S. Department of Agriculture, Bureau of Forestry as Bulletin 34. Washington, DC: Government Printing Office, 1902.

Goode, James M. *Capital Losses: A Cultural History of Washington's Destroyed Buildings.* Washington, DC: Smithsonian Institution Press, 1979.

Green, Constance McLaughlin. *The Secret City.* Princeton: Princeton University Press, 1967.

Hedrick, Ulysses P. *A History of Agriculture in the State of New York.* Printed for the New York State Agriculture Society, 1933. New York: Hill and Wang, 1966.

Hendrick, George, and Willene Hendrick. *The Creole Mutiny.* Chicago: Ivan Dee, 2003.

Horne, Field. *Index to News of Saratoga Springs, New York 1819–1900.* Privately printed, 1998.

Jensen, Amy LaFollette. *The White House and its Thirty-Five Families.* New York: McGraw–Hill, 1970.

Johnson, Walter. *Soul by Soul: Life inside the Antebellum Slave Market.* Cambridge: Harvard University Press, 1999.

Jones, Howard. *Mutiny on the Amistad.* New York: Oxford University Press, 1987.

Kelly, Charles Suddarth. *Washington, D.C., Then and Now.* New York: Dover Publications, 1984.

Kolchin, Peter. *American Slavery 1619–1877.* New York: Hill and Wang, 2003.

Larkin, F. Daniel. *Pioneer American Railroads: The Mohawk and Hudson and the Saratoga and Schenectady.* Fleishmanns, New York: Purple Mountain Press, 1995.

McInnis, Maurie D. *Slaves Waiting for Sale.* Chicago and London: The University of Chicago Press, 2011.

Pellet, Elias Porter. *History of the 114th Regiment, New York State Volunteers.* Norwich, New York:Telegraph & Chronicle Power Press, 1866.

Randall, Samuel S. *The Common School System of the State of New York.* Troy: Johnson and Davis, 1851.

Reed, Robert. *Old Washington, D.C. in Early Photographs 1846–1932.* New York: Dover Publications, 1980.

Ricks, Mary Kay. *Escape on the Pearl: The Heroic Bid for Freedom on the Underground Railroad.* New York: William Morrow, 2007.

Schafer, Judith Kelleher. *Slavery, the Civil War, and the Supreme Court of Louisiana.* Baton Rouge: Louisiana State University Press, 1994.

Shad, William G., and Roy C. Herrenkohl (eds.). *Seven on Black: Reflections on the Negro Experience in America.* Philadelphia: Lippincott, 1969.

Shelton, William Henry. *The Jumel Mansion.* Boston: Houghton Mifflin, 1916.

Siebert, Wilbur Henry. *Vermont's Anti-slavery and Underground Railroad Record.* Columbus Ohio: The Spahr and Glenn Company, 1937.

Sterngass, Jon. *First Resorts.* Baltimore: Johns Hopkins University Press, 2001.

Stewart, L. Lloyd. *A Far Cry from Freedom: Gradual Abolition, (1790–1827), New York State's Crime against Humanity.* Bloomington, Indiana: AuthorHouse, 2006.

Stone, William L. *Reminiscences of Saratoga and Ballston.* New York: Worthington and Company, 1890.

Stowe, Harriet Beecher. *A Key to Uncle Tom's Cabin.* London: Samson Low, 1853.

Taylor, John. *William Henry Seward, Lincoln's Right Hand.* Washington and London, Brassey's, 1991.

Torrey, Jesse. *American Slave Trade.* London: J.M. Cobbett, 1822.

Trammell, John. *The Richmond Slave Trade: The Economic Backbone of the Old Dominion.* Charleston: History Press, 2012.

Van Deusen, Glyndon G. *William Henry Seward.* New York: Oxford University Press, 1967.

Wilson, Carol. *Freedom at Risk: The Kidnapping of Free Blacks in America, 1780–1865.* Lexington, Kentucky: The University Press of Kentucky, 1994.

Wyckoff, Edith Hay. *The Autobiography of an American Family.* Fort Edward, New York: Washington County Historical Society, 2000.

B

The Northup story takes place over more than half a century and throughout the northeast, mid-Atlantic region and the south. Original sources relevant for presenting the tale are therefore very diverse in nature and geographically scattered. The following is an outline of the original-source materials upon which this book is based.

1. There is an extensive unpublished genealogy of the descendants of Stephen Northup, the first American ancestor of Henry Northup. This impressive work was prepared, in part, by John Northup, and was shared with the authors. It includes the family tree from Stephen Northup down to the present generations. Another highly important source is *The Autobiography of an American Family,* largely based on an extraordinary collection of family letters compiled by the late Edith Hay Wyckoff, a descendent of Henry Northup. There is no formal genealogy of the Mintus Northup line, but family records and recollections have been shared with the authors. All descendants known to the authors are of Alonzo Northup (Solomon's son), although much effort was made to trace the lines of Solomon's two daughters.

2. Official records of legal and notarial proceedings provide a major component of our evidentiary base and tie the story's chronology to other documentary evidence. These include: wills; deeds; notarial records of property transfers in Louisiana; court records in both New York and Louisiana (including petitions, affidavits, interrogatories, sequestration orders, foreclosure orders, indexes to convictions, bail certification documents, records of indictments, court orders,

arbitration decisions, and court decisions); and legislative and gubernatorial acts. In the private sector, hospital records in New Orleans and church records in New York have provided important supporting evidence.

3. The records of public bodies are also important sources to verify and elucidate events in the story. These include legislative documents of the Senate and Assembly of the State of New York; the New York Annual Register; the Congressional Journal; municipal tax and property records, especially in Sandy Hill and Washington, D.C.; Civil War pension files and military service records in the National Archives; ship registers and manifests, also from the National Archives; and Washington, D.C., city proclamations.

4. Valuable in locating the Northup families and their movements (and determining their evolving occupations) are: 18th-century Rhode Island census reports, Federal Census Reports from 1790 to 1880, and New York State census reports from 1815 to 1875. Also useful for this purpose and for establishing familial relations are cemetery records from cities and towns in Rhode Island, New York, the District of Columbia, and Virginia.

5. Also useful in piecing together the details of events, especially those surrounding the kidnapping, are City Directories and Registers and period municipal maps for communities in Saratoga, Warren, and Washington Counties, New York; in the District of Columbia, including Washington, Georgetown, and Alexandria (part of the district until 1846); and New Orleans, Louisiana.

6. The following regional histories and biographies provided useful contextual material:

Bascom, Robert O. *The Fort Edward Book.* Fort Edward, NY: J. D. Keating, 1903.

Dowd, Patrick (ed.). *Warren County (New York): Its People and their History over Time.* Virginia Beach, VA: Donning Company Publishers, 2009.

Frothingham, Washington. *History of Fulton County.* Syracuse: D. Mason, 1892.

Gresham Publishing Company. *History and Biography of Washington County and The Town of Queensbury, New York.* New York: Gresham Publishing Co., 1894.

Johnson, Crisfield. *History of Washington Co., New York.* Philadelphia: Everts & Ensign, 1878.

Jones, Mable. *Minerva, Essex County, N.Y.* Minerva: np, 1957.

Moore, Charles B (compiler). *Cemetery Records of the Township of Kingsbury, Washington County, New York.* Queensbury, New York: Historical Data Services, 1996.

Smith, H. Perry (ed.). *Essex County: History of Essex County with Illustrations and Biographical Sketches of Some of its Prominent Men and Pioneers.* Syracuse: D. Mason & Co., 1885.

Smith, H. Perry. *History of Warren County.* Syracuse: Mason & Co., 1885.

Stone, William L. *Washington County, New York, Its History to the Close of the Nineteenth Century,* np: New York History Co., 1904.

Sylvester, Nathaniel Bartlett. *History of Saratoga County.* Philadelphia: Everts and Ensign, 1878.

Watson, Winslow C. *Military and Civil History of the County of Essex, New York.* Albany, J. Munsell, 1869.

7. Extensive use has been made of archival materials to shed light on the culture of period, the institution of slavery, and specific events in Northup's life. These include documents, rare books, period maps, prints, photographs, broadsides, artifacts, and interpretive materials in the possession of national, state, and local libraries, colleges, historical societies, and museums, including the National Archives; the New York State Library; the New York State Archives; the Rhode Island Historical Society; the Historical Society of Washington, D.C.; the Office of Historic Alexandria; the Historic New Orleans Collection; the Fort Edward Historical Society; the Washington County Historical Society; The Old Fort House; the Rensselaer County Historical Society; the American Antiquarian Society; the Vermont Historical Society in Montpelier; the Special Collections of Schaffer Library, Union College; the Special Collections of the University of Virginia Library; Houghton Library at Harvard; the Martin Luther King Library in Washington, D.C.; the Saratoga Room of the Saratoga Public Library; the Farmers Museum at Cooperstown, New York; and Old Sturbridge Village.

8. Newspaper accounts and advertisements are a critical source for information on public aspects of the story such as the rescue, the trial of Birch, Northup's public appearances, the arrest and trial of the kidnappers, reviews of the book and plays, obituaries, etc. The following newspapers were valuable resources:

Albany Argus, Albany Evening Journal, Alexandria [Virginia] Gazette, Amsterdam Evening Recorder, Ballston Journal, Buffalo Dailey Courier, [St. Johnsbury, Vermont] Caledonian, [Janesville, Wisconsin] Daily Morning Gazette, Essex County Republican, Frederick Douglass' Paper, [Elyria, Ohio] Independent Democrat, Keesville Republican, Lewis County [New York] Republican, The Liberator, [Washington, D.C.,] National Daily Intelligencer, National Era, New Orleans Daily Picayune, New York Daily Times, New York Daily Tribune, New York Evening Telegram, New York Herald, New York Herald Tribune, Northern Christian Advocate, Northern Star and Freeman's Advocate, Richmond Whig, Rochester Democrat and Chronicle, Rome [New York] Citizen, Salem Press, Sandy Hill Herald, Saratoga Republican, Saratoga Sentinel, Saratoga Whig, Saratogian, [Rome, New York] Sentinel, Springfield [Massachusetts] Republican, St. Albans Messenger, Syracuse Daily Standard, Syracuse Evening Chronicle, Syracuse Evening Journal, Syracuse Post-Standard, Temperance Helper, Utica Daily Observer, Utica Morning Herald, Washington Daily Evening Star, [Montpelier, Vermont] Watchman & State Journal, The Wesleyan, Wilmington [North Carolina] Commercial.

9. The authors have discussed this story at length on several occasions with members of Solomon Northup's family and descendants of other people mentioned in the story, including those of Henry Northup and Cephas Parker. The authors have also interviewed many historians, who have been a source of important information, interpretation and criticism. These include: Kenneth Aslakson from the History Department at Union College (who gave valuable feedback on the manuscript), Warren Cardwell, Tom Colarco, Eileen Hannay, Field Horne, Paul McCarty, Gail Redmann, Sonia Taub, and Kay Tomasi.

10. The authors visited many relevant sites in Saratoga, Warren, Fulton, Montgomery, Washington, and New York Counties in New York State; in Washington, D.C. and Alexandria VA; in New Orleans, and in the Red River Valley region of Louisiana, including many sites in Rapides and Avoyelles Parishes mentioned in the narrative.

Index

ABOUT THE AUTHORS

DAVID FISKE (MLS, University at Albany, 1978) is a librarian and a genealogical and history researcher. He has had many local history articles published in *Ballston Spa Life* and is the author of *Solomon Northup: His Life Before and After Slavery* (2012). He has given presentations (on Solomon Northup, and Nate Salsbury's Black America show) at the Researching New York conference.

CLIFFORD W. BROWN, PhD, is the Robert Porter Patterson Professor of Government at Union College, Schenectady, NY. His published works include the co-authored *Struggles in the State: Sources and Patterns of World Revolution, Jaws of Victory: The Game-Plan Politics of 1972, A Campaign of Ideas,* and *Serious Money: Fundraising and Contributing in Presidential Nomination Campaigns.* Brown holds a doctorate from Harvard University.

RACHEL SELIGMAN, MA, is Assistant Director for Curatorial Affairs at the Frances Young Tang Teaching Museum and Art Gallery at Skidmore College, Saratoga Springs, NY. She was one of the principal organizers of a major exhibition on the life of Solomon Northup at Union College's Mandeville Gallery in 1999. She has organized numerous historical and interdisciplinary exhibitions. She holds a master's degree in art history from George Washington University.